Prophecies of the Cross

Prophecies of the Cross:
The Preaching of Christ Crucified according to the Scriptures

Timothy L. Fan

Published by
God-centered Universe Press
www.gcupress.com

Copyright © 2021 by Timothy L. Fan
All rights reserved.

ISBN-13: 978-0-9981369-3-6

Library of Congress Control Number: 2019917101

All Scripture quotations, unless otherwise indicated, are taken from the World English Bible® (WEB), a modern, public domain translation based on the American Standard Version 1901 Bible, Biblia Hebraica Stuttgartensia Old Testament, and Byzantine Majority Text New Testament. However, the (WEB) Scripture quotations have been adapted in the following manner: (i) the use of the divine name, Yahweh, has been quoted in its traditional English rendering, "the LORD"; (ii) contracted English words have been expanded into their formal equivalents (e.g. "don't" is quoted as "do not"); and (iii) pronouns representing God have been capitalized (e.g. "him," when referring to God, is quoted as "Him").

Scripture quotations marked (KJV) are taken from the King James Version of the Bible.

Scripture quotations marked (NKJV) are taken from the New King James Version®. Copyright © 1982 by Thomas Nelson. Used by permission. All rights reserved.

Scripture quotations marked (NASB) are taken from the New American Standard Bible®, Copyright © 1960, 1962, 1963, 1968, 1971, 1972, 1973, 1975, 1977, 1995 by The Lockman Foundation. Used by permission. (www.Lockman.org)

Scripture quotations marked (ESV) are taken from The Holy Bible, English Standard Version® (ESV®), copyright © 2001 by Crossway, a publishing ministry of Good News Publishers. Used by permission. All rights reserved.

Cover Image: Pixabay License: Free for commercial use; no attribution required.

He said to them, "Foolish men, and slow of heart to believe in all that the Prophets have spoken! Did not the Christ have to suffer these things and to enter into His glory?" Beginning from Moses and from all the Prophets, He explained to them in all the Scriptures the things concerning Himself. (Luke 24:25-27)

CONTENTS

PREFACE: A PRAYER FOR THE READER   i

INTRODUCTION: THE CHURCH'S PULPIT HAS LOST ITS POWER   iii

PART ONE
THE CROSS IN THE BOOKS OF MOSES

1 You Shall Bruise His Heel   3
The Cross in Genesis 3:11-15

2 God Will Provide Himself the Lamb   17
The Cross in Genesis 22:1-19

3 The Passover Lamb   31
The Cross in Exodus 12:1-13

4 The Day of Atonement   45
The Cross in Leviticus 16:1-34

5 The Bronze Serpent   61
The Cross in Numbers 21:1-9

6 Curses on Mount Ebal   77
The Cross in Deuteronomy 27:1-26

PART TWO
THE CROSS IN PSALM 22

7 Why Have You Forsaken Me?   95
The Cross in Psalm 22:1-21

8 I Will Declare Your Name to My Brethren   111
The RESURRECTION in Psalm 22:22-31

PART THREE
THE CROSS IN ISAIAH 53

9 God's Hidden Servant   127
The Cross in Isaiah 52:13 – 53:4

10 He Was Pierced   141
The Cross in Isaiah 53:5-9

11 It Pleased the Lord to Crush Him   157
The Cross in Isaiah 53:10

12 He Shall See Light   165
The RESURRECTION in Isaiah 53:11-12

PART FOUR
THE CROSS IN THE BOOK OF ZECHARIAH

13 Me, Whom They Have Pierced   181
The Cross in Zechariah 12:1-14

14 Awake, O Sword!   197
The Cross in Zechariah 13:7-9

PART FIVE
THE GLORY OF THE CROSS OF CHRIST

15 Now the Son of Man Is Glorified   213
The Glory of THE CRUCIFIED CHRIST in John 13:31-35

16 Peace Be to You   229
The Glory of THE RISEN CHRIST in John 20:19-29

17 The Seven-sealed Scroll   245
The Glory of THE LAMB, SLAIN in Revelation 5:1-14

CONCLUSION: "I HAVE FINISHED THE WORK" (JOHN 17:4)   259

TO DR. AND MRS. CHEN

Valiantly God-centered. Nobly humble.
Unwavering in obedience to the Gospel of God.

AND TO MY BELOVED WIFE & CHILDREN

You have suffered with me through many tribulations.
You have loved Christ as faithful pilgrims.

"But far be it from me to boast, except in the cross of our Lord Jesus Christ, through which the world has been crucified to me, and I to the world."

GALATIANS 6:14

PREFACE

Dear Reader,

God Himself is the Gospel, since the Gospel is, *"Behold! Your God!"* (Isaiah 40:9). Jesus Christ Himself is the Gospel, since the Gospel is, *"Behold! The Lamb of God, who takes away the sin of the world"* (John 1:29). The Holy Spirit Himself is the Gospel, since the Gospel is, *"But you are not in the flesh but in the Spirit, if it is so that the Spirit of God dwells in you. But if any man does not have the Spirit of Christ, he is not His"* (Romans 8:9). Therefore, the Gospel is infinitely valuable, since God is infinitely worthy. Thus the Gospel is worth suffering for [2 Timothy 1:8], contending for [Jude 3], and dying for [Acts 21:13].

Yet what does it mean to preach the Gospel in the very manner in which the Apostles preached it, namely, that Christ died for our sins *"according to the Scriptures"* (1 Corinthians 15:3)? Since the *manner* of preaching the Gospel in today's churches has become so very unbiblical—so dominated by mere words of *"human wisdom"* (1 Corinthians 2:4) and so wanting in rich Scriptural content—this question of how to preach *"Christ crucified"* as *"according to the Scriptures"* is one of the most important and urgent questions of our day. Therefore, as we approach this great question with much fear and trembling before the never-sleeping eyes of our God, allow me to pray thus, on your behalf, as a pastor of Christ's Church, as an unworthy servant of the Master, and as your fellow bondservant of our Lord Jesus Christ:

> "O Sovereign LORD, You who are mighty have done great things for Your people, and holy is Your name. Please sanctify these servants of Yours, even all of those who will read this book with hearts that fear You, by making them holy in Your truth—Your Word is truth. Righteous Father, let Your teachings drop like rain, and Your speech distill as the dew, even as

raindrops on the tender herb, and as showers on the grass. I pray for these, my dear Brethren, that You would count them worthy of this calling, and fulfill in them all the good pleasure of Your goodness, and the work of faith with power, that the name of the Lord Jesus Christ may be glorified in them, and they in Him, according to Your grace, O Father, and the grace of our Lord Jesus Christ. Blessed Father, strengthen their hearts to know the love of Christ which surpasses knowledge. I pray that You would fill them with the knowledge of Your will, in all wisdom and spiritual understanding, that they would walk worthy of You, fully pleasing You, being fruitful in every good work, and growing in the knowledge of You. And through the blessing of Your Spirit, may Your Word, which is sent out through this present work, run swiftly and be glorified both in them and through their witness to Jesus Christ, to the saving of many lost souls, by the power of the Holy Spirit, and to the eternal glory, majesty, and honor of Your precious and praiseworthy Name. To You, our holy God and Father, and to the Lamb who was slain, be all power and riches and wisdom, and strength and honor and glory and blessing, both now, and forevermore. Amen."

May the Spirit of the Lord give you utterance to open your mouth boldly to make known the mystery of the Gospel, on behalf of which so many of the blessed Prophets and Apostles and saints have given their blood, and for which even many today are in chains, so that you may speak it boldly, as you ought to speak.

In Christ's Covenantal Love,

Timothy L. Fan
Christmas, 2021

INTRODUCTION:
The Church's Pulpit Has Lost Its Power

He took the twelve aside, and said to them, "Behold, we are going up to Jerusalem, and all the things that are written through the Prophets concerning the Son of Man will be completed. For He will be delivered up to the Gentiles, will be mocked, treated shamefully, and spit on. They will scourge and kill Him. On the third day, He will rise again." They understood none of these things. This saying was hidden from them, and they did not understand the things that were said. (Luke 18:31–34)

GOD warns His servants *beforehand* of the coming sufferings of the Gospel. He announces these sufferings to His true servants *beforehand*, so that they will not be dismayed at them. The offense of the cross, which is a staggering offense to the wicked pride of sinful man, is so high and lofty and dangerously jagged as to seem, to the eyes of unbelief, to be an impossible ascent. The cross smells to the reprobate like the aroma of death. It prophecies pain to a world that worships only pleasure.

The world desires life to be all hedonistic glory and self-exalting victory. It cannot, therefore, put up with a God who suffers. The false god of this world, rather, is a god of good-fortune-telling, and prosperity forecasting, and flattery, and lies, and progress, and manifest success. Being thus deceived by Satan, this present world hates Christ, for Christ is the Son of God who suffers. That is, if the Gospel of Christ is the Gospel of the Man of Sorrows, complete with all of His bitter rejections, stinging tears, and vehement cries to God for salvation from His earthly sufferings, then this current, prosperous world wants nothing to do with such a Gospel, and thus hides its face, in disgust, from such a Christ.

Yet if true handsomeness is found only in the scars of the crucified Christ, and if the true strength and power of divine glory is revealed only in the utter weaknesses of the suffering Christ, then we praise God, our Father, that He announces beforehand the sufferings of His children. In this manner, He revealed to Abraham, long before the actual events came to pass, that his descendants, though vast in number, would be strangers in a land not their own, and would serve as slaves to their captors, and would be in affliction under their captors for a span of four hundred years [Genesis 15:13-14].

Likewise, the Lord, speaking through Moses, announced beforehand to the children of Israel that, after they had been brought forth from the fiery furnace of Egypt, and yet subsequently had rebelled against the commandments of her God, even by worshipping the gods of the peoples around them, they would be uprooted from the land of their inheritance and cast into another land, even the land of a new captivity [Deuteronomy 29:28].

Our Lord Jesus, then, announces the sufferings of the Gospel well before they actually come about. He tells His disciples that the Son of Man will be scourged and killed by evil men. He warns them that they themselves will be delivered up to tribulations by their persecutors, who will kill them, and that they will be hated by all nations for His name's sake [Matthew 24:9]. Jesus warns His disciples beforehand, saying to them:

> *"I have said these things to you so that you would not be caused to stumble. They will put you out of the synagogues. Yes, the time comes that whoever kills you will think that he offers service to God. They will do these things because they have not known the Father, nor Me.* **But I have told you these things, so that when the time comes, you may remember that I told you about them.** *I did not tell you these things from the beginning, because I was with you."* (John 16:1–4)

He is a praiseworthy God, then, and a good Shepherd of our souls, since He warns us *beforehand* of the sufferings of the cross:

INTRODUCTION: THE CHURCH'S PULPIT HAS LOST ITS POWER

*"Now **I have told you before it happens** so that when it happens, you may believe."* (John 14:29)

O dear Church of the living God, contrary to the false prosperity hopes of those who have deceived themselves into believing the doctrine of *Post*-millennialism—which is the unbiblical hope that there will be a Millennium of Christian global conquest and security and ease *prior to, and not after* the Second Coming of our Lord Jesus Christ—the truth of the Gospel, as handed down to us from the earliest Church Fathers, has always been *Pre*-millennial. That is, our Lord has warned us beforehand of many bitter and unprecedented persecutions that will immediately precede His Second Coming. The truth, then, is not that we should expect a massive, global revival unto righteousness just prior to Christ's return to earth, but rather that we ought to brace ourselves for the bitter and cruel times of the end, even the times of the Antichrist, in which the sufferings and torments of the elect will prove to be so severe that only a very small remnant of saints will be found faithful to Christ up until the very Day of His return.

Is yours, then, a gospel of immediate prosperity, which is a different gospel, or else the true Gospel of immediate suffering, which only afterwards shall be followed by Heavenly glory? If you, dear Church, confess the true Gospel, which is the Gospel of immediate suffering, then you will do well to prepare yourself for endurance through tribulations. Yet as you gird up the loins of your mind for such suffering, there is, here, in the Eighteenth Chapter of Luke's Gospel, a Word of great comfort to you, namely, that Christ told His disciples *beforehand* of His impending cross.

This is an unspeakable comfort to us as we suffer for His name, since the Christ who suffered on the cross had sovereign power over His own sufferings. That is, if He, in His divine sovereignty, *foretold* the cross, then He must have had divine sovereignty over the cross itself. But if He had divine sovereignty over the cross, then the cross was not able to overcome Him, but rather He overcame the world through the cross. And yet if He had divine sovereignty over the cross, then He also, in the present time, has divine sovereignty over the sufferings of His children, which He likewise has foretold. But if, in the present time, He has divine sovereignty over our own sufferings, then He will not allow our sufferings, endured for the sake of His name, to overcome us, but instead will make us more than conquerors through our sufferings, so that His name will be glorified through our tribulations. So then, dear Church, both your present and future sufferings, which He has warned you about beforehand, only shall be for your glory.

Therefore, be sober-minded as you meditate upon these things, and encourage one another with these words.

WRITTEN BY THE PROPHETS

However, when our Lord Jesus warns the disciples beforehand of the coming sufferings of the cross, it is not as though He is telling them something altogether new. Instead, these things already were *foretold in the Law and the Prophets*. Our Lord Jesus, then, in announcing this new thing, which is, the sacrificial dying of the Son of Man and His being raised to life, subsequently, on the third day, is only announcing *that which already was announced long ago* in the writings of the Prophets of Israel:

> *Surely the Lord GOD will do nothing,* **unless He reveals His secret to His servants the Prophets***.* (Amos 3:7)

And,

> *Behold, the former things have happened and I declare new things.* ***I tell you about them before they come up.*** (Isaiah 42:9)

Our Lord's Words to the disciples, then, are not new, but rather very ancient. For, God warned beforehand of the sufferings of the Christ, even in the ancient Scriptures of Israel:

> *He took the twelve aside, and said to them, "Behold, we are going up to Jerusalem,* ***and all the things that are written through the Prophets concerning the Son of Man will be completed****. For He will be delivered up to the Gentiles, will be mocked, treated shamefully, and spit on. They will scourge and*

Introduction: The Church's Pulpit Has Lost Its Power

kill Him. On the third day, He will rise again."
(Luke 18:31–33)

Do you see the condescending love of God and the pains which He has taken to ensure that His Gospel has been announced beforehand, such that all men, everywhere, are without excuse? For, it is not only that Jesus warned His disciples beforehand of His impending passion, but also that the Lord God of Israel announced such things hundreds, or in some cases thousands of years in advance, so that the whole world might see the astounding sovereignty with which He executed His purposes for the redemption of fallen man out from his bondage to sin and death. Thus God announced the Gospel of Christ's cross, and also His subsequent victory over death through His resurrection from the grave, from the most ancient of times, through His holy Prophets.

What, then, does our Lord Jesus mean when He says, *"And all the things **that are written through the Prophets concerning the Son of Man** will be completed?"* He is referring to the Old Testament prophecies of the Christ. And these prophecies come in two forms. First, there are types. And then, second, there are direct, verbal foretellings.

Regarding the *types* of Christ in the writings of the Law and the Prophets, they are so numerous that we lack sufficient time even to categorize them, much less name them one by one.[1] Yet we will mention Isaac as a type of Christ. For, just as Isaac, who was Abraham's only-begotten son by Sarah, was led to the altar of sacrifice while riding on a donkey, so too did Christ offer Himself as the true atoning sacrifice for our sins on the cross, yet only after riding into Jerusalem on a donkey, even a colt, the foal of a donkey [Genesis 22:1-5; Matthew 21:4-7].

Likewise, we remember the Passover Lamb, eaten as a sacrifice every year in Israel, as a memorial of the First Passover in the land of Egypt. For, just as the Law commands concerning the

---

[1] Thus John Chrysostom, in *Homilies on First Corinthians* 38.3 (*NPNF*[1] 12:228), says, "And [in] many other instances [of Old Testament prophecy], too, not to name all one by one, partly in words and partly in types, one may see in them [the cross of Christ] stored up, setting forth His slaughter in the flesh and that He was slain for our sins."

Passover Lamb, *"Do not break any of its bones"* (Exodus 12:46), so it is recorded of the Lord Jesus when He was crucified, *"But when they came to Jesus, and saw that He was already dead, they did not break His legs"* (John 19:33).

Lastly, we mention Jonah, as a type of the coming Christ. For, just as Jonah was cast down into the waters of death, so that his guilt might be removed from the mariners' ship, and thus the mariners were not charged by God with innocent blood, and thus God calmed the storm of His wrath against Jonah's sin that threatened to sink their ship, so too was Jesus plunged into the waters of death on the cross, and yet He was, by contrast, the innocent One, and not the guilty one. And thus innocent blood was on the hands of all men, and yet Jesus, by His death, took our guilt in His own body on the tree, so that the storm of God's wrath against us, who were guilty, might be calmed by the sinless blood of the sacrificial death of Christ Jesus in our stead [Jonah 1:14; Matthew 27:24].

Yet the Law and the Prophets also contain *direct, verbal foretellings* regarding the death and resurrection of the Christ. Thus it is written of the sufferings of the Christ:

For dogs have surrounded Me. A company of evildoers have enclosed Me. **They have pierced My hands and feet.** *I can count all of My bones. They look and stare at Me.* **They divide My garments among them. They cast lots for My clothing.** (Psalm 22:16–18)

And,

Because of all My adversaries I have become utterly contemptible to My neighbors, a horror to My acquaintances. Those who saw Me on the street fled from Me. **I am forgotten from their hearts like a dead man. I am like broken pottery.** *For I have heard the slander of many, terror on every side, while they conspire together against Me,* **they plot to take away My life.** (Psalm 31:11–13)

And again,

INTRODUCTION: THE CHURCH'S PULPIT HAS LOST ITS POWER

*They also gave Me [gall] for My food. In My thirst, **they gave Me vinegar to drink**.* (Psalm 69:21)

And also, in the book of the Prophet Isaiah:

*He was taken away by oppression and judgment. As for His generation, who considered that **He was cut off out of the land of the living** and stricken for the disobedience of My people?* (Isaiah 53:8)

However, these direct, verbal foretellings in the Law and the Prophets are not concerning the sufferings of Christ only, but also concerning His subsequent resurrection from the dead. For, just as Jonah was three days and three nights in the belly of the fish, so too was the Son of Man three days and three nights in the heart of the earth, but then came His glorious resurrection from the grave:

*For You will not leave My soul in Sheol, **neither will You allow Your Holy One to see corruption**.* (Psalm 16:10)

And again,

*After two days He will revive us. **On the third day He will raise us up**, and we will live before Him.* (Hosea 6:2)

This, then, is how we must read the Law and the Prophets, for this is how our Lord Jesus has instructed us to read them:

*He said to them, "**Thus it is written**, and thus it was necessary for the Christ to suffer and to rise from the dead the third day...."* (Luke 24:46)

It is no wonder at all, then, that we find the Apostle Paul, in the book of Acts, preaching the Gospel of Christ in this very manner. For, Paul did not declare Christ to lost souls using mere reason, arguing from the reason of man alone, as the unbelievers do, but rather Paul preached Christ *as the fulfillment of all things that are written by the Prophets concerning Him*:

PROPHECIES OF THE CROSS

*Paul, as was his custom, went in to [the Jews in Thessalonica], and for three Sabbath days reasoned with them **from the Scriptures, explaining and demonstrating that the Christ had to suffer and rise again from the dead**, and saying, "This Jesus, whom I proclaim to you, is the Christ."* (Acts 17:2–3)

Just as Apollos, who was commissioned by the brethren as an evangelist, *"refuted the Jews, **publicly showing by the Scriptures that Jesus was the Christ**"* (Acts 18:28), so too did Paul, perhaps the greatest of evangelists, explain to the Jews in Rome and solemnly testify of the Kingdom of God to them by *"**persuading them concerning Jesus, both from the Law of Moses and from the Prophets**, from morning until evening"* (Acts 28:23). Evangelism, then, must not preach Jesus as a philosophical ideal, but rather must preach Jesus as the very Christ to whom all of the Law and the Prophets bear witness:

*But now apart from the Law, a righteousness of God has been revealed, **being testified by the Law and the Prophets**....* (Romans 3:21)

And,

*For I delivered to you first of all that which I also received: that Christ died for our sins **according to the Scriptures**, that He was buried, that He was raised on the third day **according to the Scriptures**.* (1 Corinthians 15:3–4)

Yet preaching in the Evangelical Church today falls ever so short of such Apostolic demonstrations of the authority and power of the Old Testament Scriptures, and especially when expounding upon the Gospel of Jesus. Instead, contemporary Evangelical preaching has become the kind of preaching which Richard Baxter, the great Puritan pastor of pastors, said that he loathed:

Of all the preaching in the world (that speaks not stark lies), I hate that preaching which tends to make the hearers laugh, or to move their minds with trickling levity, and affect them as stage-

INTRODUCTION: THE CHURCH'S PULPIT HAS LOST ITS POWER

plays used to do, instead of affecting them with holy reverence for the name of God.[2]

Again, today's sickly and compromised Evangelical preaching is not the preaching of the Gospel in all of the fearful majesty and holy splendor of the breadth and depth of the Old Testament types and verbal utterances which find their fulfillment in the coming of the Son of Man. To the contrary, today's Evangelicalism is fueled by the kinds of doctrinal cowardice, cultural fashionableness, and psychological flattery that Wang Mingdao, the father of the Underground Church in China, would certainly decry as a syncretistic form of idolatry:

> Today the Church is in a sad state, burning incense to all kinds of "golden calves" and worshipping at strange altars. *Many preachers who should be rebuking sin with God's Word have become silent.* Among them, some are afraid to risk danger and calamity, and so they dare not open their mouths for God. Others are out for their own benefit, which requires that they please men. Therefore they cannot speak the truth of God.[3]

O weak and worldly Evangelical Church, why is it that your pulpits have lost their power? How does it so happen that although you have filled your pulpits with doctors of leadership, and doctors of knowledge, and doctors of entertainment, and doctors of trendy fashionableness, there still is no more authentic outpouring of the Holy Spirit among you? Why is there no more deep conviction of sin amongst the congregations, and no more weeping over idolatry, and no more burning of the expensive magic books of Ephesus, and no more fear of God falling upon the people of God? Why is there a Tabernacle, and an altar, but no more fire coming out from the presence of the Lord to consume the sacrifices? Why is there a

---

[2] Richard Baxter, *The Reformed Pastor* (first published 1656; ed. and abr. William Brown, 1829; repr. Edinburgh: The Banner of Truth Trust, 2001), 119-120.

[3] Wang Mingdao, *A Call to the Church: 20 Pre-prison Messages of Conviction and Courage* (trans. Theodore Choy; ed. Leona F. Choy; Fort Washington, PA: Christian Literature Crusade, 1983), 150, emphasis added.

Temple, and a sanctuary, but no more cloud of glory filling the Temple, such that the priests of the Temple cannot continue ministering in the sanctuary because of the glory of the Lord filling the House of the Lord? Why is the Gospel said to be preached to millions, and yet the millions to whom it is preached are no longer cut to the heart, with tear-soaked repentance, by it? For what reason do we have so many preachers today, but so little true revival of God-centered, God-fearing Christianity today?

Is this not because there are so few pastors in the world today who truly are afflicted, and struck of spirit, and who tremble at God's Word? And thus lacking truly God-fearing men in the pulpit, are not today's pulpits themselves experiencing a veritable famine of God's Word? For, they have preached their own version of Jesus *in place of* what is written in the Law and the Prophets, rather than preaching the true Jesus *as foretold and proved by* what is written in the Law and the Prophets. That is, instead of preaching Christ from the Law and from the Testimony, they have preached a Christ severed from the Old Testament Scriptures. In doing so, they have gained the applause of men, but they have forfeited the very authority, history, context, and doctrine of the Gospel. For, God is not God-in-the-abstract, but the God of Scripture, the God of Abraham, Isaac, and Jacob, and thus Christ, who is God, must be preached as *the Christ of the Scriptures, the Christ of the Prophets*, or else the gullible, itching-eared congregations, so steeped in their love of the world, shall only continue to hear of an altogether different Christ, and thus of an altogether different Gospel.

Yet we hope for much better things for our sons and our daughters. We pray that the Lord will raise up new Josiah's to lead His churches into a new Reformation, and we pray for new Elijah's in the churches who will preach the full offense of the cross of Christ—with the prophecies of the cross contained within the Law and the Prophets, as explained by the Apostolic writings, being their source of authority—such that the hearts of fathers will be turned to the sons, and the hearts of the sons to their fathers, lest the Lord strike the land with a curse [Malachi 4:6]. Unto this end the present author presents this work, which itself is the fruit of many personal sufferings (both in body and in spirit) for the sake of the Gospel, as a gift to Christ's Church, for the equipping of His saints, so that the Lord of the Church may be glorified in the rising generation. For, as it is written, *"We will not hide them from their children, telling to the generation to come the praises of the LORD, His strength, and His [miraculous] deeds that He has done"* (Psalm 78:4). The grace of the Lord Jesus Christ be with all the saints. *Soli Deo Gloria.* Glory to God alone.

Part One:

THE CROSS
in the Books of Moses

1

YOU SHALL BRUISE HIS HEEL
The Cross in Genesis 3:11-15

God said, "Who told you that you were naked? Have you eaten from the tree that I commanded you not to eat from?" The man said, "The woman whom you gave to be with me, she gave me fruit from the tree, and I ate it." The LORD God said to the woman, "What have you done?" The woman said, "The serpent deceived me, and I ate." The LORD God said to the serpent, "Because you have done this, you are cursed above all livestock, and above every animal of the field. You shall go on your belly and you shall eat dust all the days of your life. I will put [enmity]¹ between you and the woman, and between your [seed] and her [seed]. He will bruise your head, and you will bruise his heel." (Genesis 3:11–15)

GOD has a love for sinful mankind that is incomprehensibly vast and deep. Being three times holy, He has the divine prerogative to strike down Adam and Eve, even at this instant in the Garden, and to cast them directly into Hell. They have violated His holy commandment. Both of them, man and woman alike, have committed spiritual adultery with the Serpent. In their wicked pride, they have traded their spiritual coverings of glory for the shameful nakedness of sin. The Lord God would be perfectly just if He were to give the sentence to condemn them to an everlasting,

---

¹ Throughout this current work, the present author, only when necessary, has chosen to insert his own Hebrew-to-English or Greek-to-English translation improvements on the World English Bible's translation of the Holy Scriptures by putting his own translation words or phrases in [brackets].

conscious torment in a sulfurous, ever-burning fire, right at this moment, in the divine courtroom of the Garden.

Yet He does not do this. Instead, He acts as a loving, longsuffering Father towards His image bearers. Instead of bringing down the death sentence, right away, He asks these very first image bearers, whom He loves, a set of heart-piercing questions. He asks the man, *"Have you eaten from the tree from which I commanded you not to eat?"* Then, He asks the woman, *"What have you done?"*

Do we not hear, in these questions, the voice of a loving Father in Heaven? Do not even earthly fathers, when they love their children, confront their children's sins with convicting, yet tearful questions? Can you not hear an earthly father confronting his precious, youthful son, who has committed a grave sin when his father was not home, with the question, "Did you think that you could sin in this horrific way simply because I was not home?" Or, can you not hear the same earthly father, asking his beloved, toddling daughter, who is munching on a piece of explicitly forbidden candy, "Did you really petition *a stranger* to give you that candy, the very candy that I, your father, forbid you to eat?" Does not even the earthly father, who himself fears God, ask such questions with a delicate mixture of righteous indignation and heartbroken tears?

Of course, sinful pride refuses to be truthful about the utter sinfulness of sin. Proud sinners want to pass the blame onto someone else. Adam says, *"**The woman**... she gave me fruit from the tree, and I ate it"* (v. 12). Eve says, *"**The serpent** deceived me, and I ate"* (v. 13). Much later in Israel's history, King Saul will say to the prophet Samuel, *"But **the people** took of the plunder, sheep and cattle, the chief of the devoted things, to sacrifice to the LORD your God in Gilgal"* (1 Samuel 15:21). In fact, this pattern repeats itself innumerable times in world history. For, in world history, it is the king who says, "It is *the Parliament's* fault," and the Parliament who says, "It is *the people's* fault," and the people who say, "It is *the king's* fault."

In today's crooked world that is ever so wanting in justice, the acknowledgement of the exceeding sinfulness of sin is almost all but evaded. A pastor says, "The need to fit in with the culture made me alter the Apostolic prohibitions on all immodesty of dress in the Church." A mother says, "Peer pressure from other mothers made me hand my own child over to the public schools to be indoctrinated in Secular Humanism." A university professor says, "My requirements for tenure pushed me into being silent about the Gospel." And a murderer says, "I stopped taking my depression medication, and thus my psychological disorder made me commit the murder," or else the murderer will say, "A child would ruin my sports scholarship, and I cannot afford college without that sports scholarship, so I simply had to have the abortion."

Dear Reader, you who have been endowed with a soul that is created in the image of God, do you feel, in the stirrings of your heart, the horror of the guilt of your own sins before God? Have you committed in the darkness the unfruitful deeds of darkness—even sexual immorality, and uncleanness, and covetousness, and dishonoring your parents, and the telling of lies, and utterances uttered to idols—and has God, who knows all and sees all, not seen these things? Do you, then, feel undone and shamefully exposed in the nakedness of your sins? Before the holy, holy, holy eyes of the Judge of all, the Lord of Heaven who sits upon the throne of Heaven, do you cry out, "Woe is me! For, I have sinned against my holy Creator, whose eyes are too pure to look upon evil! And thus I am unworthy even to lift my eyes to Heaven!"? Do you weep over the truth that your sins of denying Christ through disobeying His holy commandments, with every single sin being a wicked betrayal of God's tender love towards you, are the same sins that condemned Jesus on the cross? (For, they were your sins, and not His own, which demanded His torment on the cross.) If not, then your heart is quite dead to the Holy Spirit of God, and you remain under His just wrath. Yet if you do so weep and lament over your sins, then your glorious hope of redemption and forgiveness shall be found in the Lamb of God who was slain on Calvary's cross in your stead.

ENMITY BETWEEN TWO KINGDOMS

God is a loving Father, but He will not accept the prideful excuses of Adam and Eve. His judgments will fall upon them. They will be severe, as Genesis 3:16-19 painfully demonstrates.

However, since God, in His righteous anger, is also merciful, He does not expend His wrath on Adam and Eve. Instead, He pours out the fiercest heat of His anger upon the Serpent. In dealing with Adam and Eve, the Judge of all employs convicting, but still very much merciful questions. Yet in dealing with the Serpent, God asks no questions. There is no mercy for the Serpent. Instead, for the Serpent there is only the curse of God's fierce wrath:

> *The* LORD *God said to the serpent, "Because you have done this, you are cursed above all livestock, and above every animal of the field. You shall go on your belly and you shall eat dust all the days of your life.* ***I will put [enmity]*** *between you and the woman, and between your [seed] and her [seed]. He will bruise your head, and you will bruise his heel." (Genesis 3:14–15)*

God's curse upon the Serpent is a declaration of war against the Serpent. There will be *"enmity"* between the Serpent and the woman. That is, the whole world is now divided into two Kingdoms. There is the Kingdom of the world, which is ruled by the Serpent and populated by the Serpent's children. Then, there is the Kingdom of God, which is ruled by God and populated by the true, spiritual descendants of Eve. And these two Kingdoms, says God, never shall be at peace with one another. There shall be enmity between them, perpetually, until one of them is completely destroyed by the other.

This is an ancient enmity. It reaches all the way back to the events of the Fall that took place in the Garden of Eden. Ever since then, it has played out on the battlefields of human history. The children of Satan always have been at war with the children of God. There is enmity between the Serpent and the woman. In like manner, there is enmity between Esau and Jacob:

> *"Because you* [Edom, the descendants of Esau] *have had **a perpetual [enmity]**, and have given over the children of Israel* [the descendants of Jacob] *to the power of the sword in the time of their calamity, in the time of the iniquity of the end; therefore, as I live, says the Lord* GOD, *I will prepare you for*

blood, and blood shall pursue you: since you have not hated blood, therefore blood shall pursue you." (Ezekiel 35:5–6)

The nations of this earth are constantly at war with each other. Yet in truth even the warring nations are still fighting for the same cause. All nations that hate Christ, even the ones that hate each other, are on the side of the Serpent. They find common ground in their hatred of the Lord Jesus:

*Herod and Pilate **became friends** with each other that very day, for before that they were **[at enmity]** with each other.* (Luke 23:12)

Of course, the Gospel proclaims the astonishing news that ancient enmities can be overturned. By the power of the Gospel, men who formerly were at war with God can be made to lay down their weapons, in repentance, and to beg clemency from Christ, by turning towards Him, in faith. Once this happens, through the miraculous rebirth of the Holy Spirit, the believer experiences peace with God. War ceases in the sinner's heart once that heart surrenders itself to the conquering love of God, demonstrated by the death of Jesus Christ in our place.

However, there is also a social dimension to this. In the Gospel, the enmity that used to exist between peoples is abolished. Newly converted spouses, who formerly were on the verge of divorce, reconcile with one another. Christian parents reconcile with their once estranged, but now fully reborn Christian children. Christian Jews reconcile with Christian Palestinians. The former enmity is removed between Christian master and Christian slave. Christ, graciously, has brought us His peace, and so we now become peacemakers in His Church:

*...having abolished in the flesh **the [enmity]**, the Law of commandments contained in ordinances, that he might create in himself one new man of the two, making peace; and might reconcile them both* [Jew and Gentile] *in one body to God through the cross, having killed the **[enmity]** thereby.* (Ephesians 2:15–16)

Yet while the Gospel brings peace amongst true believers, it also maintains its enmity with the world. God is still at war with the Serpent. The Kingdom of God is still at war with the Kingdom of this world. There is still a great enmity between the Serpent and the woman. Satan hates the Church, and the Church wars against Satan.

This means that there is no such thing as an unbeliever who is at peace with God. All unbelievers demonstrate their unbelief through idolatry. And all idolaters hate God. They do not love God, as some of them like to claim, "in their own way." Rather, all idolaters are at war with God. They hate His Law, and seek to dethrone His Christ:

> ...*because the mind of the flesh is **[at enmity]** towards God; for it is not subject to God's Law, neither indeed can it be.* (Romans 8:7)

There is, then, no unbeliever who perishes in Hell by accident. The way that some preachers talk about unbelievers, one might think that they are essentially good people. Some preachers want you to look at your neighbor, who is an idolater, and to say of him, "Well, he is a really great guy. He has a good heart. His niceness towards others shows what a noble heart he has. It's just too bad that he has forgotten—or else has not been told—to pick up his free ticket to Heaven at the will-call box. I hope that he, being the good guy that he is, does not forget—or else is told by someone—to pick up his free ticket before he dies."

This is not the true Gospel, as it speaks to the state of unbelievers. The true Gospel is that there is no such thing as an unbeliever who has a good heart. Rather, the heart of every unbeliever is deceitful above all things, and incurable, and none can truly know it [Jeremiah 17:9]. This means that your neighbor might be good at flattery, and so come across as a really nice fellow, but in truth he is wicked. He hates God. He is at war with God, and his heart is vile. Until he repents, no matter how cheerful or polite he may act, his heart is vile.

This also means that Christians need to stop forging spiritual friendships with the world. The Church today is grossly compromised on account of its friendship with the world. Today's Church members want to sing the music of the world, enjoy the entertainments of the world, tattoo their bodies, just like the world, live in the luxuries of the world, and receive the plaudits of the world. Yet if Christ is at enmity with the world, then Christians are forbidden from seeking these sinful things.

We are commanded, as the Church, to be at war with the spiritual allegiances and immoral cravings of the world. Therefore, the warning from James, the brother of Jesus, is that if we seek to join forces with the world, then we shall find ourselves at war with God:

*You adulterers and adulteresses, do you not know that friendship with the world **is [enmity] toward God**? Whoever therefore wants to be a friend of the world makes himself **an enemy of God**.* (James 4:4)

There is no such thing as neutrality in this world. In the heart of the individual, every thought and every deed is either for Christ, or against Him. Even in the broader culture, there is no neutrality. Classrooms either worship Christ with the explicit language of ascribing glory to Him, or else (even by their culpable silence on the subject of Christ) they war against Him. Scientists either believe the six, literal days of Genesis, thus affirming that the earth is approximately six thousand years old—in accordance with the creation account, the biblical genealogies, and Noah's global flood—or else they war against the authority of Genesis. Museums, courtrooms, and legislatures either honor God's Word by actively quoting it and seeking to obey it, or else they rage against God's Word. There is no neutrality.

The problem with Evangelicals in the contemporary Church is that they have not been willing to live in this realm of Christian antithesis to the world. They have ceased to embrace biblical holiness. They do not view estrangement from the world as a normative part of biblical faith. They have, instead, sought to look like the world, act like the world, and think like the world. Is it any mystery at all, then, that today's Evangelicals are anything but the salt and light of the world?

According to our Lord, the world, by definition, is at enmity with Christians. It hates us. The world belongs to the Serpent, so it hates the ways in which we live. The world hates our vision for educating our children, in which we confess biblical authority above secular authority. It also hates the ways in which we spend our money and our time, investing them in Heavenly things, and not patronizing the world's immodest retail stores and frivolous entertainment centers. The world plays its own, godless music, but we do not dance to it. It sings its own, godless dirge, but we do not mourn with it. We love the lost, unsaved people of this world with a compassionate, God-centered love. We even love those who persecute us. But they hate us, and so they should. For our King is at war with theirs.

Dear Christian, have you experienced the horrible pain and rejection of being hated by the world? Have you suffered under the afflictions of being persecuted by the world? If so, do not lose heart, but rather rejoice and be glad, for in the same way they persecuted the Prophets who were before you, and, therefore, great is your reward in Heaven. But if not, then have you considered the biblical truth that you, therefore, must not be living in true Christian godliness and authentic Christian holiness?

ENMITY BETWEEN TWO SEEDS

Thus there is enmity between the Serpent and the woman. This means that there is also enmity between two Kingdoms. The Kingdom of the Serpent is in a perpetual war with the Kingdom of God. Yet this ancient enmity is not only between two Kingdoms. For, God's pronouncement against the Serpent in Genesis 3:15 also involves enmity between two *"seeds"*:

> *"I will put [enmity] between you and the woman, and between **your [seed]** and **her [seed]**. He will bruise your head, and you will bruise his heel."* (Genesis 3:15)

There are two warring Kingdoms. There are also two warring seeds. There is the godly seed. There is also the Satanic seed:

*Adam knew his wife again. She gave birth to a son, and named him Seth, saying, "For God has given me **another [seed]** instead of Abel, for **Cain** killed him."* (Genesis 4:25)

Cain is of the Serpent's seed. Seth is of the woman's seed. One is a child of the Devil. The other is a child of God. The difference between the two is saving faith. It is the children of the promise who are of the woman's seed:

*The LORD appeared to Abram and said, "I will give this land **to your [seed]**." He built an altar there to the LORD, who had appeared to him.* (Genesis 12:7)

Still, the seed of Abraham is not just the bloodline descendants of Abraham. The Pharisees, who hate Jesus, think that they are Abraham's seed simply because they are Jews. Yet Jesus says that Abraham's seed consists of all those who fear God and worship His only-begotten Son. If they do not love Jesus, then they are not Abraham's seed:

*"I know that you are **Abraham's [seed]**, yet **you seek to kill Me**, because My Word finds no place in you....**You are of your father, the Devil**...."* (John 8:37, 44)

The Apostle Paul makes this explicit:

*That is, it is not the children of the flesh who are children of God, but the children of the promise are counted as **[the seed]**.* (Romans 9:8)

And again,

*If you are Christ's, **then you are Abraham's [seed]** and heirs according to promise.* (Galatians 3:29)

Thus we see a great enmity between the seed of Satan and the seed of Christ. Christ, Himself, is the Seed of the promise. His offspring, then, are His seed. Yet this means that all those who are outside of Christ are not the godly seed. And this, in turn, explains why Satan does not persecute all people. The Serpent knows the difference between those who are his own seed, and those who are Christ's seed. And he, the Serpent, rages against the seed of Christ:

The dragon grew angry with the woman, **and went away to make war with the rest of her [seed]**, *who keep God's commandments and hold Jesus' testimony.* (Revelation 12:17)

We are of *"the seed"* of Christ because Christ is *"the Seed"* of Eve. He is the Seed who was prophesied by Moses in Genesis 3:15. Satan was told, all the way back in the Garden of Eden, that one of Eve's *"seed"* would arise to conquer him. A virgin would be with Child. A Baby would be born. He, the promised *"Seed,"* would be the one to conquer the Serpent.

The Gospel obligates us to believe, then, that it was necessary for Christ to come in the form of *human* seed. That is, He took on full humanity. He is not an angel, sent from Heaven, lacking a human nature. He is not merely a wise teacher, telling us how to be saved. Rather, Christ is God in human flesh. The Son of God took on full humanity when He was conceived in the womb of Mary.

It had to be this way. It was necessary for Him to come in the form of *human* seed. For, the Serpent had beguiled *humans*. Having deceived Adam and Eve, the Serpent now held the power of death over their heads. They, the humans, had defiled God's glory and thus condemned themselves. Animal sacrifices would be made for them, in order to provide clothing for them, but only a *truly human* sacrifice, and a *sinless, divine* one at that, would ever be able to make satisfaction for their sins.

Yet there is more. Just as the Serpent *defeated* the first Adam, a *human*, so did God ordain that the Serpent would *be defeated* by the second Adam, *the Son of God in human flesh.* He, the Serpent, preyed upon man. By a Man, then, the Son of Man, was his demise predestined. The Serpent outwitted the first Adam, who was created *in* God's image. Yet the Serpent would, in time, be crushed by the second Adam, who is *the very Image* of God.

You Shall Bruise His Heel

An Enmity that Leads to Two Wounds

In the Gospel of God, there are two Kingdoms, and two Seeds. There is the Kingdom of the Serpent, whose citizens are the Serpent's seed. There is also the Kingdom of God, whose citizens are of the seed of Christ. And these foes are always at enmity with each other. The Kingdom of God is always at war with the Kingdom of Satan. And the Serpent's seed is always at enmity with Christ's own seed.

Where, then, does this enmity lead? If this is a war, then what casualties come forth from it? There are, as we have said, two warring kingdoms, and two warring seeds. And out of these cosmic sets of two come two horrible wounds. Two kings clash in battle. Two horrible wounds come out of that clash:

*"I will put [enmity] between you and the woman, and between your [seed] and her [seed]. He will **bruise your head**, and you will **bruise his heel**."* (Genesis 3:15)

The Serpent strikes at the heel of Christ. He, the belly-crawler, is condemned always to strike *from the dust*. He deceived Adam and Eve into *eating* the forbidden fruit. Therefore, he must crawl on his belly, and *eat* the dust of the earth. Even at the end of the age, it must be so:

*"The wolf and the lamb will feed together, and the lion will eat straw like the ox. **Dust will be the serpent's food**. They will not hurt nor destroy in all My holy mountain," says the LORD.* (Isaiah 65:25)

That cursed Serpent, God says, must eat dust. Yet from the dust, he strikes upwards, at the Christian heel. He brings sicknesses upon men, and pierces them with thorns in the flesh. He stops missionaries from arriving at their planned destinations, and casts the faithful into prison. He is sly, and crafty, injecting his poison into the Church body through the deadly fangs of his false preachers and teachers. Ultimately, with his sending of the Antichrist, the Serpent will disguise his evil nature in the form of a man who pretends to be Jesus, but is not [Revelation 13:11].

At Calvary, then, two kings clashed in battle. The Serpent, who is the king of this world, clashed with Christ, who is King of Heaven and earth. And the Serpent wounded Christ with a horrible wound. He crushed His heel. He sent an iron spike through the very heels of Jesus, nailing Him to a Roman cross. God, the Father, wept as the Serpent crushed the heel of His beloved Son. The Serpent struck Him, even to death on a cross.

Yet Christ, the King, struck back. On the cross, Christ lifted up His heel over the head of the Serpent, and stamped down upon that diabolical head with all of His divine might. On the cross of Calvary, Jesus crushed the Serpent's head.

Then, on the third day, when God raised Him from the dead, Jesus triumphed over the Serpent. He showed the Serpent that only one of the kings that had clashed in battle had received a timeless wound. The heel of Christ, which had been crushed, was now fully healed, restored to life and immortality through His resurrection from the dead. But the Serpent's wound remained. It was a mortal wound that would never heal. So Christ, and not the Serpent, was the Victor.

Therefore, in this present evil age, which is ruled by Satan, Christians have an imperishable hope. Our hope is founded upon the irrefutable truth that Christ has vanquished the Serpent for us. Our Lord Jesus has, in the words of Irenaeus, the great second-century bishop of Lyons, "trampled upon his head."[2] He has broken the power of the Devil's grip upon us:

> *He who sins is of the Devil, for the Devil has been sinning from the beginning.* ***To this end the Son of God was revealed: that He might destroy the works of the Devil.*** *Whoever is born of God does not commit sin,* ***because His seed remains in him;*** *and he cannot sin, because he is born of God.* (1 John 3:8–9)

Christians, then, need not fear the Serpent any longer:

> *You will tread on the lion and cobra. You will trample the young lion* ***and the serpent underfoot.*** (Psalm 91:13)

---

[2] Irenaeus, *Against Heresies* 5.21.1 [*ANF* 1:548].

And, in the Words of our Lord from the Gospels:

*"Behold, I give you authority **to tread on serpents and scorpions**, and over all the power of the enemy. Nothing will in any way hurt you."* (Luke 10:19)

God has prepared an everlasting fire for the Devil and his angels. Christians, today, need this truth. For we live in a world in which it seems that Satan is winning. We feel the horrific pain of the Serpent biting the Church, and crushing the heels of the Church. Our brothers and sisters in Eritrea and Pakistan languish in prison, separated for many years from their families and their churches, and no liberation comes to them. Christian mothers in China live through the indescribable horror of having their beloved babies forcibly aborted by Chinese government authorities, and yet the horror of forced family planning in China does not end. False teaching and carnal compromise are rending and destroying the Church in the West. In all of this, then, it becomes rather easy to despair and to think to oneself, "It feels as if Satan is going to win."

Yet the remnant, the seed of Christ, which perseveres through all trials and tribulations, no matter the cost, knows certain things about the future, as foretold by the Scriptures, which promise the defeat of Satan. Christ came the first time to inflict a mortal wound upon the head of the Serpent. But Christ also has promised to return to earth, to finish the good fight. This time, upon the Second Coming of Christ, He will crush the Serpent's head completely.

Dear Christian, whose side are you on? Are you trying to hide yourself amongst the ranks of the Serpent's seed, so that you do not stand out from the crowd and thus face persecution? Are you afraid to declare war, publicly, on the wicked ways of this world, since you know, deep down, that waging war against the Devil will cost you dearly? Are you ashamed to call yourself a soldier of Christ Jesus, since you know that identifying with Christ, in a bold and outspoken fashion, but always with meekness, will bring the hatred of the world against you?

Or instead, dear Christian, are you, right now, in the very throes of suffering and persecution? Have you sided with Christ, and taken up your sword in battle, and are you now suffering as a good soldier of Christ Jesus? Is the pain greater than you had anticipated that it would be? Are the financial hardships worse than you had estimated? Do the losses of loved ones feel like wounds that will never heal? Does the loneliness of the fight seem too much for you to bear?

If this is your case, beloved Brother or Sister in Christ, then hold fast to the hope that He who is the Victor over the Serpent is also your coming Savior. He died for you. He has loved you, and does now love you beyond ineffably more than you can know—for His love surpasses knowledge. And He who loves you in such an immeasurable way also collects your tears and gathers them into His wineskin. As you commit your soul to Him, as to a faithful Creator, while you suffer, the Father of glory commissions His risen and ascended Son to prepare a place for you in His own Heavenly abode. Therefore, Christ Jesus shall come, indeed, to rescue you, and to bring you into His everlasting glory:

And the God of peace **will quickly crush Satan under your feet**. *The grace of our Lord Jesus Christ be with you.*
(Romans 16:20)

And thus Christ Jesus shall be praised and adored as the Victor of Heaven, unto the glory of God the Father, forever and ever, ages unto ages, world without end. Amen.

2

GOD WILL PROVIDE HIMSELF THE LAMB
The Cross in Genesis 22:1-19

After these things, God tested Abraham, and said to him, "Abraham!" He said, "Here I am." He said, "Now take your son, your only son, Isaac, whom you love, and go into the land of Moriah. Offer him there as a burnt offering on one of the mountains which I will tell you of." Abraham rose early in the morning, and saddled his donkey; and took two of his young men with him, and Isaac his son. He split the wood for the burnt offering, and rose up, and went to the place of which God had told him. On the third day Abraham lifted up his eyes, and saw the place far off. Abraham said to his young men, "Stay here with the donkey. The boy and I will go over there. We will worship, and come back to you." Abraham took the wood of the burnt offering and laid it on Isaac his son. He took in his hand the fire and the knife. They both went together. Isaac spoke to Abraham his father, and said, "My father?" He said, "Here I am, my son." He said, "Here is the fire and the wood, but where is the lamb for a burnt offering?" Abraham said, "God will provide Himself the lamb for a burnt offering, my son." So they both went together.
(Genesis 22:1–8)

GOD tests Abraham. He interrupts Abraham's affairs, intrudes upon his situational serenity, and initiates a great test for His servant. For, it is not God's way to allow His bondservants to stroll through life untroubled by trials. Instead, the Lord Himself, being zealous for the proving of our faith—which is *"more precious than gold that perishes even though it is **tested by fire**"*

(1 Peter 1:7)—constantly trains our faith by testing both its purity and its persevering strength.

Thus God tests Abraham, just as He will later test the children of Israel. In the wilderness, at Marah, God will test Israel with the bitter waters that are made sweet by a tree, once Moses casts the tree into the waters, and He will call Israel to give ear to His commandments and to keep all His statutes. Again in the wilderness, this time at the Wilderness of Sin, God will test Israel with hunger. He will see whether or not they will be obedient to gather the miracle bread from Heaven on six days only, and to rest on the seventh day. The test, then, will be whether Israel will walk in His Law, or not.

Around seven hundred years after Moses, God will test Hezekiah, King of Judah. When the ambassadors of the princes of Babylon, that wicked land, come to make an alliance with Hezekiah, bringing him gifts, God will surely *"[withdraw] from him, **in order to test him**, that He might know all that [is] in his heart"* (2 Chronicles 32:31, NKJV). Yet Hezekiah, full of that foolish pride that always comes before a fall, will fail this particularly test.

To be sure, God tempts no one to sin: *"for God cannot be tempted by evil, and He Himself tempts no one"* (James 1:13). Yet the Lord does indeed test us for our own good:

Examine me, O LORD, and prove me.
Try my heart and my mind. (Psalm 26:2)

Precious Brethren, do you, then, count it all joy whenever you fall into various kinds of testing? Does not tribulation work out perseverance for you? And does not perseverance finish its work only by making you perfect and complete, and lacking nothing? So if the Devil were to test you by throwing some of you into prison, giving you tribulation for ten days, would you be completely bewildered by such a test? Would you not, rather, accept the test as being from God, and allow it to sanctify you in order to prepare you for the coming, everlasting crown of life?

Biblical faith is not stationary. By its very nature, it cannot accommodate the sinful flesh. Therefore, God tests our faith in order to keep it actively exercised and strengthened. This precious, saving faith is that very faith which is constantly tested by God, and even severely so, for our own good, our own sanctification. It is, then, God's love for us that tests our faith, and it is our love for God that clings to Him throughout the duration of the cross-bearing, pain-soaked test.

ABRAHAM'S MIGHTY FAITH

Without faith it is impossible to please God, and Abraham's aim is to please God. Therefore, this present account of Abraham and Isaac, as towering as it is amongst the Gospel prophecies of Christ in the history of the ancient Hebrews, is not about Abraham as a particular man of courage, or of daringness. Instead, this present account is concerned, in the main, with Abraham's *faith*. It is, no doubt, the holy record of the mightiness of the *faith* of this special servant of God:

After these things, God tested Abraham, and said to him, ***"Abraham!"*** *He said,* ***"Here I am."*** (Genesis 22:1)

This is the language of mighty faith, namely, the response of Abraham, *"Here I am."* For, whenever God summons a man by name, it is only the man of mighty faith who responds with these words, *"Here I am."* This is how Abraham responds to Isaac, even in the hottest part of this fiery test:

Isaac spoke to Abraham his father, and said, ***"My father?"*** *He said,* ***"Here I am***, *my son." He said, "Here is the fire and the wood, but where is the lamb for a burnt offering?"*
(Genesis 22:7)

This is also how Abraham responds, once again, to the Lord, even when Abraham has grasped the knife in preparation for slaughtering his only son, Isaac:

The LORD's Angel called to him out of the sky, and said, ***"Abraham, Abraham!"*** *He said,* ***"Here I am."***
(Genesis 22:11)

Abraham, then, is most certainly the Father of Faith. This is not to say that Adam, Seth, Enoch, and Noah, before him, were not mighty men of faith. It is, however, a historical declaration that because of Abraham's great test, here, with knife in hand, and how Abraham responded to the test by saying to God, *"Here I am,"* he has become the father of all those who believe:

God spoke to Israel in the visions of the night, and said, ***"Jacob, Jacob!"*** *He said,* ***"Here I am."*** *He said, "I am God, the God of your father. Do not be afraid to go down into Egypt, for there I will make of you a great nation."* (Genesis 46:2–3)

And, in the call of Moses:

When the L*ORD* *saw that he came over to see, God called to him out of the middle of the bush, and said,* ***"Moses! Moses!"*** *He said,* ***"Here I am."*** (Exodus 3:4)

And also, this time in the case of Samuel,

...the L*ORD* ***called Samuel****. He said,* ***"Here I am!"***
(1 Samuel 3:4)

And again, yet now in the life of the Prophet Isaiah:

I heard the Lord's voice, saying, ***"Whom shall I send****, and who will go for us?" Then I said,* ***"Here I am****. Send me!"* (Isaiah 6:8)

And once more, this time concerning Ananias, called by God to baptize Saul of Tarsus:

Now there was a certain disciple at Damascus named Ananias. The Lord said to him in a vision, ***"Ananias!"*** *He said,* ***"[Here I am], Lord."*** (Acts 9:10)

Abraham is the father of all of these mighty men of faith. He says to God, *"Here I am,"* and all of these great men simply follow in his footsteps.

Yet consider how great a test it is to which Abraham is here subjected. For, the Lord previously had promised him a countless multitude of descendants, and that only through Isaac, the miracle-child of the promise. However, now the Lord God has commanded Abraham to offer up Isaac as a whole-burnt offering to Him, and this even long before Isaac himself has any children of his own. How, then, can the promise of God be fulfilled? If Abraham is to sacrifice his only-begotten son by Sarah, his beloved son, how can Isaac ever father a countless multitude of sons?

Again, we witness the mightiness of Abraham's faith here. For, he leaves his young men behind, taking Isaac alone to the place of sacrifice. However, when he bids farewell to the young men, he promises that both he *and Isaac* will return to them:

> *And Abraham said to his young men, "Stay here with the donkey; the lad and I will go yonder **and worship*** [Do you see? Worship is about sacrifice, since we are to present our bodies to God as living sacrifices, holy and acceptable to Him!], ***and we*** [not "I," but "we"!] ***will [return] to you."*** (Genesis 22:5, NKJV)

How does Abraham know that both he *and Isaac* will return from the sacrifice? He only knows this by faith, since God already has promised him, saying, *"For **your [seed]** will be named **through Isaac"*** (Genesis 21:12). Does Abraham, then, foresee that God will intervene and not allow him to go through with the sacrifice? Not at all, but rather the book of Hebrews says:

> ***[Abraham reasoned] that God is able to raise up even from the dead.*** *Figuratively speaking, he also did receive him back from the dead.* (Hebrews 11:19)

This is mighty faith, that Abraham both believes God's promise regarding Isaac and, at the same time, is willing to sacrifice Isaac on the altar of God before that promise has been fulfilled. Therefore, since Abraham exercises such mighty faith in

God, obeying God contrary to all earthly-mindedness, the Lord honors his faith by allowing him to fulfill his word to the young men, namely, that both he *and Isaac* would *"return"* to them:

> *So Abraham **returned** to his young men* [that is, with Isaac beside him!], *and they rose up and went together to Beersheba. Abraham lived at Beersheba.* (Genesis 22:19)

How blessed, then, is Abraham's name in the Kingdom of Heaven! For, his name means, "Father of a Multitude."[1] The Lord God promised him that if he was able to count the stars in the heavens, only then would he be able to count his seed. And he believed this Word from the Lord, and the Lord *"credited it to him for righteousness"* (Genesis 15:6). Also, God promised Abraham that his descendants would be as innumerable as the dust of the earth. Abraham believed this, even when the Lord called him to sacrifice Isaac on the altar, and so now God reaffirms His promise to Abraham:

> ***"...I will bless you greatly, and I will multiply your offspring greatly like the stars of the heavens, and like the sand which is on the seashore.*** *Your offspring will possess the gate of his enemies. All the nations of the earth will be blessed by your offspring, because you have obeyed My voice."*
> (Genesis 22:17–18)

Abraham believes God and obeys God, being willing even to offer up his *only seed*, his *beloved seed*, Isaac, as an offering to God. Therefore, God, in the subsequent history of mankind, *multiplies Abraham's seed immeasurably*. He first multiplies the seed of Abraham through Israel, such that the seed of Israel cannot be numbered, and then he multiples the seed of Abraham through the Gentiles, by calling so many Gentiles into the mystery of the Gospel of Christ that the Gentile believers become as numerous as the sand of the seashore. In this way, Abraham, by faith, has

---

[1] The present author's view is that *'Abrāhām* is a contraction of *'Abrām* ("Exalted Father") and *Hāmôn* ("Multitude"), or, in Hebrew: (אַבְרָהָם ← הָמוֹן + אַבְרָם).

become *"the father of us all"* (Romans 4:16), in which the *"all"* represents the entirety of the elect of God, or *"all"* who are saved by faith in the Son of God.

O dear Church of the living God, there is the great problem of the diminishing *"godly seed"* in the midst of our local churches. The Prophet Malachi says that the Lord *"seeks godly seed"* (Malachi 2:15, NJKV), and yet such a *"godly seed"* is diminishing in our churches both because of the cowardly, faithless sin of contraception in the churches, and also because of the generational apostasy that is taking place amongst the younger generations in the churches.

What, then, is the answer to this great problem of the diminishing *"godly seed"* in the churches? It is *the God-fearing faith* of Abraham. For, once Abraham has put his faith in God by readying himself to sacrifice Isaac as an offering to the Lord, God says to Abraham, *"For now I know that **you fear God**...."* (Genesis 22:12). Therefore, it is Abraham's *God-fearing faith* which brings the blessing of the *"godly seed"* of faith to the nations.

Not at all implying that all God-fearing parents will automatically have regenerate adult children, since many God-fearing parents are asked by God to bear the heavy cross of betrayal which Christ first bore when Judas betrayed Him, we nevertheless gravely warn the members of the Church, with tears, that without a God-fearing faith being taught to them by their own parents, the children of our churches will certainly become the plunder of Satan's violent armies. We are commanded by Holy Scripture, then, both to pray for an overflowing abundance of children of our own, and also to call our own children, by the calling of a truly *God-fearing* faith, out from the midst of Babylon, out from the corrupting ways of a sinfully corrupt world, and onto the sacrificial altar of the Gospel, on which they must learn how to become *"living sacrifice[s], holy [and] acceptable to God"* (Romans 12:1). It is then, and only then, that the promise will apply to us, as God-fearing parents of faith, and to our seed, as God-fearing children of faith:

> *For most certainly, He does not give help to angels, **but He gives help to the [seed] of Abraham**.* (Hebrews 2:16)

PROPHECIES OF THE CROSS

HIS ONLY-BEGOTTEN SON

Yet the substance of a God-fearing faith must behold the Lamb of God. Since all have sinned and fallen short of the glory of God, all are in need of the wrath-appeasing Lamb of God. Being children of wrath prior to our conversion, even all of us who are now in Christ were in need of the Lamb to bear the Lord's wrath against sin, in our stead.

Abraham has taken hold of the knife. Isaac is about to bear the deadly pain of the sharp tip of the knife. Yet God will provide for Himself the lamb for the burnt offering *in Isaac's stead*:

Abraham took the wood of the burnt offering and laid it on Isaac his son. He took in his hand the fire and the knife. They both went together. Isaac spoke to Abraham his father, and said, "My father?" He said, "Here I am, my son." He said, "Here is the fire and the wood, **but where is the lamb for a burnt offering?***" Abraham said,* **"God will provide Himself the lamb** *for a burnt offering, my son." So they both went together.* (Genesis 22:6–8)

And,

Abraham lifted up his eyes, and looked, and saw that behind him was **a ram** *caught in the thicket by his horns. Abraham went and took the ram, and offered him up for a burnt offering* **instead of** *his son.* (Genesis 22:13)

Do you see in this precious verse, Genesis 22:13, these colossal, Gospel Words, *"instead of"*? The lamb is slaughtered *"instead of"* Abraham's son, Isaac. The lamb, then, is a "substitutionary" sacrifice. This is the great, colossal doctrine of the "substitutionary atonement" of Christ Jesus:

For Him who knew no sin **He made to be sin on our behalf***; so that in Him we might become the righteousness of God.* (2 Corinthians 5:21)

And also,

> ***He Himself bore our sins in His body on the tree***, *that we, having died to sins, might live to righteousness. You were healed by His wounds.* (1 Peter 2:24)

Substitutionary atonement, which is the doctrine that Christ *substituted* His own, *sinless* body in the place of our own, *sinful* bodies, on the cross, in order to quench the fire of God's wrath against our sins with the fire-quenching flow of His own blood, is not peripheral to the Gospel, but rather at its very heart. Abraham lifts his eyes, and, the Scripture says, **"Behold!"** Abraham sees **"a ram"** caught in a thicket by its horns. Likewise, John the Baptist sees Jesus coming towards him, and says, **"Behold! The Lamb of God who takes away the sin of the world!"** (John 1:29).

Moreover, Isaac is Abraham's *"only-begotten"* son, and this carries us, like a straight arrow shot, swiftly and directly to the Gospel of Christ:

> *By faith Abraham, when he was tested, offered up Isaac, and he who had received the promises offered up **his only-begotten son**....* (Hebrews 11:17, NKJV)

Abraham's love for Isaac is extremely deep, for Isaac is his only-begotten son. Yet God's love for Jesus Christ is *infinitely* deep, for the Lord Jesus is God's *eternally-only-begotten* Son. If Abraham's love for Isaac is a gushing river, then the Father's love for Jesus Christ is an infinite ocean. If Abraham's tears for Isaac are flowing streams, then the Father's tears for His only-begotten Son are celestial torrents of flooding rain:

> *For God so loved the world that **He gave His only-begotten Son**, that whoever believes in Him should not perish but have everlasting life.* (John 3:16, NKJV)

And,

In this the love of God was manifested toward us, **that God has sent His only-begotten Son into the world**, *that we might live through Him.* (1 John 4:9, NKJV)

To get at the divine love of this, think upon Mount Moriah. Abraham takes his only-begotten son, Isaac, atop Mount Moriah. There, he obeys God and prepares to sacrifice Isaac as a whole-burnt offering. Yet later on in Israel's history, Solomon builds the Temple of the Lord at Jerusalem *"on Mount Moriah"* (2 Chronicles 3:1). Thus in Jesus' day, the Passover lambs are sacrificed in the Temple, on Mount Moriah, even while Jesus is crucified outside of the city gates, on Mount Calvary, as the true Lamb of God who takes away the sins of the world.

Even more, think upon God's love for His only-begotten Son in this way, that Isaac spoke to Abraham his father and said, *"My father!"* How sharply did Abraham's heart break to hear these words! How tellingly did his voice tremble with love when he answered, *"Here I am, my son"*! When Isaac obeyed Abraham, and voluntarily stretched himself out to be bound by the cords, how tenderly and overflowingly did Abraham marvel at his son! The same eyes that he had seen when he held his baby boy in his arms, he now saw trusting him, even as he raised the knife over him. Who, then, can describe the magnitude of this love between such a God-fearing father and such a God-fearing son?

Yet now think upon Jesus, nailed to the cross, with no lamb to take His place, for He is the Lamb of God. He is screaming in pain. His body is convulsing in pain, and His soul is in greater anguish than the sum total of all suffering and pain that has ever been known by all other men in all of world history. For, He feels forsaken by His Father, His glorious Father whom He has known for an eternity, and with whom He shared eternal glory before the foundation of the world.

Then, when the work of suffering for the sins of the world is finished, and the Father's wrath against those sins is satisfied, He cries out and His Father hears Him. The Father's Son, His only-begotten Son, whom He loves with a love that far exceeds the bounds of all human comprehension and understanding, being a love that is beyond immeasurably greater than the sum total of all of the true, godly love between husbands and wives, fathers and sons, mothers and daughters, and fellow brothers and sisters, that ever has existed since the creation of man, cries out to His Father and says, *"Father! Into Your hands I commit My spirit!"* and the Father's heart roars with ten million times the volume of ten million giant waterfalls full of love for His only-begotten Son, and He opens His bosom to Him, and receives Him back into Paradise, and, after the resurrection and the ascension, seats Him upon His own Throne, at His right hand of majesty, with all of the angels bowing before His holy Divinity and Kingship, and all of the saints of ancient Israel who are in Heaven—including Abraham, Isaac, and Jacob!—falling down upon their faces to pay trembling, joy-soaked homage to their Lord and their God.

ABRAHAM'S REWARD

We are pierced by this love! The Gospel pierces our hearts with God's love! Abraham has been willing to offer Isaac, and God has provided for Himself the Lamb, in Isaac's stead. All that remains, then, is to taste of the sweetness of Abraham's reward:

> *The LORD's Angel called to Abraham a second time out of the sky, and said, "'I have sworn by Myself,' says the LORD, 'because you have done this thing, and have not withheld your son, your only son,* **that I will bless you greatly, and I will multiply your [seed] greatly like the stars of the heavens, and like the sand which is on the seashore. Your [seed] will possess the gate of his enemies. All the nations of the earth will be blessed by your [seed], because you have obeyed My voice.**'" *So Abraham returned to his young men, and they rose up and went together to Beersheba. Abraham lived at Beersheba.* (Genesis 22:15–19)

Psalm 127 says that the fruit of the womb is a reward, that the man who has his quiver full of them is blessed, and also that they shall not be ashamed, but shall *"speak with their enemies in the gate"* (v. 5). What shall we say, then, of Abraham, whose seed shall *"possess the gate of his enemies"* (Genesis 22:17)? If the man with a full quiver is blessed, what about the man whose seed is multiplied *"like the stars of the heavens, and like the sand which is on the seashore"* (v. 17, again)?

More than that, Abraham's reward is a missionary's reward. For, God says that in his seed *"all the nations of the earth will be blessed"* (v. 18), which is the fulfillment of God's earliest blessing upon Abraham in Genesis 12:

> *Now the* LORD *said to Abram, "Leave your country, and your relatives, and your father's house, and go to the land that I will show you. I will make of you a great nation. I will bless you and make your name great. You will be a blessing. I will bless those who bless you, and I will curse him who treats you with contempt.* ***All the families of the earth will be blessed through you****."* (Genesis 12:1–3)

The seed of Abraham is a countless seed. As a missionary seed, it has won worshippers of God from all of the nations of the earth. How much more, then, is Christ Jesus deserving of His reward, and of His seed amongst all the nations!

> *Yet it pleased the* LORD *to bruise Him. He has caused Him to suffer. When You make His soul an offering for sin,* ***He will see His [seed]****. He will prolong His days and the* LORD*'s pleasure will prosper in His hand. After the suffering of His soul, He will see the light and be satisfied. My righteous servant will justify* ***many*** *by the knowledge of Himself; and He will bear their iniquities.* (Isaiah 53:10–11)

And also,

> *His name endures forever. His name continues as long as the sun. Men shall be blessed by Him.* ***All nations will call Him blessed****.* (Psalm 72:17)

Abraham's reward, then, is very much about world missions. For, in world missions, we gather Abraham's seed from all the four corners of the earth. Therefore, world missions, no matter how costly or how painful, is certainly worth the expenditure of one's strength and one's very life:

If you are Christ's, **then you are Abraham's [seed]** *and heirs according to promise.* (Galatians 3:29)

    Yet again, if world missions brings in the harvest of Abraham's seed, once it has been sown, has sprouted, and has grown fully ripe for the harvest, how much more shall the Second Coming of Christ bring in the final harvest of Christ's own seed, which is His own reward! For, our Lord Jesus Christ shall have His reward. The Lamb who was slain, who loved us and washed us from our sins in His own blood, shall have His seed as His reward. Even as the stars of the heavens or the sand on the seashore, the offspring of Christ, the little lambs of Heaven who follow the Lamb of God wherever He leads them, allowing Him to shepherd them in perfect love, shall be His reward. And as His reward, they shall praise Him forever and ever, a countless multitude, singing of His exaltation, majesty, worthiness, and glory:

After these things I looked, **and behold, a great multitude, which no man could count, out of every nation and of all tribes, peoples, and languages, standing before the throne and before the Lamb***, dressed in white robes, with palm branches in their hands. They cried with a loud voice, saying, "Salvation be to our God, who sits on the throne, and to the Lamb!"* (Revelation 7:9–10)

    And this song shall go on in Heaven forever and ever, world without end. Amen.

3

THE PASSOVER LAMB
The Cross in Exodus 12:1-6

The LORD spoke to Moses and Aaron in the land of Egypt, saying, "This month shall be to you the beginning of months. It shall be the first month of the year to you. Speak to all the congregation of Israel, saying, 'On the tenth day of this month, they shall take to them every man a lamb, according to their fathers' houses, a lamb for a household; and if the household is too little for a lamb, then he and his neighbor next to his house shall take one according to the number of the souls; according to what everyone can eat you shall make your count for the lamb. Your lamb shall be without defect, a male a year old. You shall take it from the sheep, or from the goats: and you shall keep it until the fourteenth day of the same month; and the whole assembly of the congregation of Israel shall kill it at evening.'" (Exodus 12:1–6)

GOD makes the Passover month the *first* month of the year in ancient Israel. Time is important to the Lord our God. He created the sun, moon, and stars on the fourth day of the creation week to mark signs and seasons, and also days and years. God keeps an orderly calendar of world history through the earth's yearly revolutions around the sun, and thus annual calendar markers, such as seasons and holiday festivals, are very important in the Holy Scriptures.

In the Israelite calendar, as commanded by Scripture, there are holy feasts that serve to commemorate and define God's covenant with His people Israel. There are the golden-white fields of grain and the oven-baked aromas of barley cakes that signify the Feast of

Pentecost, in the third month. Then, after the summer is over, there are the crowded clusters of grapes and bright, blushing pomegranates spilling out of harvest baskets—and also the olive presses dripping with fresh, juicy oil, and the wine presses flowing with dark-crimson streams—all of which mark the end of the harvest season through the celebration of the Feast of Tabernacles, in the seventh month of the year.

Yet the *Passover* feast is so uniquely important that it marks the very beginning of the year. Its presence in the Israelite month of *'Abib* is of such tremendous weight that it makes the month of *'Abib* the very first month of the year for the Israelites. Thus God has chosen the Passover to be the sign of the beginning of all saving faith. That is, true faith, which is the only saving faith, begins not with harvest blessings or ripe thanksgivings. Burgundy tree leaves and hot ciders cannot, in themselves, awaken the sinful human heart to God. Instead, it is *blood*, the blood of a perfect, unblemished sacrifice for sins, which alone *must come first*. Passover is about slaughter and death. It is a sign of blood on the doorposts and doorframes of the elect. This, and nothing else, marks the beginning of new life in Israel.

The Gospel, then, must come first. The Gospel of *"Christ crucified"* marks the beginning of life for the Christian. Without the Gospel, all are alienated from God, being enemies of God on account of their wicked works, and thus are dead in their sins and trespasses. Unless a man is born again, and thus made new—*"born not of blood, nor of the will of the flesh, nor of the will of man, but of God"* (John 1:13)—He cannot enter into the Kingdom of God. Yet in the Gospel, there is a new beginning. All of life begins anew for the broken-hearted, repentant man who has learned to die to sin and to live for righteousness through the Gospel:

*Therefore if anyone is in Christ, he is **a new creation**. The old things have passed away. Behold, all things **have become new**.* (2 Corinthians 5:17)

In ancient Israel, Passover marks the beginning of faith. In the Church, the Gospel marks that beginning. For, how can we describe the miracle of our souls being made alive to God, without marking the cross of Christ as the beginning of that miracle? We have been brought out of darkness, out of Egypt, and thus out of slavery to Satan. God has called us into His Kingdom, into His priesthood, and thus into His very Kingdom of light. We who formerly were not His people, are now called His people. We who had not received His Gospel mercy, now are the recipients of that mercy. Yet did this not begin, in our lives, at the cross? Was it not Christ lifted up, Christ crucified, that drew us to bow down and worship His glory? Was it not the blood sacrifice of Jesus Christ that preceded our new nature and our new heart, with which we now have a new love for all of the things of our new life in God?

O precious Church, this is the difference between death and life to us! For, according to the darkened understanding of the sons of this world, life begins by being dead to God and alive to sin. Satan said to the woman, *"You will not surely die"* (Genesis 3:4), and ever since then sinful man has believed the lie that sin brings life. Yet being dead to God and alive to sin is not the path to life. It is, rather, the path to everlasting judgment and torment in Hell. Sin brings death, not life, to those who love it and practice it.

Yet according to the Gospel, life begins by being dead to sin and alive to God. The beginning of everlasting life is not found in the world, for the world is steeped in sin, and sin leads to death. Rather, the beginning of everlasting life, which alone contains the very first things of true light and true hope, is found at the place of Christ's blood-soaked cross. Everlasting life *begins here*, and nowhere else, and thus no matter how horribly the world may threaten us, or what diabolical lies and deadly instruments it may use to persecute us, we shall never stop preaching, *"Jesus Christ and Him crucified"* (1 Corinthians 2:2). For, this alone is the wisdom of God, and this alone is the power of God, namely, that Christ was *"led as a lamb to the slaughter, and as a sheep before its shearers is silent, so He opened not His mouth"* (Isaiah 53:7).[1]

EATING THE FLESH OF THE PASSOVER LAMB

Where does everlasting life begin for us? It begins in the springtime of the heart of the broken, repentant sinner. It sprouts

---

[1] NKJV translation.

and blooms only with the Gospel. True life begins only with the *death* of the Passover Lamb, and the *eating* of the Passover Lamb:

> *"Speak to all the congregation of Israel, saying, 'On the tenth day of this month, they shall take to them every man a lamb, according to their fathers' houses, a lamb for a household; and if the household is too little for a lamb, then he and his neighbor next to his house shall take one according to the number of the souls; according to what everyone can eat you shall make your count for the lamb. Your lamb shall be without defect, a male a year old. You shall take it from the sheep, or from the goats: and you shall keep it until the fourteenth day of the same month; and the whole assembly of the congregation of Israel* **shall kill it** *at evening..... They shall* **eat the flesh** *in that night, roasted with fire, and unleavened bread. They shall* **eat it** *with bitter herbs.'"* (Exodus 12:3–6, 8)

Still, we ask: how is it that eating the lamb that has been slain brings life to the eater? To understand this, we must first remember that it was the act of *"eating"* that originally brought *"death"* to Adam and Eve:

> [God warns Adam:] *"...but you shall not eat of the tree of the knowledge of good and evil;* **for in the day that you eat of it, you will surely die.***"* (Genesis 2:17)

And yet,

> *The serpent said to the woman, "You* **will not surely die***, for God knows that in the day* **you eat it***, your eyes will be opened, and you will be like God, knowing good and evil."* (Genesis 3:4–5)

It was that original sin of eating from the Tree of the Knowledge of Good and Evil that brought death into the world. Eve took of the fruit of sin, *and ate*. Then, she gave some of it to her husband, who was with her, and *he ate*, and thus both Adam and Eve died. Ever since then, all of the descendants of Adam have been eating of sin, and thus have been subjecting themselves to death through the eating of it. Yet in his sinful madness, the depraved mind of depraved man thinks that the eating of the fruits of sin is a delightful act, even a jovial act, assuming that such a life of sinful indulgence ends in a peaceful death, rather than a death of judgment and everlasting suffering in fire and brimstone:

> *In that day, the Lord, GOD of Hosts, called to weeping, and to mourning, and to baldness, and to dressing in sackcloth: and behold, joy and gladness, killing cattle and killing sheep, **eating flesh** and drinking wine: "**Let us eat** and drink, **for tomorrow we will die**." The LORD of Hosts revealed Himself in my ears, "Surely this iniquity will not be forgiven you **until you die**," says the Lord, GOD of Hosts.* (Isaiah 22:12–14)

It was a *sinful eating* that brought *death* into the world. Therefore, redemptively, God has ordained that it is only a *sacrificial eating* that brings *life* into the world. By eating of the fruit of sin, man died. Yet by eating of the true Passover Lamb, man may live forever:

> *On the first day of Unleavened Bread, **when they sacrificed the Passover**, His disciples asked Him, "Where do You want us to go and prepare that You may **eat the Passover**?"* (Mark 14:12)

This is a wondrous thought, that Jesus would eat the Passover lamb with His disciples. For, the animal, the lamb, was merely a sacrifice to nourish the flesh and to be a type of the true Lamb of God, sacrificed for the sins of the world. Yet Jesus *is* the Lamb of God who takes away the sins of the world. Therefore, in order to eat the Passover in true faith, for the saving of our souls, we must eat of the true Passover Lamb, who is Jesus Christ Himself:

> *Jesus therefore said to them, "Most certainly I tell you, **unless you eat the flesh of the Son of Man** and drink His blood, you do not have life in yourselves. **He who eats My flesh** and drinks My blood **has eternal life**, and I will raise him up at the Last Day."* (John 6:53–54)

And,

> *...knowing that you were redeemed, not with corruptible things, with silver or gold, from the useless way of life handed down from your fathers,* **but with precious blood, as of a faultless and pure lamb, the blood of Christ.** (1 Peter 1:18–19)

How, then, do we keep the true Passover of God? We do so only by faith in Jesus Christ as the true, uncreated, eternal Son of God:

> *Purge out the old yeast, that you may be a new lump, even as you are unleavened.* **For indeed Christ, our Passover, has been sacrificed in our place.** (1 Corinthians 5:7)

By eating of the fruit of sin, we all died. Yet by eating of Christ, our Passover Lamb, we can be made alive. He tasted death for us, in our place. Moreover, having risen from the dead on the third day, He has abolished death for us, and brought life and immortality to light through His glorious Gospel. Therefore, whenever we think upon the Lamb, slain for our sins, we who are born of His Holy Spirit are compelled to bow down and worship Him. We follow the example of those ancient Israelites who feared God, who, upon hearing of the commandments concerning the Passover, responded to the humbling news of the slaughter of the Passover lamb by bowing down in worship before the Lord:

> *"It will happen, when your children ask you, 'What do you mean by this service?' that you shall say, 'It is the sacrifice of the LORD's Passover, who passed over the houses of the children of Israel in Egypt, when He struck the Egyptians, and spared our houses.'"* **The people bowed their heads and worshiped.** (Exodus 12:26–27)

In like manner, we bow before God and worship the Lamb who was slain for our everlasting redemption:

*Now when he had taken the book, **the four living creatures and the twenty-four elders fell down before the Lamb**, each one having a harp, and golden bowls full of incense, which are the prayers of the saints. They sang a new song, saying, "You are worthy to take the book, and to open its seals: for You were [slain], and bought us for God with Your blood, out of every tribe, language, people, and nation, and made [them] kings and priests to our God, and [they] will reign on earth."*
(Revelation 5:8–10)

    Thus we say to the unconverted, "O faithless and unbelieving generation, why are you still feeding upon sin, thinking that by it you may attain to life? Do you not know? Have you not heard? Has it not been told to you that those who eat of the Tree of the Knowledge of Good and Evil, habitually, without true, heart-rending repentance, but instead with a happy, godless appetite for sin, shall surely die? Do you not know that the worship of the creature, rather than the Creator, is both the essence of idolatry and the blasphemy of unbelief? Yet do you remain unblushing in your shameful acts of feeding upon the creature, rather than upon the Creator? If so, if you are feeding upon the creature, even as the unbelieving Jews eat the Passover lamb without worshipping Jesus Christ, and as the Muslims eat their sacrificial meat at their Festival of Sacrifice without ascribing divine glory to the incarnate Son of God, then you are feeding upon *death*! This is not life, but *death*! For, this is not feeding upon the blood sacrifice of Jesus Christ upon the cross, feeding upon it by faith. Instead, it is eating from the tables of the antichrist religious ceremonies and pagan mystic rites that only serve to feed the insatiable appetite of human pride and rebellion against God.

    "What, then, O faithless generation, shall you eat? Shall you feed at the table of the goddess Hedonism, seeking to suck the pleasures out of the tree roots of sin to the very last drop, only to find your souls sickened and diseased by the eating of it? Or shall you eat of the meaningless tree of the false god Existentialism, seeking to create your own meaning in life by yourself defining good and evil, as if you can be your own god? Is the fruit poisonous, even mortally so, and will you continue to lust after it? Is the flesh of the fruit deadly, even everlastingly so, and will you foolishly join the multitudes of perishing souls by tearing it with your teeth and devouring it upon impulse? O senseless man or woman, even you who have been created in the image of God, when will you come to your senses? When will you be honest with yourself and say to yourself, 'It tastes of death! All this time, despite all of my proud, lying, intellectual excuses for doing so, I have been deceiving myself! I have loved sin, and by loving sin, I have been feeding upon death! Death! Death! Therefore, I am just now beginning to loathe all of this poisonous fruit, which I have eaten to my own condemnation!'?

"O wayward Sheep, since God graciously has granted you the time to do so, patiently sparing you from death even to this hour, will you repent before Him? Even this very day, while you are still breathing, and thus have not yet been summoned before the Judgment Throne of the Holy One of Heaven to receive that irrevocable sentence of everlasting damnation—even this very day of salvation, will you confess before His throne of majesty in Heaven that He would be just and right to cast you, body and soul, into Hell, for so you deserve to be thrust into the fire? And yet will you also confess that you now repent before Him, begging the forgiveness of your crimes against Him, and you now believe that He, in His love for you, sent His Lamb to die your death in your stead, on the cross, so that you might, by faith, eat of Him—of His sacrifice and His righteousness—and thus live forever?"

THE PASSOVER MEAL MUST BE EATEN IN HASTE!

The Gospel, then, demands that we eat of the one, true Passover Lamb, Jesus Christ, since there is no other name under Heaven by which we must be saved. However, the Gospel also demands our departure from this world of sin, our hasty departure out of the kingdom of this world, and thus demands that our feet make speed into the wilderness, hasting after holiness, on our way to the Promised Land of Heaven:

They shall eat the flesh in that night, roasted with fire, and unleavened bread. They shall eat it with bitter herbs. Do not eat it raw, nor boiled at all with water, but roasted with fire; with its head, its legs, and its inner parts. You shall let nothing of it remain until the morning; but that which remains of it until the morning you shall burn with fire. This is how you shall eat it: with your belt on your waist, your shoes on your feet, and your staff in your hand; **and you shall eat it in haste***: it is the LORD's Passover.* (Exodus 12:8–11)

The roasting of the meat in the fire, the eating of the meal with belts on their waists and with sandals on their feet, and the sharing of the meal with staffs in their hands—all of these things speak of haste. The Passover is eaten *with haste*; it demands the departure of the Israelites out of Egypt, and that in great haste:

They baked unleavened cakes of the dough which they brought out of Egypt; for it was not leavened, **because they were thrust out of Egypt, and could not wait, and they had not prepared any food for themselves***.* (Exodus 12:39)

To eat of the Passover sacrifice with true faith and hope in God is to depart from Egypt. For, a true Israelite cannot have his sins forgiven by the blood of the lamb, and yet desire to stay in Egypt and share in all of the hideous fornications and idolatries of Egypt. Instead, a true Israelite, in whom there is no falsehood, will be moved by the Spirit of God to flee with Moses, and thus to depart from Egypt, in order to follow Moses out into the wilderness, wherein he can be free to sacrifice to the one, true God. This is the Gospel summons. It summons the disciples of the Lord out of the world, out of sin, and thus onto the pilgrim's path that leads through the wilderness of Christian sanctification:

Leave Babylon! Flee from the Chaldeans! *With a voice of singing announce this, tell it even to the end of the earth: say, "The LORD has redeemed His servant Jacob!"* (Isaiah 48:20)

And,

Flee out of the middle of Babylon, and save every man his life; *do not be cut off in her iniquity: for it is the time of the*

LORD's vengeance; He will render to her a recompense. (Jeremiah 51:6)

And again,

*"'**Come! Come! Flee from the land of the north**,' says the LORD; 'for I have spread you abroad as the four winds of the sky,' says the LORD. '**Come, Zion! Escape, you who dwell with the daughter of Babylon**.'"* (Zechariah 2:6–7)

And, as the New Testament summons the Church,

*I heard another voice from Heaven, saying, "**Come out of her, My people**, that you have no participation in her sins, and that you do not receive of her plagues."* (Revelation 18:4)

The Gospel is a departure from this world of sin. It is a leaving behind of all that belongs to the world, a forsaking of father or mother, sister or brother, son or daughter, or of anyone who still clings to the idols of this present world, in order to follow Christ. It is letting the dead bury their own dead. The Gospel demands that Noah leave the world behind him by entering into the ark. It beckons to Lot, calling him out of Sodom, lest he die in the fire that will rain down from Heaven upon that wicked city of sodomy. It calls the faithful in Jesus' day to flee idolatrous Jerusalem, the city that crucified her own Christ, such that him who is on the housetop should not go down to take anything out of his house, and him who is in the field should not go back to get his clothes. The Gospel demands of us our departure from global Babylon, the city of harlotry, and it commands us to make this departure with all haste.

O dear, suffering Christian, now is not the time for your bodily rest. You live in a Babylonian world. You wake up every morning in the city of Sodom. You go to sleep every night with the agents of the kingdom of the Beast hunting for the true saints of God, seeking ways to persecute them, and thus to silence their preaching of the Gospel, or else to kill them. Shall you, then, seek to find your rest here? Shall you try to make peace with Babylon, so that you might rest in her idolatrous entertainments and commercial luxuries? Would not such an attempt be counted as treason against Christ Jesus, your King? As Richard Baxter says:

> Should the mariner choose his dwelling on the sea, and settle his rest in the midst of rocks, and sands, and raging tempests? Though he may adventure through all these for a commodity of worth, yet I think he takes it not for his rest. Should a soldier rest in the midst of fight, when he is in the very thickest of his enemies, and the instruments of death compass him about? I think he cares not how soon the battle is over.[2]

O suffering Friend, how, then, can you seek to find rest in the midst of this world of struggle and contest against the lies of Satan and the sinful ways of the flesh? Should you really be found by God laboring for your "dream house" in this present life, seeking your rest somewhere amongst the estates and amenities of Babylon? O no! Do not do it, dear Christian! Instead, flee from the midst of Babylon—and that with much haste, with your belt on your waist, with your shoes on your feet, and with your backpack strapped to your back—by putting into practice the Scriptural Words of the blessed Apostle Paul:

Having therefore these promises, beloved, **let us cleanse ourselves from all defilement of flesh and spirit,** *perfecting holiness in the fear of God.* (2 Corinthians 7:1)

THE ATONING BLOOD OF THE PASSOVER LAMB

Due to the carelessness of our souls, we recklessly forget that in God's relation to sinful humanity, the Gospel is as serious to Him as death itself. The biblical Gospel is not "try it out, and see if it doesn't make your life better" Christianity. That is an altogether different gospel, a heretical, man-flattering gospel. Instead, the true Gospel warns of the fierce judgment that awaits all who reject it. Regarding the Passover, it says that the sufferings of the wicked in

---

[2] Richard Baxter, *The Saints' Everlasting Rest, Unabridged* (Geanies House, Fearn, Scotland, UK: Christian Focus Publications, 1998), 458.

Hell are as awful and sharp as the shrill sounds of the entire land of Egypt crying out in lamentation over the deaths of all of the firstborn sons of Egypt:

> *For I will go through the land of Egypt in that night,* ***and will strike all the firstborn in the land of Egypt****, both man and animal. Against all the gods of Egypt I will execute judgments: I am the LORD.* (Exodus 12:12)

Judgment is upon Egypt. God's anger against her false gods and her hard-hearted unrepentance cannot be assuaged any longer. The volcano of God's fury is about to erupt. The plague of God is about to go forth and strike dead every firstborn in Egypt. And, for the Israelites, and also for all of those Egyptians who would repent and believe the Word of the God of the Israelites, there is only one way to prevent the plague of God's wrath from striking one's own home, namely, to apply the blood of the Passover lamb to the doorposts of one's own house:

> *You shall take a bunch of hyssop,* ***and dip it in the blood that is in the basin, and strike the lintel and the two door posts with the blood that is in the basin;*** *and none of you shall go out of the door of his house until the morning.* (Exodus 12:22)

The hyssop applies the blood of the lamb to the doorframes of the houses with swift, striking motions, first up-and-down, and then side-to-side, and thus in cross-shaped fashion. In this way, the houses of those who fear God are marked, or sealed, by the blood of the lamb, and thus are made exempt from the coming slaughter of the fury of God's righteous vengeance:

> *The blood shall be to you for a token on the houses where you are:* ***and when I see the blood, I will pass over you, and no plague will be on you to destroy you****, when I strike the land of Egypt.* (Exodus 12:13)

However, in Egypt, at the time of the Passover event, the land was full of idolatrous, hard-hearted Egyptian households who would not heed the commandment to celebrate the Passover, and thus to put the seal of the blood on the doorframes of their houses. Therefore, God's wrath struck, with the plague against the firstborn, across the entire land of Egypt:

At midnight, **the LORD struck all the firstborn in the land of Egypt, from the firstborn of Pharaoh who sat on his throne to the firstborn of the captive who was in the dungeon; and all the firstborn of livestock.** *Pharaoh rose up in the night, he, and all his servants, and all the Egyptians;* **and there was a great cry in Egypt, for there was not a house where there was not one dead.** (Exodus 12:29–30)

O little Flock, O precious Church of the Living God, do not forget that God's holy nature requires God's righteous wrath to go forth against all ungodliness and unrighteousness of men, who suppress the truth in their unrighteousness [Romans 1:18]. Once out in the wilderness, Moses says to Aaron of rebellious Israel, **"for wrath has gone out from the LORD! The plague has begun!"** (Numbers 16:46), and also much later in history the Prophet declares, **"Behold, the day of the LORD, cruel, with wrath and fierce anger;** *to make the land a desolation, and to destroy its sinners out of it"* (Isaiah 13:9). In the New Testament, the Apostle Paul warns, *"for which things' sake"* [fornication, uncleanness, passion, evil desire, and covetousness] **the wrath of God comes on the children of disobedience"** (Colossians 3:5–6), while the book of Revelation foresees the final outpouring of God's wrath upon the wicked in this manner:

I saw another great and marvelous sign in the sky: **seven angels having the seven last plagues, for in them God's wrath is finished.** (Revelation 15:1)

What, then, is the Gospel? With what specific message does the "Glad Tidings" of salvation come to us through God's evangelists? The Gospel, which alone has the divine power to cause the human heart to flow with tears of true repentance before God, is the eternal truth that the sign of blood, the blood of the true Passover Lamb, shall cause the coming wrath of God to *"pass over"* all broken, pleading sinners who call upon the name of Christ for salvation from that wrath:

By faith, [Moses] **kept the Passover, and the sprinkling of the blood, that the destroyer of the firstborn should not touch them.** (Hebrews 11:28)

And,

Much more then, being now ***justified by His blood****, we will be saved from God's wrath through Him.* (Romans 5:9)

Therefore, the true Passover is celebrated only when the blood of Jesus Christ, the Lamb of God, is applied to the guilty human soul, and that by way of the spiritual hyssop of believing upon His name as Lord over all. For He, Jesus Christ, is *the Firstborn of God*, and yet He was slain in our place. As the Passover Lamb of God, none of His bones were broken on the cross, but rather one of the soldiers pierced His side with a spear, such that blood and water flowed out, proving that He had died [John 19:34]. Yet as the Firstborn of God, it is He who has loved us and washed us from our sins in His own blood [Revelation 1:5]; and it is He for whom the house of David shall mourn when they look upon Him whom they have pierced and grieve for Him as one grieves for a firstborn [Zechariah 12:10]; and thus it is He whom God raised from the dead. And being raised from the dead, He, the Lord Jesus Christ, is now *the Firstborn from the dead*, and the Ruler over the kings of the earth [Revelation 1:5, again]—even He who shall come again on the clouds, with the holy angels, to gather His elect from the four winds, and whose Kingdom shall have no end. And He shall reign forever and ever, world without end. Amen.

4

THE DAY OF ATONEMENT
The Cross in Leviticus 16:1-34

The LORD spoke to Moses, after the death of the two sons of Aaron, when they came near before the LORD, and died; and the LORD said to Moses, "Tell Aaron your brother, not to come at all times into the Most Holy Place within the veil, before the mercy seat which is on the Ark; lest he die: for I will appear in the cloud on the mercy seat. Aaron shall come into the sanctuary with a young bull for a sin offering, and a ram for a burnt offering. He shall put on the holy linen coat. He shall have the linen breeches on his body, and shall put on the linen sash, and he shall be clothed with the linen turban. They are the holy garments. He shall bathe his body in water, and put them on. He shall take from the congregation of the children of Israel two male goats for a sin offering, and one ram for a burnt offering." (Leviticus 16:1–5)

GOD is not to be approached without fearful trembling. He says to Moses that unless Aaron, Moses' brother, comes before Him in the proper, holy manner, he shall surely die. Therefore, God gives Moses these commandments concerning Aaron so that Aaron may approach Him and yet not die:

*The LORD spoke to Moses, after **the death** of the two sons of Aaron, when they came near before the LORD, **and died**; and the LORD said to Moses, "Tell Aaron your brother, not to come at all times into the Most Holy Place within the veil, before the mercy seat which is on the Ark; **lest he die**: for I will appear in the cloud on the mercy seat."* (Leviticus 16:1–2, again)

45

To approach God, in His holy, holy, holy habitation, in any kind of unholy manner, is a deadly act. In the tenth chapter of the book of Leviticus, Nadab and Abihu, Aaron's sons, offer profane fire before the Lord, right in the Lord's holy presence, and, as a result, fire goes out from the Lord and consumes them, such that they die right there, in the presence of the Lord. Similarly, even in the age of the New Covenant, Ananias and Sapphira, having lied to God by lying to the Holy Spirit concerning the price of the land which they sold, claiming that they were giving the full amount of the proceeds to God, yet all the while holding back some of the proceeds for themselves, both fall down dead before Peter, such that great fear comes upon all the Church and all who hear of these things [Acts 5:1-11]. Moreover, the Apostle Paul says that there are some in Corinth who are weak and sickly in their midst, even with many of them dying, and all because they have dared to approach the Lord's Table with defiled hearts, even eating of the bread and drinking of the cup of the Lord in an unworthy manner [1 Corinthians 11:27-34]. The Lord our God, then, is He who is to be feared.

In what manner should a man approach God? The Prophet Isaiah, one of the holiest of men in all of history, approaches God's holy throne by crying out, *"Woe is me! For I am undone, because I am a man of unclean lips, and I dwell among a people of unclean lips: for my eyes have seen the King, the L*ORD *of Hosts!"* (Isaiah 6:5). Ezekiel, another one of the greatest of the Prophets, sees, in a vision, God seated upon His throne, and promptly falls down upon his face, terrified and almost lifeless [Ezekiel 1:28]. Daniel, upon seeing a vision of the pre-incarnate Christ, loses all strength and falls with his face to the ground [Daniel 10:7-9]. Even John, the beloved Apostle, whom Jesus loves, and who is so close to Jesus that the Lord allows him to recline on His bosom, upon seeing a vision of the resurrected and glorified Christ does not stay upright, but rather is compelled to fall upon his face in holy fear and trembling at the sight of the majesty of Christ's holiness:

When I saw Him, ***I fell at His feet like a dead man****.* (Revelation 1:17)

The Day of Atonement

O beloved Brothers and Sisters, we must, therefore, beware the many idolatries of the Contemporary Church. For, the Contemporary Church has been built upon what it calls "contemporary worship," and yet such worship has been defined by an ethos of casualness. "Come casually to worship," they say. And then they boast by saying, "Ours is a church where you can feel safe in coming to God without any fear of feeling judged or condemned." Is this not, then, the very *opposite* of the sixteenth chapter of Leviticus? Should we not, therefore, recognize the hidden, crafty hand of Satan at work in such stark redefinitions of Christian worship?

If we are to approach the living God in worship, we must come with tears of repentance over our sins, and we must come fearing Him on account of His infinite holiness. That is, true worship in the Church requires a spiritual tearing of our clothes, since we are guilty of offending God with our many sins, and it also demands a spiritual wearing of sackcloth and ashes, because we have grieved the Holy Spirit of God by our transgressions. The songs of the Church should be joyful, for our faith in Jesus Christ as the Son of God has overcome the world. Yet our songs also should be filled with lamentation, mourning, and weeping, since our sins have wounded and grieved the very One who was willing to be afflicted for us. We praise our God, but only by first coming to Him with tears of repentance. We rejoice before our Lord Jesus Christ, yet not without first humbling ourselves before Him with deep, trembling confessions of our sins against Him.

SPECIAL GARMENTS FOR THE DAY OF ATONEMENT

How, then, should the Church return to God in a manner that is befitting His incomprehensible holiness? We must begin by confessing before Him that we have forgotten—have intentionally turned our backs on—the Gospel significance of the ancient Israel holiday (and, instead of "holiday" we actually should say "Holy Day") of the Day of Atonement. That is, in the ancient Israelite calendar, once a year, on the tenth day of the seventh month, the Israelites were to afflict themselves with a day of fasting and repentance. This day, known as the Day of Atonement, is, literally in Hebrew, the *"Day of Atonements,"* plural (Leviticus 23:27ff.), possibly because the verb for *"making atonement"* is used no less than sixteen times throughout the sixteenth chapter of Leviticus (e.g. 16:6, 10, 11, 16, etc.). Yet it is fine for us to use the singular, and thus to call it the *"Day of Atonement,"* since this entire chapter is concerned with making the necessary atonement for the people of Israel, so that they do not die whenever they approach the holy sanctuary of God in worship.

Yet what is required of God's children on the Day of Atonement? First, there are the fearful statutes regarding *the undefiled garments* of the high priest, for use in making atonement both for himself and for his people:

> *"Aaron shall come into the sanctuary with a young bull for a sin offering, and a ram for a burnt offering. He shall put on **the holy linen coat**. He shall have **the linen breeches** on his body, and shall put on **the linen sash**, and he shall be clothed with **the linen turban**. They are **the holy garments**. He shall bathe his body in water, and put them on."* (Leviticus 16:3–4)

Aaron, the high priest, is not allowed to go into the Most Holy Place, otherwise known as the Holy of Holies, which is the innermost chamber of the Tent of Meeting, on just any day of the year. Instead, he is only to enter into the Holy of Holies, inside the veil and thus before the very Ark of the Covenant, once a year, on the Day of Atonement. For this occasion, he must wear special, holy garments. He is to put them on before entering into the Holy of Holies on the Day of Atonement, and then, once he is finished making atonement within, he is to take these special garments off before resuming with his priestly work at the altar, outside:

> *"Aaron shall come into the Tent of Meeting, **and shall take off the linen garments, which he put on when he went into the Holy Place, and shall leave them there.** Then he shall bathe himself in water in a holy place, and put on his garments, and come out and offer his burnt offering and the burnt offering of the people, and make atonement for himself and for the people."* (vv. 23–24; see also vv. 32-33)

The Day of Atonement

The garments of the high priest in Israel must be holy and undefiled. They must be special, linen garments. For, linen garments keep them clean, undefiled, and without sweat:

*It shall be that, when they enter in at the gates of the inner court, they shall be clothed **with linen garments**; and no wool shall come on them, while they minister in the gates of the inner court, and within. They shall have **linen tires on their heads**, and shall have **linen breeches on their waists**; they shall **not clothe themselves with anything that makes them sweat**.* (Ezekiel 44:17–18)

Still, why is the subject of clothing so important here? If God does not judge by external appearances, but rather judges the heart, why should He be concerned with the pristine cleanness of the clothing of the high priest on the Day of Atonement? All of this is a pattern, a figure of holiness. For, in the Bible, the clothing of the high priest, whether clean or defiled, signifies his moral state, whether clean or defiled:

*Now Joshua [who was the high priest of Israel at the time] **was clothed with filthy garments**, and was standing before the Angel. He answered and spoke to those who stood before Him, saying, **"Take the filthy garments off of him."** To him He said, "Behold, I have caused your iniquity to pass from you, and I will clothe you with rich clothing." I said, "Let them set **a clean turban** on his head." **So they set a clean turban on his head, and clothed him**; and the LORD's Angel was standing by.* (Zechariah 3:3–5)

It is the duty of the high priest in Israel, on the Day of Atonement, to approach God in worship in a way that gives him special access to the presence of the glory of God. Therefore, the garments of the high priest must be spotless and undefiled, for no one can approach the Lord, the Holy One of Israel, in filthy garments, without being cast out of His presence, and into outer darkness:

*"But when the king came in to see the guests, **he saw there a man who did not have on wedding clothing, and he said to him, 'Friend, how did you come in here not wearing wedding clothing?'** He was speechless. Then the king said to the servants, **'Bind him hand and foot, take him away, and throw him into the outer darkness**; there is where the weeping and grinding of teeth will be.' For many are called, but few chosen."* (Matthew 22:11–14)

All of this beckons us to consider the defiling nature of sin, and how even the sin of the high priest in ancient Israel brought defilement upon the nation. Our great need, therefore, is for a sinless High Priest. For, all of us have become like one who is unclean, and all of our acts of righteousness, including the righteous acts of the sin-stained high priests in ancient Israel, are like *"a polluted garment"* (Isaiah 64:6). Thus whenever we meditate upon the Gospel significance of the Day of Atonement, we must, with much trembling, think upon *the garments of Jesus Christ at the cross*, splattered with His own blood and divided, for sport, by the soldiers who mocked Him, even as they bludgeoned Him and crucified Him:

*They divide **My garments** among them. They cast lots for **My clothing**.* (Psalm 22:18)

Yet Christ Jesus, our High Priest, is no longer upon the cross. Having died a sinless death—and yet He became sin for us [2 Corinthians 5:21]—He rose from the dead on the third day. Being thus victorious over sin and death, He wears the High Priestly vestments of the very Holy of Holies in Heaven, ministering on behalf of His elect in the very Holy of Holies in Heaven:

*I saw until thrones were placed, and One who was Ancient of Days sat: **His clothing was white as snow** [that is, whiter than the whitest of fine linen!], and the hair of His head like pure wool; His throne was fiery flames, and its wheels burning fire....* (Daniel 7:9)

And,

And among the lamp stands was one like a Son of Man, **clothed with a robe reaching down to his feet** [that is, the High Priestly garment of the High Priest of Heaven] *and with a golden sash around His chest.* (Revelation 1:13)

Thus what shall we say of the spiritual garments of true Christians? If the holiness of God demands that we approach Him with all fearful trembling, and if Christ, our High Priest, is clothed with such radiant holiness and purity that the mere sight of Him is as intense as the sun shining in all of its strength, then in what condition should our own spiritual garments be found on the Day of Judgment? Should we take the righteous robes of Christ, given to us by faith in Christ's own righteousness, and defile them with a prostitute? Shall we drag them through the refuse piles of worldly ambitions and idolatry? Shall we soil them with false doctrines, and stain them with all of the gluttonous feastings of the flesh? Shall we parade them through the spiritual trash heaps of covetousness, greed, and all manner of friendship with the world?

He has washed us in His own blood for this sole purpose: to make us a Kingdom, it is true, but also *priests* to serve His God and Father. Thus if we are a kingly priesthood, we ought to wear the pure and undefiled garments of the priests of the everlasting Kingdom. We put on, therefore, the linen tunic of righteousness, being clothed with Christ and thus abhorring all false gods. We wear the linen trousers of modesty, not for a moment being found amongst those who practice the shameless, unblushing immodesty of dress and immodesty of speech of the world. We gird ourselves with the linen sash of boldness, being ready to call all men, everywhere, to repent of their wicked idols and evil notions of God. Also, we wear the linen cap of sound doctrine, of true Gospel truth, contending earnestly for the faith that was once for all delivered to the saints. Moreover, skillfully woven into the fabrics of all of these priestly garments is the crimson thread of love, since love is the bond of perfection and the unmistakable mark of the Christian priesthood.

Thus as Christ Jesus is our High Priest, and we are His little priests, we clothe ourselves in holiness. Being clothed with the righteousness of Christ, we strive, by His Spirit's might striving within us, to keep our garments undefiled. We walk in the fear of Him, in white garments, walking in His holy commandments, lest we be found unclean and defiled on His coming Day of Judgment.

THE SIN-BEARING "SEND-AWAY GOAT"

How shall we approach the living God in prayer and in worship? We cannot do so without the righteous garments of the righteousness of Christ. For, He became flesh in order to fulfill the righteous requirements of the Law in our stead. Yet wherever there is sin, it must be atoned for, or else there can be no salvation. Thus in order to approach the Holy One of Israel, we must have a sin-bearer—one who bears our sins for us, carrying them for us, even carrying them *away from us*. This we find only in the biblically prescribed sending away of the *"scapegoat"* during the Day of Atonement:

> *"He shall take from the congregation of the children of Israel two male goats for a sin offering, and one ram for a burnt offering. Aaron shall offer the bull of the sin offering, which is for himself, and make atonement for himself and for his house. He shall take the two goats, and set them before the LORD at the door of the Tent of Meeting. Aaron shall cast lots for the two goats; one lot for the LORD, and the other lot **for the scapegoat**. Aaron shall present the goat on which the lot fell for the LORD, and offer him for a sin offering.* ***But the goat, on which the lot fell for the scapegoat, shall be presented alive before the LORD, to make atonement for him, to send him away for the scapegoat into the wilderness.*** *"* (Leviticus 16:5–10)

And,

> *"When he has finished atoning for the Holy Place, the Tent of Meeting, and the altar, he shall present the live goat.* ***Aaron shall lay both his hands on the head of the live goat, and confess over him all the iniquities of the children of Israel, and all their transgressions, even all their sins; and he shall***

put them on the head of the goat, and shall send him away into the wilderness by the hand of a man who is in readiness. The goat shall [bear] all their iniquities on himself to a solitary land, and he shall let the goat go in the wilderness."
(Leviticus 16:20–22)

What is the scapegoat? In Hebrew, the goat is designated as the *'Azā'zēl* goat, which is, in English, the *"Send-away-goat."* That is, this is the goat that is *"sent away,"* sent to be cut off, way out in the wilderness. The sins of the sons of Israel are, by the high priest's confession of them over the head of the live goat, symbolically or spiritually transferred to the goat. Then, since the goat now carries or bears in its body the curses of God for the sake of those sins, it is sent away, by the hand of a timely and trustworthy man, out into the cursed wasteland of the wilderness.

We believe, therefore, that Jesus has become the *"Send-away-goat"* for us, since it is He, and not a mere animal, who carries away our sins:

Everyone who sins also commits lawlessness. Sin is lawlessness. You know that He was revealed **to take away our sins**, *and in Him is no sin.* (1 John 3:4–5)

Moreover, just as the *"Send-away-goat"* was to *"bear"* all of the iniquities of the peoples, and thus be released in the *"solitary land"* (Leviticus 16:22), or, more literally, *"land of cutting off,"* so too did the Lord Jesus *"bear"* our iniquities, and so was He *"cut off"* for our sins:

"The goat **shall [bear]** *all their iniquities on himself to a solitary land [that is, the 'land of* **cutting off**'*]; and he shall let the goat go in the wilderness."* (Leviticus 16:22)

This, then, is fulfilled in the death of our Lord Jesus Christ on our behalf:

He was taken away by oppression and judgment; and as for His generation, who considered that He was **cut off** *out of the land* *of the living and stricken for the disobedience of my people?* (Isaiah 53:8)

And also,

*...yet **He bore** the sin of many, and made intercession for the transgressors.* (Isaiah 53:12)

    O Christian, should this not soften your heart towards God? Should it not quicken your spiritual pulse, and cause your affections to rush towards God, like a racing river? If He has sent your sins away from you, removing your transgressions as far as the east is from the west, should this not awaken your soul to love Him with all of your strength? If the spotless, precious Lamb of God has taken away your sins, having borne them Himself, such that He was cut off from the land of the living on your behalf, should not such divine love pierce your heart with love unto Him?

    Your sins, O Christian, are not light, but exceedingly heavy, even as heavy as the wooden cross which He Himself bore for you. At the cross, God the Father pronounced *your* sins over *His* head. He carried your sins for you out into the wilderness of the cross. He bore the curse of sin for you. Our Lord Jesus Christ was cut off from the land of the living. His own life was pure. His was a perfect righteousness and a perfect love. Yet for you He was stricken, and cut off.

    Therefore, should not your love for Him be exceedingly loyal? If persecutors come and threaten you, wanting you to deny Him, shall you do it? Shall you not, rather, say to them, "What, shall I deny my Lord, even He who bore my sins out of His inestimable love for me?" O Christian, draw near to God with a loyal love unto Him. Do not allow your flesh, which shrinks back from suffering, cause you to look away from the cross of Christ. Instead, gaze upon the cross. Look straight upon the face of the crucified Christ, bludgeoned by the Roman soldiers beyond recognition, and wearing the crown of thorns, and see God's love for you. For, if you will gaze rightly upon the Lamb, keeping your eyes fixed upon Him, you will learn to love Him more than all others, and will never be content or at rest with anything or anyone other than God Himself.

THE BLOOD AND THE MERCY SEAT

There must be atonement. In order to approach the holy, holy, holy presence of God, there must be blood, sacrificial in nature, in order to cover over our sins. For, without the shedding of blood, there can be no forgiveness of sins [Hebrews 9:22]. Therefore, even as the *"Send-away-goat"* gives us one type or shadow of the atonement of Christ, so too does the other Day-of-Atonement goat, the slaughtered one, teach us about the true nature of the blood of Jesus:

*"Then he shall kill the goat of the sin offering, that is for the people, **and bring his blood within the veil**, and do with his blood as he did with the blood of the bull, **and sprinkle it on the mercy seat, and before the mercy seat.**"* (Leviticus 16:15)

This is a terrifying venture. For, will the high priest dare to enter inside the veil? And yet he is commanded by God to do so on the Day of Atonement. Therefore, he must come *with blood*, with the blood of the other goat, to sprinkle on the mercy seat and before the mercy seat. Also, he must come *with smoke of sweet incense*, since the smoke will hide him and shield him, a sinner, from the holy gaze of such a holy God:

*"Aaron shall present the bull of the sin offering, which is for himself, and shall make atonement for himself and for his house, and shall kill the bull of the sin offering which is for himself. He shall take a censer full of coals of fire from off the altar before the LORD, and two handfuls of sweet incense beaten small, and bring it within the veil: **and he shall put the incense on the fire before the LORD, that the cloud of the incense may cover the mercy seat that is on the testimony, so that he will not die**."* (Leviticus 16:11–13)

Here, then, is the heart of the Day of Atonement, and also the heart of the historic-Christian doctrine of the atonement of Christ, namely, that the blood of the other goat, the slaughtered one, is to be sprinkled upon the very *"mercy seat"* that is on the Ark of the Covenant:

> ***"He shall take some of the blood of the bull, and sprinkle it with his finger on the mercy seat on the east; and before the mercy seat he shall sprinkle some of the blood with his finger seven times."*** (Leviticus 16:14)

Yet if this is the heart of the Day of Atonement, and thus the doctrine of atonement, what does it mean? What is this *"mercy seat"* on the Ark of the Covenant, before which the high priest is to sprinkle the blood seven times? The *"mercy seat,"* as Luther called it, is, straight from the Hebrew, the *"atonement cover."* Thus the Day of *Atonement* has the *atonement cover* as its focal point. The blood is to be sprinkled there.

However, if we want to get at the meaning of this—but only with hearts that tremble at His holy Word—then we must understand the sacrificial significance of the Ark of the Covenant, itself. For, the atonement cover is simply the top, or the lid of the Ark. Yet the Ark is not merely the special chest used to house the tablets of the Ten Commandments, along with the golden pot of manna and Aaron's rod that budded [see Hebrews 9:4]. Instead, the Ark speaks to us of the very presence of the glory of God behind the veil, within the Holy of Holies. For, what is it that the Ark signifies? If it is an earthly shadow of a Heavenly reality, of what Heavenly object is it a type?

We tremble at the thought of where this actually leads us. For, the earthly Ark is overshadowed by two cherubim of gold. It must be shrouded in smoke when the high priest comes before it, lest he die, and its cover, the *"mercy seat"* or *"atonement cover,"* must be sprinkled with blood on the Day of Atonement. All of this, then, is a shadow of God's throne room in Heaven.

For, in Heaven, God's throne is guarded by four fierce and mighty cherubim, burning with glory, as if on fire, each having six wings, and each covered with eyes all around and within. And, according to David, God's Prophet, the earthly Ark is a shadow of the very *footstool* that rests beneath God's throne in Heaven. And it is before this Heavenly footstool that the four living creatures in Heaven fall down and cry, *"Worthy is the Lamb who was slain!"* (Revelation 5:8, 12, NKJV). The earthly Ark, then, is the type of *the Heavenly footstool* that rests beneath God's Heavenly throne:

> *Then David the king stood up on his feet, and said, "Hear me, my brothers, and my people! As for me, it was in my heart to build a house of rest for* **the Ark of the LORD's covenant**, *and for* **the footstool of our God**; *and I had prepared for the building."* (1 Chronicles 28:2)

And also,

> *We will go into His dwelling place. We will worship* **at His footstool**. *Arise, O LORD, into Your resting place; You, and* **the Ark of Your strength**. (Psalm 132:7–8)

We are, then, to see, by faith, the *Heavenly* Day of Atonement. That Day of Atonement does not occur once every year, but rather occurred only one time, only once, on the Day on which Jesus died. On that Day, after Jesus gave up His spirit, He entered into Paradise as the High Priest of Heaven. Wearing the High Priestly garments of both the Son of Man and the Ancient of Days, He approached the Father's throne not with the blood of a bull or a male goat, but rather with His own blood—fully divine and fully human. This blood of the Son of God, which is the blood of the Son of Man, is so worthy that even a single drop of it is worth more than all of the valuable things of the creation put together, even the sum value of all of the souls of all men from all epochs of world history combined. And so He entered into the throne room of His Father with this blood, and there, before the footstool of His Father's throne, He sprinkled some of this blood with His divinely worthy finger, even seven times. Thus we are to see it:

> *This hope we have as an anchor of the soul, a hope both sure and steadfast* **and entering into that which is within the veil; where as a forerunner Jesus entered for us**, *having become a High Priest forever after the order of Melchizedek.* (Hebrews 6:19–20)

And,

> *Having therefore, brothers, boldness* **to enter into the holy place by the blood of Jesus, by the way which He dedicated for us, a new and living way, through the veil, that is to say, His flesh**.... (Hebrews 10:19–20)

And again,

> *But Christ having come as a High Priest of the coming good things,* **through the greater and more perfect Tabernacle, not made with hands, that is to say, not of this creation,** *nor yet through the blood of goats and calves,* **but through His own blood, entered in once for all into the Holy Place,** *having obtained eternal redemption.* (Hebrews 9:11–12)

Who, then, shall dare to pray to God while dishonoring the blood of Jesus? Shall a woman dare to baptize, or to occupy the pulpit, or to officiate at the Lord's Table, in violation of the holy Law of Christ? Shall a man dare to take upon himself the holy mantle of the pastorate, and thus to pray in the office of a pastor, even claiming the blood of the Lamb for his congregation, and yet at the same time refuse to decry homosexuality as an utter abomination unto God? Shall baptized children, baptized under their own public profession of faith, take from the Lord's Table and then go home and dare to dishonor their parents? Shall the adult members of the congregation share in the cup of the Lord on the Lord's Day, and then go to the houses of their neighbors in the middle of the week and share in the cup of demons?

O how we fall to our knees in holy fear at these frightful considerations! For, those who trample the blood of Jesus underfoot, treating it is an approval to sin, are only storing up for themselves the fiery indignation of God that they shall face everlastingly in Hell. The flying eagle says to them, *"Woe! Woe! Woe to you!"* (Revelation 8:13). For, they who reject *the blood of the Lamb* have nothing else to look forward to than *the outpoured wrath of the Lamb*, and they who do not honor Christ's blood as the fulfillment of the *Day of Atonement* are being prepared by God as vessels of judgment for the everlasting *Day of Wrath*.

Yet we are not of those who shrink back, to their destruction, but rather of those who, by faith, persevere to the very end. Therefore, our hope, which is imperishable, is that since Christ sprinkled His own blood within the Holy throne room of God in Heaven, before the very footstool of God in Heaven, we may, upon our glorification, enter into that throne room, bow down before the One who sits upon the throne and before the Lamb, and worship Him who lives forever and ever, without being cast into outer darkness. Instead, we who, having been born of the Spirit of Christ, now keep God's commandments, will join that great multitude of saints in Heaven, so numerous as to be almost immeasurable, who, while falling down upon their faces, will cry out forever and ever, *"Salvation be to our God, who sits on the throne, and to the Lamb!"* and also, *"Amen! Blessing, glory, wisdom, thanksgiving, honor, power, and might, be to our God forever and ever! Amen!"* (Revelation 7:10, 12).

And thus it shall be to the praise of the glory of His grace, forever and ever, eons unto eons, world without end. Amen.

5

THE BRONZE SERPENT
The Cross in Numbers 21:1-9

The Canaanite, the king of Arad, who lived in the South, heard that Israel came by the way of Atharim. He fought against Israel, and took some of them captive. Israel vowed a vow to the LORD, and said, "If You will indeed deliver this people into my hand, then I will utterly destroy their cities." The LORD listened to the voice of Israel, and delivered up the Canaanites; and they utterly destroyed them and their cities. The name of the place was called Hormah. They traveled from Mount Hor by the way to the Red Sea, to go around the land of Edom. The soul of the people [became short] because of the journey. The people spoke against God, and against Moses, "Why have you brought us up out of Egypt to die in the wilderness? For there is no bread, and there is no water; and our soul loathes this [cursed] bread." (Numbers 21:1–5)

GOD is wondrously patient and merciful, and thus gracious and compassionate, even towards such an ungrateful and stiff-necked people. Since He is their God and they are His people, God listens to Israel when they cry out to Him after an enemy has attacked them. The king of Arad, the Canaanite, has assaulted Israel and taken some of the Israelites as prisoners. Therefore, Israel cries out to God, asking Him to deliver the people of the king of Arad into their hands, and also vowing utterly to destroy their cities if God will so come to their rescue. And in His great mercy, God listens to the voice of their prayers:

*The LORD **listened to the voice of Israel**, and delivered up the Canaanites; and they utterly destroyed them and their cities. The name of the place was called Hormah.* (Numbers 21:3)

How quickly, then, do the children of Israel forget the covenantal mercies of God! Many times in their history, He will regard their affliction, hear their cry, and deliver them from their distresses on account of the multitude of His mercies. Yet just as many times, Israel will quickly forget the lovingkindness of God, and how He has delivered them, and thus, once they are back in a state of security and ease, will forsake God, even provoking His wrath by *"speaking against"* Him:

*They traveled from Mount Hor by the way to the Red Sea, to go around the land of Edom. The soul of the people [became short] because of the journey. **The people spoke against God**, and against Moses, "Why have you brought us up out of Egypt to die in the wilderness? For there is no bread, and there is no water; and our soul loathes this [cursed] bread."* (Numbers 21:4–5)

God is merciful to rescue His people Israel out of their calamities. Yet His people Israel are ungrateful and foolish, being quick to forget God's mercies towards them the very moment that their peace and prosperity is restored to them. Thus the Exodus out of Egypt is a colossal act of deliverance by God, and yet very quickly after the Exodus, the people already are found making a god for themselves in the form of a golden calf. Also, during the times of the Judges, even as God raises up judge after judge in order to deliver Israel from her oppressors, each time the people promptly forget God's merciful deliverances on their behalf and rapidly return to their evil practices of intermarrying with the Canaanites and serving the gods and goddesses of the Canaanites. Even in the days of Nehemiah, after God has shown such great mercy to His people, bringing them out of the land of Babylon, restoring them to Jerusalem, and enabling them to complete the rebuilding of the wall of Jerusalem—even so the people quickly forget God, fix their eyes on commercial trade, and begin to tread wine presses on the Sabbath, and also to load donkeys with wine, grapes, figs, and all kinds of merchandise to be brought into Jerusalem and sold on the Sabbath [Nehemiah 13:15]. Israel, then, is an ungrateful and shameful people, ready to forget God the very moment that He has rescued her, and her troubles have ended. As it is written in the book of the Prophet:

According to their pasture, so were they filled; they were filled, and their heart was exalted. **Therefore they have forgotten Me**. (Hosea 13:6)

    What shall we do, then, O Brothers and Sisters, to curb this sinful folly in our own, sinful hearts? For, how quickly do we, too, become ungrateful towards God! How speedily do we forget the mercies of God! We face distresses, and they threaten to swallow us up. Therefore, we cry to God for deliverance, and in His mercy He delivers us from them. Yet the fact that we respond all too quickly by forgetting God, and turning our gaze back upon the world, shows that the impulses of our sinful flesh within us are still too strong, and so in great need of being crucified. That is, we desire the prosperity of the flesh more than we desire God Himself, and this is why we forget God so easily after our flesh has been rescued from destruction, and restored to health.

    Precious Brothers and Sisters, let us humble our hearts and crucify the flesh by not allowing ourselves to forget the many kindnesses of deliverance which God has shown us. Yet in order to do this, in order to wage war against the pride of our flesh by keeping the remembrances of God's mercies ever before our eyes, we need a vast arsenal of spiritual weapons. We need prayer journals, to be sure, to remind us of those former, lowly depths of despair, up from which God has raised us. Yet we also need personal testimonies, Christian biographies, written histories of different epochs of Church history, historical poems, well-framed Ebenezer stones, and many church gatherings of remembrance and thanksgiving unto God. For, unless we humble ourselves by way of the disciplines of Christian remembrance and thanksgiving, instead of raising our children in the worldly norms of sensational entertainments, romantic pursuits, and vain sports, we will fail to tell the generation to come—speaking to them directly from the Scriptures—all of the praiseworthy deeds of our God. And if we fail to recount to them the multitude of God's excellencies and covenantal mercies, and also the sheer helplessness out of which He has saved us, then both we and our children will, indeed, bring upon ourselves the horrible, corporate epitaph of being a people who forgot God.

"BECOMING SHORT" WITH GOD

The Israelites in the wilderness, then, are collectively (though there are plenty of individual exceptions) a people who do not truly love God for His own sake. The proof of this is that they forget Him immediately after He has delivered them from the hand of the king of Arad, the Canaanite, since their victory restores their peace and thus puts their minds back on fleshly matters. Yet as if this is not insulting enough to the divine majesty of God, they now go so far as to *"become short"* with Him. They dare to accuse God, and to be vexed towards God, as if the creature has the right to *"become short"* with the Creator:

> *They traveled from Mount Hor by the way to the Red Sea, to go around the land of Edom.* **The soul of the people [become short] because of the journey** *[that is, they dared to "become short" with God Himself!]. The people spoke against God, and against Moses, "Why have you brought us up out of Egypt to die in the wilderness? For there is no bread, and there is no water; and our soul loathes this [cursed] bread." The* LORD *sent fiery serpents among the people, and they bit the people. Many people of Israel died.* (Numbers 21:4–6)

Even in general, a short-tempered people is a foolish people, and the individual who is quick to anger exalts his own folly. Yet to *"become short"* with God Himself is a cursed act of rebellion. It is much more than the child raging at his father, or the subject raging at his sovereign. This is even worse than the pot raging at the potter, or the donkey biting its master. For, this is the image bearer raging at God, and thus the human being shaking his fist at the very divine majesty and divine honor of God. It is no marvel at all, then, that God immediately judges the rebels with the poisonous bites of fiery serpents.

Still, the insult to the divine honor of God is even greater here, since the people not only become short with God, but also speak of His gracious gift of manna—that miracle bread of angels with which He feeds them—with gross ingratitude and wickedness. In their prideful raging, they even go so far as to call this gracious, life-giving bread of God a *"cursed bread"*:

> *The people spoke against God, and against Moses, "Why have you brought us up out of Egypt to die in the wilderness? For there is no bread, and there is no water;* **and our soul loathes this [cursed] bread.*"* (Numbers 21:5)

This is an outrageous sin. For, if *"anyone who curses his father or his mother shall surely be put to death"* (Exodus 21:17), and if *"whoever curses his father or his mother"* shall have his lamp *"put out in blackness of darkness"* (Proverbs 20:20), then to curse God Himself is surely a capital crime of the highest degree:

> **You shall not blaspheme God**, *nor curse a ruler of your people.* (Exodus 22:28)

And,

> **Therefore the LORD heard, and was angry**. *A fire was kindled against Jacob, anger also went up against Israel,* **because they did not believe in God, and did not trust in His salvation**. (Psalm 78:21–22)

How sinful the human heart is, such that it can despise the best gifts of God! In Eden, He gives His image bearers a plethora of trees—even pleasant to the sight and good for food—from which to eat, and yet, wanting to be their own gods, they despise those good trees, and go after the one tree that is forbidden. In the wilderness, He sends them bread from Heaven, and they call it bland. He provides for them the food of angels, even so that they do not starve and die in the wilderness, and they rage against it and call it a *"cursed bread."* Then, much later in history, He sends His only-begotten Son in the flesh to be the Bread of Life for His spiritually emaciated people, and yet even this Bread, this incarnational Bread of everlasting life, they despise. Since they love their sinful cravings more than God, and worship Mammon instead of God, they despise Christ Jesus Himself:

> **The Jews therefore [grumbled] concerning Him**, *because He said,* **"I am the bread which came down out of Heaven."** *They said, "Is this not Jesus, the son of Joseph, whose father and mother we know? How then does He say, 'I have come down out of Heaven?'"* (John 6:41–42)

Those who dare to *"become short"* with God are those who *"curse"* the gifts and provisions of the Gospel of God. They despise God's miracle manna in favor of worldly meats and flesh-pleasing treats. They rage against the Gospel demands of submission to God and obedience to Him, which are the very demands of all true, saving faith. Such cursed men want to control their own food supply themselves, rather than to be humbled into depending upon Christ Jesus for their daily provision of miracle-bread. In their rebellious pride, they would gladly feed themselves according to their own works of the Law and their own fleshly appetites, but to be fed with the sacrificial flesh of Jesus Christ for the forgiveness of their sins, and also for the fulfillment of the righteous requirements of the Law in their stead, is far too offensive to their pride even to come under their own consideration. Also, they will not delight in the manna of the Gospel, since it demands the crucifixion and death of their former, sinful appetites. Jeshurun would rather grow fat and kick, growing obese in sin [Deuteronomy 32:15], than die to sin and live upon that healthy, healing, holy Bread of Life which comes down from Heaven and gives life to the world.

Fellow Christian, is not the Gospel manna wholesome enough to satisfy your soul? Since you are not of the hypocrites, but, rather, are truly regenerate, truly born of the Holy Spirit, do you have any valid reason for allowing the manna of the Gospel to become bland to you? If it is becoming bland to you, is this not an alarming indication of the hardening plaque of sin in your heart, and of the multiplying of the fat cells of covetousness in your belly? Does not such a state call for your immediate repentance, lest you face a collapse of spiritual health and fall into a spiritual heart attack?

To the palate of the wicked, the manna of the Gospel of God is always bland, if not bitter. For, a lack of humility, gratitude, and a true love for God will always cause the manna of Christ to taste rancid and repulsive to the soul. Thus the wicked, when they taste the manna, oftentimes say that it tastes like death to them—and so it should, since their eating of it in an unworthy manner will surely sentence them to an everlasting death, even everlasting, conscious punishment in Hell. This is why they call it, so blasphemously, a *"cursed bread."*

Yet for the righteous, this Gospel manna should be always sweet, and never bland. Since theirs is humility in Christ, and unceasing gratitude towards Christ, and a true love for God and fear of God in Christ, the manna is always delightful and delicious to them. It smells of the sweetness of Christ's righteousness. It tastes of the honey-sweetness of His imperishable Word. For those who hunger and thirst for righteousness, it satisfies. For the meek, the eating of it grants them the glorious, Spirit-revealed revelation from God that, having eaten of it in humble repentance and with authentic faith in Jesus Christ as the Son of God, they will live forever.

THE LORD SENDS FIERY SERPENTS!

The children of Israel have spoken against God, have grown short with Him, and even have called the miracle bread, which is His gracious manna, a *"cursed bread."* These are not only daring, but also egregious crimes against the Most High. Therefore, the Israelites can only expect the most terrifying of judgments to fall upon them. And, for such an affront to God's holy honor, it is, indeed, a stinging, burning judgment which comes upon them very suddenly:

The LORD sent fiery serpents among the people, and they bit the people. *Many people of Israel died. The people came to Moses, and said, "We have sinned, because we have spoken against the LORD, and against you. Pray to the LORD, that He take away the serpents from us." Moses prayed for the people.* (Numbers 21:6–7)

These fiery serpents, the ones that now bite and kill many of the people, are, apparently, indigenous to the wilderness in which they are travelling. For, the wilderness is described by Moses elsewhere as being full of many dangers, including these fiery serpents:

Beware lest you forget the LORD your God...who led you through the great and terrible wilderness, ***with fiery serpents*** *and scorpions, and thirsty ground where there was no water; who poured water for you out of the rock of flint.* (Deuteronomy 8:11, 15)

Up until this point, God's sovereign power graciously has restrained these fiery serpents from striking His people Israel. Yet now that Israel has dared to curse God's gift of manna, the Lord removes His gracious, restraining hand. He now allows the fiery serpents to enter into the camp of Israel, to strike, and to kill. This is a burning judgment of God, namely, the sending of fiery serpents to bite and to slay the people:

"For, behold, ***I will send serpents****, adders among you, which will not be charmed;* ***and they shall bite you****," says the LORD.* (Jeremiah 8:17)

And also,

Though they hide themselves in the top of Carmel, I will search and take them out there; and though they be hidden from My sight in the bottom of the sea, ***there I will command the serpent, and it will bite them****.* (Amos 9:3)

God takes no pleasure in the death of the wicked, but He does give the wicked over to their own wicked desires. If they listen to the voice of Satan, that ancient Serpent, then they will be bit with the fatal bite of the Serpent. If they choose to lash out at God like fiery serpents, even cursing God, and thus proving themselves to be a cursed brood, then they shall be bit by fiery serpents:

But if you bite and devour one another, *be careful that you do not consume one another!* (Galatians 5:15)

And again,

...let us not test Christ, as some of them tested, ***and perished by the serpents***. (1 Corinthians 10:9)

The serpent is poisonous! In the Garden, it was the word of the Serpent that poisoned Eve's mind by twisting the Word of God in her hearing. The Serpent deceived Eve, and thus both Adam and Eve believed the lie of the Serpent—the lie which said that it was *evil* of God to withhold from them the right to eat from the tree of knowledge of good and evil. The Serpent said to them, in essence, "God is cruel to enslave you by His commandments. He is lying to you when He says to you that if you eat from the good tree, the one tree that He calls evil, then you will surely die. No, no! You will not surely die! For evil is actually good, and good is actually evil. God knows this, but He is lying to you about all of this, for He does not want you to figure out that if you eat of the tree, your eyes will be opened, and you will be like God, knowing good and evil."

Do you see just how poisonous Satan, the Serpent, really is? Therefore, whoever makes himself a disciple of Satan also invites upon himself the horrific judgment of being bitten by serpents:

*Thus I saw the horses in the vision, and those who sat on them, having breastplates of **fiery red**, hyacinth blue, and sulfur yellow; and the heads of lions. Out of their mouths proceed fire, smoke, and sulfur. By these three plagues were one third of mankind killed: by the fire, the smoke, and the sulfur, which proceeded out of their mouths. For the power of the horses is in*

their mouths, and in their tails. ***For their tails are like serpents, and have heads, and with them they harm.***
(Revelation 9:17–19)

    When will the wicked heed the warning? How long will they continue on in their wanton pleasures, having no fear of God before their eyes? After all of the divine judgments that have been poured out upon the world thus far, do they not see that the greatest judgments are still yet to come? Shall they willfully forget that this event, in which many of the Israelites were bitten by fiery serpents and subsequently died, was a true, historical event? And shall they also deliberately forget that it was sent upon the Israelites not by chance, but rather from God, according to His wrath that burned against their sin of taking His holy Name in vain? And shall they also forget, ever so hard-heartedly, that Jesus of Nazareth, whom they falsely claim was placid, actually preached extremely often about the torments of the burnings of the fires of Hell?

    Thus we warn unbelievers, in love, "O foolish, unbelieving souls! Do you not know that you are snake-bitten? Do you not perceive the poison within the Satanic bites of Darwinian theory and moral relativism? O proud Unbeliever, if you do not repent before God and believe upon Jesus as the Christ, you will not be so self-confident when, upon your death, you find yourself in the torments of Hades. And, on Judgment Day, your unrepentant acts of cursing of God will become part of the sure evidence of guilt that will be declared against you before the holy Judgment Seat of God, on account of which evidence you will be cast into Hell. And once in Hell, your resurrected body—that is, resurrected unto everlasting torment—will experience there what you so arrogantly denied here, namely, that God is so jealous for His eternal glory that He will send fiery serpents upon those who dare to blaspheme that eternal glory. For, in Hell, there will be serpents everywhere, even fiery serpents! We know this to be terrifyingly true, since Hell is likened in the Holy Scriptures to a lake of fire, and that fiery lake will burn, and burn with a vengeance, without the worm ever dying or the fire ever being quenched [Isaiah 66:24].

    "O Unbeliever, we plead with you to save yourself from this perverse generation! Turn away from your sin, and forsake your evil ways. Turn to God, who may yet have mercy upon you. Beg Him to save you from the future curses of Hell, even the curses of the fiery serpents that will bite the inhabitants of Hell. For why should you die, O man? Does not the Lord love to show mercy? For, He does not take any pleasure in the death of the wicked, but rather desires that you would turn—O please turn to Christ, and live! Then you will learn that your soul was created not to curse God, but to bless Him, and not to fight against God, but to worship Him."

MOSES MAKES A BRONZE SERPENT

What, then, shall a snake-bit person do? Is there any hope for him at all? Praise be to God, through Christ Jesus our Lord, that there is an antivenom, by the supernatural intervention of God:

> *The people came to Moses, and said, "We have sinned, because we have spoken against the LORD, and against you. Pray to the LORD, that He take away the serpents from us." Moses prayed for the people. The LORD said to Moses,* **"Make a fiery serpent, and set it on a pole. It shall happen, that everyone who is bitten, when he sees it, shall live."** *Moses made a serpent of [bronze], and set it on the pole. If a serpent had bitten any man, when he looked at the serpent of [bronze], he lived.* (Numbers 21:7–9)

About three decades ago, a physician, a pediatric-ICU physician, stood on the roof of Children's Hospital in Denver. His eyes were fixed on a small dot on the horizon, coming from the direction of Long's Peak. That dot was a helicopter, and the helicopter was carrying a ten-year-old boy who was suffering from seizures and experiencing kidney failure, having been bitten by an enormous rattlesnake just outside of Rocky Mountain National Park. The pediatric-ICU physician, being one of the best in the whole country—and yet I say it with an admitted bias, as I am his son—would have to oversee several life-saving procedures, including ventilation and surgery, in order to keep the child alive. Yet even so, he knew that the medical solution to preserving this young boy from death was a sufficient amount of *antivenom*. Therefore, having gathered up the entire rattlesnake antivenom supply in the whole greater-Colorado region, he steadily administered the antivenom until, by the grace of the Sovereign Lord and in answer to his pleading prayers, he was able to release the boy from the hospital, alive and well.

O how lucid and clear is the prophecy concerning Jesus contained within this historical account of the fiery serpents in the wilderness and the bronze serpent which Moses made in order to heal those who had been bitten! For, *the Gospel of Jesus Christ is the antivenom to the snakebite of human sin.* Satan, of course, is the most poisonous of all serpents. Yet even as he bruised Christ's heel, it was Christ Himself who bruised Satan's head. Also, just as Moses reached out his hand and toke hold of the serpent by the tail, such that it became a rod in his hand, so too does Christ have power over the serpent, such that he can take the bite of the serpent and turn it into the everlasting medicine of the Gospel.

When Moses made the bronze serpent and lifted it up on a pole, it must have looked like a cursed serpent hanging from a cross. Yet this marks our salvation, prophetically. For, even though that same bronze serpent later on became an object of Israelite idolatry up until the days of King Hezekiah [2 Kings 18:4], and even though the sign of the serpent on the pole later on became an object of pagan idolatry for the Greeks in their practices of medicine, and, still further, even though the very sign of the cross itself has become a superstitious idol for many unsaved, superstitious Catholics and Protestants, the true cross of Jesus Christ is our only hope for salvation. Thus just as the repentant Israelites, being snake-bitten, looked upwards towards the bronze serpent which was lifted up on Moses' pole (and they did this by faith, in order to be saved from otherwise certain death), so too do God's elect, those who are truly appointed for eternal life, look upwards to Jesus on the cross, bleeding on the cross for their sins, and receive, by faith, the healing power of God unto everlasting life:

> "And I, **if I am lifted up from the earth**, will draw all people to Myself." (John 12:32)

The Bronze Serpent

And similarly,

*Christ redeemed us from the curse of the law, **having become a curse for us**. For it is written, "Cursed is everyone who hangs on a tree."* (Galatians 3:13)

And, with prophetic precision,

As Moses lifted up the serpent in the wilderness, even so must the Son of Man be lifted up, *that whoever believes in Him should not perish, but have eternal life.* (John 3:14–15)

The ancient Serpent, Satan himself, slithered on the tree in the Garden of Eden, first tempting Adam, then biting Adam, and thus slaying Adam. Yet Jesus Christ, the Second Adam, spotless and sinless, hung upon the tree, bearing the poisonous venom of sin's wretched curse in His own body, for us, on the tree. He became the curse of the serpent in our stead, bleeding and dying for us on the cross. Thus Herbert is right when he gives us imaginative ears to hear Christ's voice saying, poetically:

O all ye who pass by, behold and see;
Man stole the fruit, but I must climb the tree;
The tree of life to all, but only Me;
Was ever grief like Mine?[1]

In dealing with unbelievers, then, we have no time or place for the overly eloquent and pride-flattering apologetics of academic theology. Instead, we warn them plainly, with flowing tears of love, and so tell them plainly, "You are snake-bitten! The poison of sin within you is causing internal hemorrhaging in your soul! You have little time left to live, for your life is as a vapor, appearing today and disappearing tomorrow. Your body is dying. Your heart is already dead, being dead to God through sin. Since you have blasphemed God, you are currently under the just

---

[1] George Herbert, "The Sacrifice" in *George Herbert: The Complete English Works* (New York: Everyman's Library, 1908; ed. and repr., Ann Pasternak Slater; New York: Alfred A. Knopf, 1995), 30 (emphasis in original).

condemnation of God, being sentenced under the high-treasonous crimes of sin to everlasting stings and fiery snakebites in Hell. That is, to say it plainly, if Christ Jesus were to tear open the clouds right now, returning to earth to set up His Kingdom on earth and to judge the living and the dead, you would be sentenced to Hell forever."

Yet this is not all that we say to them. We also say, "But O Man or Woman, created in the image of God, there is a cure to this horrific snakebite of your own sin. God is merciful, and even eager to forgive your crimes against His glory. If you will but humble yourself, and repent of your pride, and look upon the Son of Man, Christ Jesus, who hung on the cross for you, suffering under the wrath of God in your stead, you can be healed. You need not die! For, the Son of God became fully Man, that He might die for men, yet He remains fully God, the very Son of the Father, eternal as the Father is eternal, and so has the divine power and authority to heal you, even you, and even right now, as you gaze upon His once-for-all wounded and bleeding frame. Having been nailed to the cross, and having suffered in your place, He died as the only true, wrath-appeasing sacrifice for your sins. See, then, His death for you! Look upon Jesus, crucified for you, and believe that God raised Him from the dead on the third day, and, therefore, through your repentance towards God, and by putting your faith and hope in God alone, be now raised to newness of life in Christ—be made alive to God, at last, to fear Him and worship Him—by His Holy Spirit! For He, the Spirit of Christ, has the divine power to raise your sin-slain heart unto new and everlasting life in Christ."

All of this, as verified in the Gospel, is accurate and true. Yet even authentic, regenerate Christians live in bodies that are preparing to die. Therefore, although we, as Christians, have looked upwards to the cross, seeing Christ hanging on the cross, and thus bearing the poisonous curse of the serpent's bite on our behalf, and have been healed by His stripes, nevertheless we still must await *the final healing* of our bodies through the resurrection from the dead.

The world is still groaning and laboring under the curse. Our own bodies are still groaning in tribulations, pains, and sufferings. Inwardly we groan, even as we eagerly await our adoption, the redemption of our bodies [Romans 8:22-23]. For, when Christ comes again, returning to earth to finish His battle with the Serpent, such that the Serpent will be bound and cast into the abyss for one thousand years [Revelation 20:1-3], only then shall He gather His elect from the four winds, and grant them their part in the first resurrection.

Then, our bodies shall be fully healed, with no more sickness, or tears, or death. Thus once this miracle of Christian resurrection breaks in upon the world, our loved ones in Christ will never again grow ill and weak. Our bodies will never again be subjected to the blood-spilling pains of the Devil's persecutions. Instead, Christ, our Lord and our God, shall be our everlasting Healer. He, whose mortal wounds on the cross were fully healed by His own resurrection from the dead, shall revive us, shall raise us immortal and imperishable, and we, in turn, shall rise up and glorify Him—being a resurrected multitude of worshippers from every nation, tribe, people, and tongue, all healed by the one, everlasting Gospel, and thus all singing in Heaven, with one accord, the one, everlasting song of the praise of the glory of the Father, and the praise of the glory of the Lamb, forever and ever, world without end. Amen.

ial text style - PROPHECIES OF THE CROSS

6

CURSES ON MOUNT EBAL
The Cross in Deuteronomy 27:1-26

Moses and the elders of Israel commanded the people, saying, "Keep all the commandments which I command you today. It shall be on the day when you shall pass over the Jordan to the land which the LORD your God gives you, that [you yourself shall raise up] great stones, and coat them with plaster. You shall write on them all the Words of this Law, when you have passed over; that you may go in to the land which the LORD your God gives you, a land flowing with milk and honey, as the LORD, the God of your fathers, has promised you. It shall be, when you have crossed over the Jordan, that you shall [raise up] these stones, which I command you today, on Mount Ebal, and you shall coat them with plaster. There you shall build an altar to the LORD your God, an altar of stones. You shall not use any iron tool on them. You shall build the altar of the LORD your God of uncut stones. You shall offer burnt offerings on it to the LORD your God. You shall sacrifice peace offerings, and shall eat there. You shall rejoice before the LORD your God. You shall write on the stones all the Words of this Law very plainly." (Deuteronomy 27:1–8)

GOD has spoken, first by His Prophets and then, in these last days, by His Son, and thus the whole world is held accountable to His holy Word. This is the divine Word, the imperishable Word that stands forever, which is the very Word that proceeds from the mouth of God. By this Word, all men from all epochs of world history will be judged. Therefore, God commands His people to *"raise up"* His Words as a witness against all within Israel who would rebel against Him:

> *"It shall be on the day when you shall pass over the Jordan to the land which the LORD your God gives you, **that [you yourself shall raise up] great stones**, and coat them with plaster."* (Deuteronomy 27:2)

And, a second time,

> *"It shall be, when you have crossed over the Jordan, **that you shall [raise up] these stones**, which I command you today, on Mount Ebal, and you shall coat them with plaster."* (Deuteronomy 27:4)

And then, a third time,

> *" 'Cursed is he **who does not [raise up] the Words of this Law** by doing them.' All the people shall say, 'Amen.' "* (Deuteronomy 27:26)

The Israelites, under Joshua, are commanded by God to *raise up* His Words, and thus to write His holy Laws on the whitewashed stones which they will *raise up* on Mount Ebal, once they have crossed the Jordan River into the Promised Land. How much more, then, are Christians required by God to *raise up* the Word of Jesus Christ, proclaiming Him to the ends of the earth! For, the Word of God, which is the very Word of the Gospel, demands a response from all men. It must be obeyed. It cannot be ignored. Since the Gospel of Jesus Christ goes out to the ends of the earth, He thus commands all men everywhere to repent. For, it is by God's holy Law, His holy Word, that all men are convicted as guilty before the Lord of Heaven and earth, and thus are summoned by their Creator to repent upon their hearing of the preaching of the cross of Jesus:

> *Now we know that whatever things the Law says, it speaks to those who are under the Law, **that every mouth may be closed,***

and all the world may be brought under the judgment of God. (Romans 3:19)

And also,

But I say, did they not hear? Yes, most certainly, **"Their sound went out into all the earth, their words to the ends of the world."** (Romans 10:18)

However, we live in the last days of the last days, and so it seems that nearly the whole world now scoffs at the holiness of God's Word. That is, when God's evangelists *raise up* the Word of Christ for all of the world to see, much like a lamp on a lampstand or a city set upon a hill, the entire world jeers at it and mocks it. In specific, the people of the world either scoff at the Bible's holy *authority*, as if they will not be judged by it on the Day of Judgment, or else they deride its holy *interpretation*, as if the practice of *God-fearing* Bible interpretation needs to be replaced by one that is much more in agreement with the world-wide idolatry of modern psychology.

Yet we, as those who do fear God, are not ashamed of the Gospel of Jesus Christ. Therefore, we assert both the holy authority and the holy interpretation of the Holy Scriptures. In doing so, we proclaim, even from the rooftops, the biblical doctrine of God's righteous wrath. For, even though a scoffing world does not want to hear it, such that they will cover their ears and gnash their teeth even at the mention of God's global flood of wrath during the days of Noah, the whole world is accountable to the Word of Christ. He has been lifted up on the cross. All men have had the opportunity to be drawn to Him by way of the cross. Therefore, all are accountable to this holy Gospel, and those who reject it shall, on the great and dreadful Day of the Lord, face all of its pronounced curses against the wicked.

MOUNT EBAL: THE MOUNTAIN OF CURSES

Mount Ebal is a mountain just inside of the Promised Land, situated about twenty miles west of the Jordan River, being adjacent to Shechem, seated on the north side of Shechem. It is one of the tallest peaks in that region of Canaan. Yet God's commandment makes Mount Ebal a place of cursing, for the Lord commands that the curses of His covenant with Israel be shouted forth from this mountain. Mount Ebal, therefore, is a landmark within Israel that serves as a perpetual reminder of all of the holy threatenings in the Bible concerning all of those who would scorn the Gospel:

> *Moses commanded the people the same day, saying, "These shall stand on Mount Gerizim to bless the people, when you have crossed over the Jordan: Simeon, Levi, Judah, Issachar, Joseph, and Benjamin.* ***These shall stand on Mount Ebal for the curse: Reuben, Gad, Asher, Zebulun, Dan, and Naphtali****. With a loud voice, the Levites shall say to all the men of Israel, '****Cursed*** *is the man who makes an engraved or molten image, an abomination to the LORD, the work of the hands of the craftsman, and sets it up in secret.' All the people shall answer and say, 'Amen.' '****Cursed*** *is he who dishonors his father or his mother.' All the people shall say, 'Amen.' '****Cursed*** *is he who removes his neighbor's landmark.' All the people shall say, 'Amen.' '****Cursed*** *is he who leads the blind astray on the road.' All the people shall say, 'Amen.' '****Cursed*** *is he who withholds justice from the foreigner, fatherless, and widow.' All the people shall say, 'Amen.' '****Cursed*** *is he who lies with his father's wife, because he dishonors his father's bed.' All the people shall say, 'Amen.' '****Cursed*** *is he who lies with any kind of animal.' All the people shall say, 'Amen.' '****Cursed*** *is he who lies with his sister, his father's daughter or his mother's daughter.' All the people shall say, 'Amen.' '****Cursed*** *is he who lies with his mother-in-law.' All the people shall say, 'Amen.' '****Cursed*** *is he who secretly kills his neighbor.' All the people shall say, 'Amen.' '****Cursed*** *is he who takes a bribe to kill an innocent person.' All the people shall say, 'Amen.' '****Cursed*** *is he who does not [raise up] the Words of this Law by doing them.' All the people shall say, 'Amen.'"*
> (Deuteronomy 27:11–26)

Curses on Mount Ebal

Mount Gerizim sits just across the valley of the city of Shechem, on the side of the valley opposite from Mount Ebal. Thus Mount Ebal sits on the north side of Shechem, while the city of Shechem, itself, rests in the valley in the middle of the two mountains, and Mount Gerizim sits on the south side of the city. The Lord, then, turns these two great mountains into echoing voices. After crossing into the Promised Land, Joshua is to build an altar to the Lord on Mount Ebal (for the curse of sin requires the atonement of blood sacrifice), and then he is to position six of the tribes of Israel on Mount Gerizim, the mountain of blessing, and the remaining six tribes on Mount Ebal, the mountain of cursing. Then, from Mount Gerizim, the Levites are to call out these curses that would so terrifyingly come upon the Israelites, if they were to forsake God by transgressing His holy statutes and commandments.

There are twelve curses listed here, probably representing the number of the tribes of Israel, with each one being a practical application of one of the Ten Commandments. For example, *"Cursed is the one who lies with his sister, the daughter of his father or the daughter of his mother,"* is a curse aimed at any man who would make himself a brazen violator of the Seventh Commandment, while the curse pronounced against *"the one who takes a bribe to slay an innocent person"* is directed against the murderer who would dare to violate the Sixth Commandment for the sake of money—even as abortionists do to this very day. The Levites, then, are to shout out these curses from their place on Mount Gerizim, causing them to echo off of Mount Ebal, which is opposite them, and then the six tribes of Israel who are positioned on Mount Ebal are to answer the Levites by shouting, *"Amen!"* such that their *"Amen!"* echoes its way back across the valley and off of the rocks on Mount Gerizim.

Mount Ebal, then, is the mountain of cursing. It is the place where Israel, being the Bride of God, reaffirms her marriage covenant with God, such that she promises to maintain her fidelity to Him, her divine Husband, by keeping His Law, and thus consents, willfully, to come under the curses of the covenant, if she were to violate it through sinful acts of idolatry (which would be spiritual adultery), Sabbath-breaking, stealing, oppressing the weak, etc. For, *God* is her Husband, and thus infidelity to this spiritual marriage covenant will bring upon Israel the worst of judgments: curses in the city, and curses in the country; curses of the fruit of the body and of the produce of the land; curses of disease, including consumption, with fever, with inflammation, and with severe burning fever; curses of the sword, including horrific acts of war perpetrated against her by her enemies; curses of disinheritance and captivity, and, as a result, the enslavement of her sons and daughters; and thus, in sum, total and complete curses, from the sole of Israel's foot to the top of her head [Deuteronomy 28:15-68]. All of these curses will come upon Israel when she does not carefully observe all the Words of the Law of her God, written for her in the book of Moses, so that she might fear this glorious and fearful name, *"THE LORD HER GOD."*

However, if Mount Ebal is such a foreboding place, filled with the warnings of such terrible curses that will come upon all of those who turn away, with hardness of heart, from God's holy commandments, then the Gospel of Jesus Christ begins with some terrifying news. That is, the Gospel proclaims that all men are guilty of transgressing God's holy statutes and commandments, and, therefore, all who are outside of Christ are headed for such terrifying curses. For, the curses of Mount Ebal are, indeed, frightening to the bones, and yet the curses of the valley of Hell, where the fire of God's wrath flows down the mountains of this wicked world and gathers into an everlasting lake of fire, are everlastingly worse. Yet the Gospel says that all men are deserving of such curses in Hell, for all men are guilty of treating God's holy commandments with great contempt:

What then? Are we better than they? No, in no way. For we previously warned both Jews and Greeks, **that they are all under sin.** *(Romans 3:9)*

Or, as Paul says it in his letter to the Galatians,

For as many as are of the works of the Law **are under a curse.** *For it is written,* **"Cursed is everyone who does not continue in** *all things that are written in the book of the Law, to do them."* (Galatians 3:10)

And, as James, the brother of Jesus, says,

For whoever keeps the whole Law, and yet stumbles in one point, **he has become guilty of all.** (James 2:10)

Nevertheless, the Gospel is still "Good News" to those who are being saved, because it declares *another mountain*, a mountain of atonement for our sins. There is, to be sure, Mount Ebal, towering above us, casting a dark shadow over our heads, and, standing beneath Mount Ebal, we all deserve the curses of Hell. Yet there is also Mount Calvary, and on Mount Calvary Jesus took the curse, including all of the curses of the covenant of the Law, upon Himself for our sins, and not for ours only but also for the whole world:

Christ redeemed us from the curse of the Law, having become a curse for us. *For it is written, "Cursed is everyone who hangs on a tree."* (Galatians 3:13)

Therefore, may it never be that we should treat Mount Calvary lightly! For, the curses of Mount Calvary were much worse, infinitely worse than the curses of Mount Ebal. And yet Jesus, in His love for the Father and His love for the whole world, bore those curses for us, His elect, in His own body on the cross.

We must, therefore, remember the curses of Mount Calvary, so that we can remember the sorrows of our Lord, who was crucified not for His own sins, but for our sins on that sacrificial Mount. He was sinless on the cross, and yet He became sin for us on the cross. Thus all of the curses of human sin—the sins of all humanity throughout all of world history—were cast upon Him on the cross. The curse of Eve's *labor pains* became His own spiritual and physical *labors of death* on the cross. The curse of Adam's *sweat* and Adam's *thorns* met together on His brow, with His *sweat* becoming drops of blood and His crown being a crown of *thorns*. If the crime of adultery demands the curse of a swelling belly and a rotting thigh, then His was the swelling belly, and His the rotting thigh upon the cross. If the curse demands that one be handed over to all of the cruel plots and abuses of one's enemies, then Jesus was so handed over to His enemies at Calvary. Our Lord Jesus Christ, our substitutionary Sacrifice, was sinless, and so the curses of Satan had no just accusation against Him, and should have been like a flitting sparrow, or like a flying swallow, unable to alight upon Him. Yet since He bore our sins, the anger of the Father in Heaven did not spare Him, but rather His jealous vengeance burned against Him, and every curse that is written in the Book of the Law settled upon Him, even Jesus, the Son of God.

Do we see this? Do we weep over this? Mount Calvary became the Mount of Cursing, even cursing the very spotless Lamb of God. There, on Mount Calvary, the King of kings became a reproach and a byword, a taunt and a curse to all men. There, at Calvary, He willingly allowed the curse of the flying scroll of the Prophet Zechariah to be sent out not into the house of the thief, but even into His own, precious body. He was perfectly meek and innocent, being infinitely more innocent than the most kind-hearted, gentle, tender, and loving little child, and yet they tortured Him and shredded His back with nail-toothed whips.

At Mount Calvary, He was poured out like water. All of His bones were out of joint. His hearted melted within Him like wax. His strength was dried up like a potsherd, and His tongue clung to the roof of His mouth. It was at Mount Calvary that He was brought down to the dust of death, and He who had the power to strike the whole earth with a curse, was Himself struck down with the curse. This is why, before crucifying Him, they previously had blindfolded Him, beaten Him, mocked Him, and struck Him mercilessly. All of this was to take the written code of the Law, and especially the written code of the curses that were to be sounded forth from Mount Ebal, and to nullify their condemning claim over God's elect by nailing them to the cross on Mount Calvary [Colossians 2:14].

O Christian, do not forget the sorrows of the curses of Mount Calvary. Do not revisit them only once per year, on Good Friday. Instead, O Christian, remember the sorrows of the cross daily. Bring them to remembrance daily. For to this you were called, even to share in those sorrows and sufferings, just as a bondslave shares in his master's business, and a son shares in his father's interests. Jesus, your Lord, bore the curses of sin for you. Therefore, you must live in continual remembrance of His suffering love for you.

Mount Gerizim: The Mountain of Blessing

If Mount Ebal, in the Law of Moses, is the mountain of cursing, then Mount Gerizim, opposite Ebal, is the mountain of blessing. The Gospel, then, speaks first of cursing, for all have sinned and fallen short of the glory of God, but then, afterwards, speaks also of blessing:

*Moses commanded the people the same day, saying, "**These shall stand on Mount Gerizim to bless the people**, when you have crossed over the Jordan: Simeon, Levi, Judah, Issachar, Joseph, and Benjamin."* (Deuteronomy 27:11–12)

In the Gospel, there are, to be sure, terrifying curses for the wicked, but there are also glorious blessings for the righteous. For, the Law of Moses sounds forth the blessings of the righteous: that they would put all of their enemies to flight; that God would cause them to be fruitful and to multiply; that their old harvest would be so plentiful that it would overlap with their new harvest; that wild beasts would cease from the land and they would dwell safely in the wilderness and sleep in the woods; that showers of blessing would fall upon their fields; that the vine would give its fruit and the ground its increase; that the heavens would give their dew; and etc. [Deuteronomy 28:1-14; Ezekiel 34:25-41]. Yet since, as we have said, there is no man who, prior to being born of the Holy Spirit, rightly obeys the Law of God, but instead all are under sin, this means that the only path to such glorious blessings from God is the path of faith in Christ Jesus. For, the righteousness of God comes to sinful man only through the righteousness of Christ Jesus, and thus comes only to those who receive that righteousness through truly repentant, saving faith in Him:

I know that, when I come to you, ***I will come in the fullness of the blessing of the Gospel of Christ****.* (Romans 15:29)

  Thus if Mount Gerizim is the mountain of blessing for Israel, then for all of those who are truly born of God, and thus who do not continue in sin, the new mountain of blessing must be the Mount of Olives. For it was there, at the Mount of Olives, that Jesus ascended into Heaven:

Then they returned to Jerusalem [that is, having just witnessed the ascension of Christ into Heaven] ***from the mountain called Olivet, which is near Jerusalem, a Sabbath day's journey away****.* (Acts 1:12)

  Yet it was here, at the Mount of Olives, near Bethany, just prior to His ascension, that Jesus lifted up His hands and blessed His disciples. The Mount of Olives, then, is the New Covenant mountain of blessing:

He led them out as far as Bethany, ***and He lifted up His hands, and blessed them****. While He blessed them, He withdrew from them, and was carried up into Heaven.* (Luke 24:50–51)

  How does the blessing of Abraham come upon the Gentiles? It comes upon them only *through Christ Jesus*. How are we blessed by our God and Father with every spiritual blessing in the Heavenly realms? We are only so blessed *in Christ Jesus*. His is the resurrection from the dead. His also is the ascension into Heaven from the Mount of Olives. Therefore, He bestows the blessing of the promise of the resurrection upon all those who are His seed, who are born of His Holy Spirit.

  However, when we speak of the Mount of Olives as the place of Christ's ascension into Heaven, and thus as the mountain of blessing for true believers, we are in no way speaking the language of the false gospel of Joseph Prince and Joel Osteen. For such men do not bless people, but rather, by their false teachings, they swiftly usher their followers into all of the curses of Hell.

Rather, we believe the New Covenant truth that those who are blessed in the Kingdom of God—and thus who shall receive all of the blessings of the coming Kingdom—are those who, in this life, are greatly persecuted, downtrodden, poor, and filled with all kinds of sorrows and tribulations:

*He lifted up His eyes to His disciples, and said, "**Blessed are you who are poor**, [yours is the Kingdom of God]. **Blessed are you who hunger now**, for you will be filled. **Blessed are you who weep now**, for you will laugh. **Blessed are you when men shall hate you, and when they shall exclude and mock you, and throw out your name as evil, for the Son of Man's sake."* (Luke 6:20–22)

Peter knew this and taught it. Speaking to New Testament believers, the great Apostle blessed his spiritual children with all of the future blessings of those who suffer, in the present time, for the sake of righteousness:

*But even if you should **suffer** for righteousness' sake, **you are blessed**. "Do not fear what they fear, neither be troubled."* (1 Peter 3:14)

And also,

*If you **are [reviled]** for the name of Christ, **you are blessed**; because the Spirit of glory and of God rests on you. On their part He is blasphemed, but on your part He is glorified.* (1 Peter 4:14)

Are you suffering, dear Brother or Sister? Do your own family members persecute you for the name of Christ? Are you under financial distress because of your obedience to the Gospel of Christ? Is your body afflicted with sickness, or weakness, and yet all under a humble submission to the commandments of Christ? Does Satan threaten to attack you? Are you scorned and rejected by the world because of your unwavering allegiance to the Word of Jesus Christ? O trembling Brother, O afflicted Sister, so hurt and alone, soaking your pillow with the tears of the Gospel, your Lord in Heaven loves you with His special, divine love. He comforts you, and even delights in you. Since you have been willing to share in His sufferings, He invites you to share in all of the blessings of the Mount of Olives—for there He ascended, and it is there that He shall descend to earth once more.

MOUNT ZION: THE HEAVENLY MOUNTAIN

Is it not becoming clear to us, then, that Mount Ebal and Mount Gerizim are, in the end, symbolic of the coming, everlasting state? For, the mountain of cursing symbolizes the burning hills of Hell, while the mountain of blessing symbolizes the glistening mountains of Heaven, full of all of the cream and honey of Paradise:

> *Moses commanded the people the same day, saying, "These shall stand **on Mount Gerizim to bless** the people, when you have crossed over the Jordan: Simeon, Levi, Judah, Issachar, Joseph, and Benjamin. These shall stand **on Mount Ebal for the curse**: Reuben, Gad, Asher, Zebulun, Dan, and Naphtali."* (Deuteronomy 27:11–13)

The mountains, then, represent the urgency of the Gospel. A man cannot waiver between the two, wanting to climb both of them at once. Life only affords one destination. Spiritually speaking, a man only has time to climb one of the two mountains before he dies. Thus either he will end his journey atop the mount of cursing, or else on the peak of the mount of blessing. Undoubtedly, it is only God's grace, the grace of the Spirit of Christ, which enables any pilgrim to ascend the mount of blessing, but nevertheless the choice between the two mountains rests upon the heart and the will of the individual:

> *"Behold, I set before you today a blessing and a curse: the blessing, **if you listen to the commandments of the LORD your God**, which I command you today; and the curse, **if you do not listen to the commandments of the LORD your God**, but turn*

aside out of the way which I command you today, to go after other gods, which you have not known."
(Deuteronomy 11:26–28)

And also,

"I call Heaven and earth to witness against you today, **that I have set before you life and death, the blessing and the curse. Therefore CHOOSE life**, *that you may live, you and your descendants."* (Deuteronomy 30:19)

What shall we say, then, of today's false-teaching hospital chaplains who, for the sake of money, give their hearty consent and submission to the secularized laws of hospital chaplaincy, including those laws that forbid them to evangelize the sick and the dying with the true, biblical Gospel of Jesus Christ? Many of them claim to be *Christian* chaplains. They say, craftily, that they evangelize silently, through their acts of love and service. Yet they refuse to call Islam a blasphemous religion of antichrist utterances, and they affirm (either verbally or by silent approbation) multiple pathways to God, and when their patients, who are dying in their sins, clearly lack the fear of God and thus the saving grace of Jesus Christ, they obey man rather than God by silently letting those sinners die in their sins, rather than risking their own necks to tell them the truth about the Gospel of righteousness, self-control, and the judgment to come. How great, then, shall be the punishment of such charlatans when they themselves cross over from death into Hell!

God's love for sinners is plain and truthful. It warns sinners not only of Mount Ebal, but of Hell itself. God's love for sinners says to them that if they sin willfully after they have received the knowledge of the truth, then *"there remains no more a sacrifice for sins, but **a certain fearful expectation of judgment**, and a fierceness of fire which will devour the adversaries"* (Hebrews 10:26–27). It also warns them of the coming curses of the coming burnings of Hell, and it does so by saying, *"For the land which has drunk the rain that comes often on it, and produces a crop suitable for them for whose sake it is also tilled, receives*

***blessing** from God; but if it bears thorns and thistles, it is rejected and near being **cursed**, whose end is to be burned"* (Hebrews 6:7–8), and also, *"Then He will say also to those on the left hand, 'Depart from Me, **you cursed**, into the eternal fire which is prepared for the devil and his angels'"* (Matthew 25:41).

However, the yearning of our hearts is to be able to tell newly born-again believers, washed in the blood of the Lamb, the glories of the blessings of Heaven. We want to tell new believers, who have received the truth of the Gospel, even in the midst of great conflict and persecution, not only about Mount Gerizim, but even more about Mount Zion, the City of our God. Our desire is to be able to tell them that on Mount Zion, *"**There will be no curse any more**. The throne of God and of the Lamb will be in it, and His servants serve Him"* (Revelation 22:3). Also, we want to have the joy of teaching them that on the Last Day, the King of glory shall say to them, *"Come, **blessed of My Father**, inherit the Kingdom prepared for you from the foundation of the world'"* (Matthew 25:34).

For, it is there, on Mount Zion, that the slopes will drip with wine, and the hills will flow with milk, and all the brooks of Judah shall rush with perfectly clean water, and a fountain shall flow from the house of the Lord and water the Valley of Acacias. It will be the Heavenly Mountain of God, a mountain of everlasting blessing, full of everlasting joy and gladness. For there, on that Mountain, we shall see God. And these are the two greatest blessings of all of the blessings which Christ has promised to His people, namely, that on Mount Zion we shall see the unveiled glory of His face, and that He shall dwell with us forever and ever:

*They shall **see His face**....* (Revelation 22:4)[1]

And,

> *"**I will set My tabernacle among you**, and My soul shall not abhor you. **I will walk among you and be your God**, and you shall be My people."* (Leviticus 26:11–12)[2]

---

[1] NKJV translation.
[2] Ibid.

And all of this shall be to the glory of the name of Jesus Christ, with all honor and adoration given to the Father of glory, everlasting ages unto everlasting ages, world without end. Amen.

Part Two:

The Cross
in Psalm 22

7

WHY HAVE YOU FORSAKEN ME?
The Cross in Psalm 22:1-21

My God, My God, why have You forsaken Me? Why are You so far from [My salvation cry], and from the words of My groaning? My God, I cry in the daytime, but You do not answer; in the night season, and am not silent. But You are holy, You who inhabit the praises of Israel. Our fathers trusted in You. They trusted, and You delivered them. They cried to You, and were delivered. They trusted in You, and were not disappointed. (Psalm 22:1–5)

GOD the Son, Jesus Christ, feels forsaken by His Father, *"My God, My God, why have You forsaken Me?"* That is to say, God the Father now puts His only-begotten Son to the greatest test. For, the greatest test is not one of feeling forsaken by God, even unto death, and then being delivered from death by God. Rather, the greatest test occurs when Jesus feels forsaken by God, even unto death, and yet there is no deliverance from death granted to Him by God.

In past ages, there were times when Israel felt forsaken by God, even unto death. Yet during such times, Israel always could cling to the promise, given to her by Moses, that the Lord her God would never forsake her:

Be strong and courageous. Do not be afraid or scared of them; for the LORD your God Himself is who goes with you. **He will not fail you nor forsake you.** (Deuteronomy 31:6)

Thus whenever Israel felt forsaken by God, she always could hold tight to this promise, and, therefore, cry out with words similar to the words of King David, **"Do not forsake me, O LORD. My God, do not be far from me!"** (Psalm 38:21). And, as God's promise is always true, since it is impossible for God to lie, Israel always could count on Him to fulfill His promise to her, and thus never forsake her:

*Behold, the LORD has proclaimed to the end of the earth, "Say to the daughter of Zion, 'Behold, your salvation comes. Behold, His reward is with Him, and His recompense before Him.'" They will call them The Holy People, The LORD's Redeemed. You will be called Sought Out, **A City Not Forsaken**.* (Isaiah 62:11–12)

Throughout her history, God subjected Israel to tests, even great tests such as: her life-threatening slavery in Egypt, during which her baby boys were mercilessly snatched out of the arms of their mothers and cast into the Nile River; her desperate lack of bread and water during her forty years of sojourning through the wilderness; her violent oppression at the hands of her surrounding enemies during the times of the Judges; and even her political bondage, much later, under the iron yokes of the Babylonians and the Persians after the burning of Solomon's Temple in Jerusalem. In all such tests, Israel felt, at times, very much forsaken by God. Yet every time, God always brought forth a supernatural deliverance. Thus Israel never was forsaken by Him.

However, it is Jesus alone who must face the greatest test. For, it is one thing to feel forsaken by God, and yet subsequently, after cries for help, to be delivered, miraculously, by the outstretched arm of God; and it is quite another thing to face feeling forsaken by God, even unto death, without any forthcoming deliverance from His Heavenly throne:

My God, My God, why have You forsaken Me? *Why are You so far from [My salvation cry], and from the words of My groaning? My God, I cry in the daytime,* ***but You do not answer****; in the night season, and am not silent.* (Psalm 22:1–2)

Why Have You Forsaken Me?

"Let Him Deliver Him, Since He Delights in Him!"

This is the greatest test. Jesus' trust in His Father is tested by this great question, "Why would the Father abandon Him, even unto death?" And what makes this test so incomparable to all others is that Jesus is the *delight* of His Father. It is not as though He is a reprobate, guilty of great crimes against God, and yet calling out to God for mercy and deliverance, not because he fears God, but only because He does not want to suffer agony in Hades. In such a case, one might understand that a reprobate deserves abandonment unto death.

Yet Jesus' righteousness is the infinite opposite of this. He is no reprobate, and He deserves no death. Rather, He is God's *greatest delight*. As the eternal Son of the Father, He is the Father's uncreated, infinite, essence-sharing *joy*. Satan mocks Jesus for this, as Jesus is dying on the cross. Satan ridicules the fact that God's beloved Son, His greatest delight, is now feeling forsaken by God upon the cross:

> *All those who see Me mock Me. They insult Me with their lips. They shake their heads, saying,* **"He trusts in the Lord; let Him deliver Him. Let Him rescue Him, since He delights in Him."** (Psalm 22:7–8)

It is true that God *"delights"* in His Son. In fact, God delights in His children, all of His children, with a special delight. Therefore, David knew that the Lord had saved him from the waters of death since God delighted in David himself:

> *He sent from on high and he took me. He drew me out of many waters. He delivered me from my strong enemy, from those who hated me, for they were too mighty for me. They came on me in the day of my calamity, but the Lord was my support. He also brought me out into a large place.* ***He delivered me, because he delighted in me.*** (2 Samuel 22:17–20)

Not only that, but God even *delighted* in Solomon, David's son, who reigned on the throne of his father:

[The Queen of Sheba speaking to Solomon:] *"Blessed is the LORD your God,* **who delighted in you***, to set you on the throne of Israel. Because the LORD loved Israel forever, therefore He made you king, to do justice and righteousness."* (1 Kings 10:9)

Yet if God *delighted* first in David, and then in Solomon, how much more does He *delight* in His only-begotten Son! For, neither David nor Solomon are spotless, sinless, eternal, uncreated, and full of divine glory. Only Jesus is these things. Thus the Father *delights* in Jesus more than any other. In turn, Jesus, His only-begotten Son, *delights* to do the Father's will:

Sacrifice and offering You did not desire. You have opened My ears. You have not required burnt offering and sin offering. Then I said, "Behold, I have come. It is written about Me in the Book in the Scroll. ***I delight to do Your will, My God****. Yes, Your Law is within My heart."* (Psalm 40:6–8)

There is no question that God the Father delights in God the Son. For, Jesus is His Servant, His Son, upon whom He has placed the seal of His Holy Spirit. For, God is, no doubt, the triune God, and the three Persons of the Trinity have delighted in each other from eternity past:

Behold, My Servant, whom I uphold; ***My Chosen, in whom My soul delights—I have put My Spirit on Him****. He will bring justice to the nations.* (Isaiah 42:1)

Who can understand how much the Father delights in the Son? If an earthly father delights in the obedience of his earthly son, how much more does God the Father delight in the obedience of His only-begotten Son? How can one possibly begin to describe the strength of love, that infinite strength of love, with which the Father in Heaven loves Jesus, His Son?

...and the Holy Spirit descended in a bodily form like a dove on Him; and a voice came [from heaven], saying ***"You are My beloved Son. In You I am well pleased."*** (Luke 3:22)

Why Have You Forsaken Me?

The cross, then, is the greatest of tests. For, on the cross Jesus feels forsaken by the very Father who has delighted in Him for all of eternity. How, then, can the One in whom God *delights* find Himself so *despised* by the people? If God *delights* in Him so, why would God allow Him to be so cruelly *despised* upon the cross?

> *But I am a worm, and no man; a reproach of men,* **and despised by the people**. (Psalm 22:6)

Is this how God treats the One in whom He most delights? Shall the royal Son, the divine Son, live His earthly life as One who is despised?

> **I am small and despised**. *I do not forget Your precepts.* (Psalm 119:141)

And,

> *The* LORD, *the Redeemer of Israel, and his Holy One, says* **to Him whom man despises, to Him whom the nation abhors**, *to a Servant of rulers: "Kings shall see and rise up; princes, and they shall worship; because of the* LORD *who is faithful, even the Holy One of Israel, who has chosen You."* (Isaiah 49:7)

What should be done for the Son of Man, whom God delights to honor? Should not a royal robe, which God Himself has worn, and a royal horse, one of God's Heavenly horses, with God's royal crest upon its head, be given to one of God's angels, so that the angel may array Jesus with all of these divine emblems of glory? Should not all of Heaven and earth see Jesus in His divine robes, riding upon His white horse, and shout, *"To Him who sits on the throne, and to the Lamb be the blessing, the honor, the glory, and the dominion, forever and ever! Amen!"* (Revelation 5:13)?

Why, then, is Jesus, who is God's own delight, not so honored? Why, instead, is He so despised?

He is despised *and rejected of men; a Man of sorrows, and acquainted with grief: and we hid as it were our faces from Him;* ***He was despised****, and we esteemed Him not.*
(Isaiah 53:3, KJV)

    Jesus, on the cross, prays Psalm 22 in great anguish of spirit, saying, *"My God, My God, why have You forsaken Me?"* He also reminds Himself of the verse from Psalm 22 that says, *"But I am a worm, and no man; a reproach of men,* ***and despised by the people.***"

    How can this be? Why has God allowed it to be so? Should the One in whom God delights the most become the most despised of men? Should the King of kings be crushed underfoot by sinful men, much like a worm? Should the King of glory, God's eternal Son, be spit upon, much in the same manner as vile men spit upon the dirt, or upon a hated foe? Why has the Father allowed the Son, in whom He delights, to be so despised? This is the greatest test for Jesus, to trust the Father, even when He feels forsaken by the Father upon the cross.

    Somehow, it was the Father's *delight* to bruise Him. Yet we do not say—may it never be!—that the Father took delight in the torments and sufferings of His Son. Rather, we say, with the Prophet Isaiah, that *the Father delighted to defeat Satan, sin, and death through the sufferings of His Son.* That is, the Father knew that Jesus' torments upon the cross, even bearing God's wrath for the sins of the world, would work out for the salvation of many souls, and thus the everlasting glory and praise of the Son:

Yet it [delighted] the LORD to bruise Him. *He has caused Him to suffer. When You make His soul an offering for sin, He will see His offspring. He will prolong His days,* **and the LORD's [delight] will prosper in His hand.** (Isaiah 53:10)

    Again, it was *not* in the torments of Jesus that the Father delighted. Once again, may it never be! To the contrary, it *delighted* the Father to bruise Him only in that the Father foreknew that the sufferings of Jesus would cause the *delight* of resurrection glory to prosper in Jesus' hand. Thus God did, does, and always shall delight in His Son, Christ Jesus, and it was *because* He delighted in Him that He delivered Him up to be so despised by the people.

O dear, suffering Christian, horrific pains and persecutions are not commonly a sign of God's displeasure towards you. Instead, in many cases, your state of being despised by the world is a sign that God delights in you:

> *Summoning the Apostles, they beat them and commanded them not to speak in the name of Jesus, and let them go. They therefore departed from the presence of the council, **rejoicing that they were counted worthy to suffer dishonor for Jesus' name**.* (Acts 5:40–41)

Do you feel despised by the people? Does it seem that you have been forsaken by God? Do you look around you and see other professing Christians living lives that are full and rich, with the world considering them to be wise, strong, distinguished, and highly honored, while you yourself are reviled, persecuted, defamed, hated by all men, weak, barren, and poor, and thus considered by the world to be foolish, dishonored, and worthy of imprisonment, or perhaps even worthy to be sentenced to death? Now if you suffer as a murderer, a thief, or an evil doer, that is of your own doing. We are not talking about that [1 Peter 4:15]. Yet if you truly are suffering for the name of Christ, then know, O precious, suffering Christian, that you are not forsaken by God! Instead, God *delights* in you! He has seen your great faith, has filled it with a great measure of the fullness of Christ, and thus has allowed Christ in you, the hope of glory, to be despised by the world. He delivers you over to be despised by the world *because He delights in you*, so that you can become a sharer in the sufferings of Christ, so that, on the Last Day, you also may become a sharer in the glory of His Heavenly Kingdom [Romans 8:17].

You Brought Me Out of the Womb

On the cross, Jesus must trust that His Father still delights in Him. Everything in His body and all of His enemies surrounding Him scream otherwise. Yet the test is whether or not He will trust that the Father delights in Him, even when He is ever so despised on the cross. Or, to put this another way, Jesus must trust the Father, who has always been His sole source of security, and that from the womb, even when the Father has allowed His bones to be pulled out of joint and subjected to the worst of torturous pains.

Somberly, we meditate upon the way in which the Father has been Jesus' sole source of security, even from His mother's womb:

> ***But You brought Me out of the womb.*** *You made Me trust at My mother's breasts.* ***I was thrown on You from My mother's womb. You are My God since My mother bore Me.*** *Do not be far from Me, for trouble is near. For there is no one to help.* (Psalm 22:9–11)

God the Father delights in His only-begotten Son. He has covered Him with divine security even from Mary's womb. In turn, Jesus has looked to His Father as His sole comfort, stronghold, and security, even from Mary's womb:

> *Rescue Me, My God, from the hand of the wicked, from the hand of the unrighteous and cruel man. For You are My hope, O Lord GOD; My confidence from My youth.* ***I have relied on You from the womb. You are He who took Me out of My mother's womb.*** *I will always praise You.* (Psalm 71:4–6)

And,

> *For You formed My inmost being.* ***You knit Me together in My mother's womb.*** *I will give thanks to You, for I am fearfully and wonderfully made. Your works are wonderful. My soul knows that very well.* (Psalm 139:13–14)

Who was it who knit together the body of Jesus when He was in Mary's womb? Who watched Jesus, with infinite delight, sucking His thumb and doing somersaults in Mary's womb? Who listened to Jesus' heartbeat in Mary's womb? And who brought Jesus forth from the womb and into the manger with such jealous, divine protection? God the Father has been Jesus' sole source of security, even from the womb:

> *This is what the LORD says,* **who made You, and formed You from the womb,** *who will help You: "Do not be afraid, Jacob My servant; and You, Jeshurun, whom I have chosen."* (Isaiah 44:2)[1]

Jesus, by His fully divine and fully human presence in Mary's womb, sanctified the womb. And the womb is known in Scripture as a refuge, a place of utmost security. For, who can tell the unspeakable love with which a godly father and mother will seek to protect and treasure their little one in the womb? Who can put into words, then, the diabolical nature of abortion, since it turns the God-ordained security of the womb inside-out, and thus makes the womb the most dangerous place on earth?

The Lord Jesus has trusted in the security of His Father's love ever since the womb. The test, then, is for Jesus to keep on trusting His Father, even on the cross, even when it *feels* as if that womb-like security of His Father's love has been removed completely:

> *I am poured out like water.* ***All My bones are out of joint.*** *My heart is like wax; it is melted within Me.* (Psalm 22:14)

And,

> ***I can count all of My bones.*** *They look and stare at Me. They divide My garments among them. They cast lots for My clothing.* (Psalm 22:17–18)

This is the physical test of the cross. Jesus has known God's womb-like security all of His life, yet now His Father has allowed His bones to be separated from each other, and pierced through with nails, such that He can count all His bones in the midst of the

---

[1] Even though the Psalm 22:9-11; 71:4-6; 139:13-14; and Isaiah 44:2 passages are interpreted here in Messianic fashion, this does not exclude their initial, historical referents and senses (that is, David in Psalm 22:9-11; the nation of Israel in Isaiah 44:2; etc.).

screaming pain of the cross. This is from Satan. It is Satan who loves to test men by striking their bones with excruciating pain:

> *Satan answered the* LORD, *and said, "Skin for skin. Yes, all that a man has he will give for his life. But stretch out Your hand now,* **and touch his bone and his flesh**, *and he will renounce You to Your face."* (Job 2:4–5)

And,

> [Job speaking:] *"Now my soul is poured out within me. Days of affliction have taken hold on me. In the night season* **my bones are pierced in me**, *and the pains that gnaw me take no rest.* (Job 30:16–17)

A woman who is in labor feels the curse of sin in her very bones. The labor pains are so immense that her bones are out of joint, and she almost can count all of her bones. Yet here, on the cross, Jesus' sufferings, by their infinite size, eclipse the suffering of labor pains. For, He not only suffers in the body—having had His back ripped to shreds by Roman whips, His face disfigured by Roman fists, and His body pierced and hung upon the cruelest instrument of torture that the Romans could invent—but even more in His spirit. Both the physical and the spiritual wrath of God are upon Him. The weight of Hell is pressing down upon His chest. The flames of Hell are burning in His lungs. He is being tormented with the cup of God's wrath that has been reserved for the necessary divine vengeance upon wicked mankind. For the salvation of the elect—and *only for the elect*, since no one who refuses to repent on account of this Gospel proclamation of Christ, and Him crucified, shall be saved—He bleeds profusely from His head, His back, His hands, and His feet.

Has God abandoned Him completely? Has the Father ceased to be good? Has the womb-like security of the Father's love been dried up, such that in its place is left only dry, hot wrath? Is Christ forsaken? This is the greatest test. It is for Jesus to trust that the womb-like security of the Father's love shall never be removed from Him, even when He suffers under the Father's wrath, as a substitutionary sacrifice for the sins of man, on the cross:

> *But Zion said,* **"The LORD has forsaken me, and the Lord has forgotten me."** *Can a woman forget her nursing child, that she should not have compassion* **on the son of her womb***? Yes, these may forget,* **yet I will not forget you!***"* (Isaiah 49:14–15)

The Father's love is stronger than maternal love. Even a mother may forget the son of her womb, yet the Father will not forget Jesus. Instead, He who formed the bones of Christ Jesus while He was in the womb shall love His Son, and not forsake His Son, even when those bones are pulled out of joint and screaming with pain upon the cross. There, on the cross, Satan taunts Jesus, "The Father has forsaken You! The Father has abandoned You!" Yet the Father has not *utterly* forsaken Him.[2] He has punished our sins in Jesus' body on the cross—thus making Him the Lamb of God who takes away the sins of the world. Yet He has not *utterly* forsaken Him. The womb-like security of the Father's love is still in place. Jesus must cling to this, even to His dying breath.

O beloved Church! Christ has conquered sin and death. He has conquered through the power of the Father's love for Him. What, then, shall we fear? (Our only fear is our fear of God. For, we only fear sinning against Him, and thus grieving Him. We only fear Him who has the power to cast both body and soul into Hell.) O Church! God's love for us in Christ Jesus is our womb-like security. It shall never be removed from us. Shall we, then, fear

---

[2] Here, theologically, we do well to distinguish between: (i) God actually "forsaking" Jesus, in the sense of giving Him over to *"be sin for us"* on the cross (2 Corinthians 5:21), such that the Father must punish our sin in Him and give Him over to the divine wrath upon the cross, in which sense God did forsake the Son, which is why the Lord Jesus cries, *"Why have You forsaken Me?"* (Matthew 27:46); and (ii) God "not utterly forsaking" Jesus on the cross, in the sense of never removing His eternal, Fatherly love for the eternal Son, even as the Son, having come in the flesh, now dies upon the cross in obedience to His will, which is why Jesus can die with the victorious cry of faith, *"Father, into Your hands I commit My spirit!"* (Luke 23:46). Yet in working out the theology of this fine-lined distinction regarding the verb "to forsake," one must be careful to guard the doctrine of the hypostatic union of Christ, in all of its Historic-Christian orthodoxy.

that tribulation, or distress, or persecution, or famine, or nakedness, or danger, or sword may somehow be able to separate us from the love of Christ [Romans 8:35]? Rather, shall we not be persuaded, following the blessed Apostle, that neither death nor life, nor angels nor rulers nor powers, nor things present nor things to come, nor height nor depth, nor any other created thing, shall be able to separate us from the love of God which is in Christ Jesus our Lord [Romans 8:38-39]?

YOU HAVE BROUGHT ME INTO THE DUST OF DEATH

Yet for Christ on the day of His crucifixion, there is no deliverance. It would be one thing if He were tested with the cross, and then cried out to the Father, and the Father delivered Him from the cross. Or it might suffice, in terms of human pride, for Him to be *willing* to go to the cross, but *never actually have to suffer* on the cross. That would satisfy the blasphemous pride of the Muslim doctrines, for example. However, this would never be sufficient for our salvation, since the wages of sin is death itself [Romans 6:23]. Therefore, it was necessary for Christ to be tested all the way to death, even true death on the cross. For, apart from shedding of blood, there is no forgiveness of sins [Hebrews 9:22].

Has God abandoned Him? What shall He think, now that dogs encompass Him and lions surround Him, and yet there is no deliverance forthcoming from God?

> ***For dogs have surrounded Me.*** *A company of evildoers has enclosed Me.... They open their mouths wide against Me,* ***lions tearing prey and roaring.*** (Psalm 22:16, 13)

Does Jesus lack faith in God? Does He have not because He asks not? Does He fail to cry out to His Father for deliverance from the dogs and from the lions? To the contrary:

> ***Deliver My soul*** *from the sword,* ***My precious life from the power of the dog....*** ***Save Me from the lion's mouth!*** *[My affliction] from the horns of the wild oxen.* (Psalm 22:20, 21)

WHY HAVE YOU FORSAKEN ME?

Why, then, must Jesus feel so abandoned by God? Why must He cry out for deliverance, but receive no answer from God? Why must they be allowed by God to pierce His hands and His feet? Is this not the only way that we can be saved from our sins? Is not Jesus, being fully God and fully Man, the only One who can die a substitutionary death for our sins?

There are two very specific and breathtakingly powerful prophecies of the cross woven into Psalm 22. Both of these majestic prophecies were fulfilled, in true history, in the death of Jesus of Nazareth on the cross. We keep in mind, then, as we read them with awe and trembling, *that they were foretold by David, under the full inspiration of the Holy Spirit, approximately one thousand years prior to their astonishing, historical fulfillment.* The first of these two prophecies concerns the manner of Christ's death at the hands of wicked men:

They have pierced My hands and feet. (Psalm 22:16)[3]

Then, the second of these two prophecies concerns the cruel, calloused mocking of Christ by His executioners during His crucifixion:

They divide My garments among them. They cast lots for My clothing. (Psalm 22:18)

These two prophecies were fulfilled in the death of Jesus Christ on the cross at Golgotha. For there, at the cross, Jesus' hands and feet were *"pierced"* by Roman soldiers, yet all under the murderous false accusations of the Jews. Also, it is at Calvary

---

[3] Here we argue, and confidently so (since the textual evidence is strongly in our favor), that the Dead Sea Scrolls preserve the correct reading of Psalm 22:16, *"They have pierced My hands and My feet,"* contrary to the Hebrew Masoretic Text, which reads, *"Like a lion, My hands and My feet."* The difference between the two readings is the difference in one letter only, a Hebrew ו (*vav*) versus a Hebrew י (*yôd*), and the witness of the Dead Sea Scrolls, being the more ancient of the two witnesses, has preserved the original reading. This fact is corroborated by the reading found in the LXX (the Greek Old Testament), ὤρυξαν χεῖράς μου καὶ πόδας, which is, *"They dug out [or 'pierced'] My hands and feet."* This agrees with the KJV, NKJV, NASB, ESV, and etc. translations.

that the soldiers made sport of Jesus' death, even casting lots for His clothing, as if His garments were mere trophies, souvenirs, or magic charms from the crucifixion of an infamous (but also miracle-working) Jewish peasant-teacher:

> **But He was pierced for our transgressions.** *He was crushed for our iniquities. The punishment that brought our peace was on Him; and by His wounds we are healed.* (Isaiah 53:5)

And,

> *Then the soldiers, when they had crucified Jesus,* **took His garments and made four parts, to every soldier a part;** *and also the coat. Now the coat was without seam, woven from the top throughout. Then they said to one another,* **"Let us not tear it, but cast lots for it to decide whose it will be,"** *that the Scripture might be fulfilled, which says, "They parted My garments among them. For My cloak they cast lots." Therefore the soldiers did these things.* (John 19:23-24)

Here, then, is the greatest test. Jesus must trust His Father, even if it means being plunged into death itself, in obedience to His Father. He must trust, even when His Father brings Him into the dust of death:

> *My strength is dried up like a potsherd. My tongue sticks to the roof of My mouth.* **You have brought Me into the dust of death.** (Psalm 22:15)

Will the Father save others from death, but not His only-begotten Son? Will He miraculously save Daniel from the mouths of the lions, but not Jesus? How can this be? Will the dead praise the Father? Will the dead be able to bear witness to the glory of the Father? Instead, will not Satan win, and Satan's children gloat, and God's name be defamed, since they have put Christ to death?

This is the greatest test. Will Jesus surrender Himself to the Father's will, and trust the Father's love, even if the Father brings Him into the dust of death? This is the test that Jesus passed, ever so gloriously, on the cross at Golgotha. For, He knew not only Psalm 22, from which He cried out, *"My God, My God, why have You forsaken Me?"* (v. 1), but also Psalm 16, which says, *"For You **will not [forsake]** My soul in Sheol, neither will You allow Your Holy One to see corruption"* (v. 10).

O Christian, so weak and afflicted, so bereaved and pierced through with mourning, the Lord only requires your trust. He is not looking for a pretend optimism as you endure your suffering. Instead, He is looking for child-like faith, and child-like trust and surrender. Will you, then, trust Him through your piercing pain and make Him your sole trust through your bitter loneliness? Will you, by faith, make the resurrection of Christ, as the first fruits of the resurrection to come, your sole hope for a complete abolishment of all of your sorrows, crying, and pain?

By perfect trust in His Father, Jesus passed the test of the cross, thus proving His divine Lordship and glory. At Calvary, He conquered. He trusted that His Father had not utterly abandoned Him, and so He proved victorious by praying to His Father, and to no other, with the full love of the eternal Son for His eternal Father, with the last drop of His dying strength:

Jesus, crying with a loud voice, said, **"Father, into Your hands I commit My spirit!"** *Having said this, He breathed His last.* (Luke 23:46)

And thus we shall sing the worthiness of the Lamb who was slain, unto the eternal majesty of God the Father, forever and ever, ages unto ages, world without end. Amen.

8

I WILL DECLARE YOUR NAME TO MY BRETHREN
The RESURRECTION in Psalm 22:22-31

I will declare Your name to My [brethren]. Among the [congregation], I will praise You. You who fear the LORD, praise Him! All you descendants of Jacob, glorify Him! Stand in awe of Him, all you descendants of Israel! For He has not despised nor abhorred the affliction of the afflicted, neither has He hidden His face from Him; but [in His salvation cry] to Him, He heard. Of You comes My praise in the great [congregation]. I will pay My vows before those who fear Him. The humble shall eat and be satisfied. They shall praise the LORD who seek after Him. Let your hearts live forever. (Psalm 22:22–26)

GOD the Son, Jesus Christ, who was afflicted, is afflicted no more. Something marvelous has happened in the midst of Psalm 22. For, at the beginning of the Psalm, Jesus the Christ, in a state of indescribable affliction, is raising His salvation cry to His God and Father, and yet feeling as if that cry is going unheard. He is not rescued by the Father from death upon the cross:

My God, My God, why have You forsaken Me? **Why are You so far from [My salvation cry]**, *and from the words of My groaning?* (Psalm 22:1)

However, by the time we arrive at verse 24 of the Psalm, things have changed in wondrous fashion. Now, He who formerly was afflicted is afflicted no longer, and He who formerly felt that

His salvation cry was forsaken by God has come to know, with joy, that His salvation cry *has been heard* by His Father:

> *For He has not despised nor abhorred the affliction of the afflicted, neither has He hidden His face from Him;* **but [in His salvation cry] to Him, He heard**. (Psalm 22:24)

This is full of marvelous wonder, that He who felt as if the Father did not hear Him crying for salvation, now rejoices in the certainty that His salvation cry has been heard. This is the wonder of the Gospel, that although the Son felt upon the cross as if He had not been heard by the Father, yet in truth He had been heard. The Father *had heard Him*, and all along had purposed to raise Him from the dead:

> *He, in the days of His flesh, having offered up prayers and petitions with strong crying and tears to Him who was able to save Him from death,* **and having been heard for His godly fear**.... (Hebrews 5:7)

This is the Gospel: not only our Lord's cry of forsakenness, issued forth from the cross, but also His shout of triumph, issued forth from the empty tomb. In the very same Psalm, we have both the terrible cross and the vacant sepulcher, both the affliction of the Holy One of God and His vindication through His resurrection from the dead. These are the twofold extremities of the Gospel about which all of the Law and the Prophets speak, namely, the extreme sufferings of Christ, on the one hand, and the extreme power and glory of His resurrection, on the other:

> *He said to them,* **"Thus it is written, and thus it was necessary for the Christ to suffer and to rise from the dead the third day...."** (Luke 24:46)

The Gospel always speaks to us in two extremes: in it there is both great *sorrow*—Christ was not spared the wrath of God when He died upon the cross for our sins—and also luminous *hope*—for He who died is risen from the grave. In the Gospel of God, Christ

Jesus embodies both the extremity of *suffering*—for who has suffered more than Christ?—and the extremity of *glory*—for who shall inherit more glory than Christ? Once again, the Gospel of Christ takes us to two polar destinations, one of *true death* and the other of *true resurrection*. In Psalm 22, we have both of these extremes. The first half of the Psalm is tremendous affliction, while the second half is unspeakable jubilation.

O Brother or Sister of many afflictions, do you find yourself encompassed and enclosed by the first half of the Psalm? Is life for you all bitter cries of forsakenness? When you look eagerly for the bright light and blooming lilies of resurrection, do you see only persecuting dogs and ravenous lions all around you? Have the pains of death hemmed you in? Have the terrors of bereavement constricted your breathing, and pierced your heart? O Christian of many afflictions, the second half of the Psalm will come, some great and everlasting Day. Though it tarries, wait patiently for it, by faith. For, your *extreme* tribulations will be translated into *extreme* rejoicings, in Heaven. It will surely come. It will not tarry much longer.

THE CONGREGATION OF THE RISEN CHRIST

What is this marvelous thing that has happened in the Psalm? Is it not the wondrous mystery of resurrection? God, who ordained the crucifixion of Christ, also has ordained His resurrection. Furthermore, God has ordained that the victory of Christ's resurrection be attested to by *a multitude of witnesses*. For, Christ shall show Himself in His flesh-and-blood body, His truly resurrected body, to the multitude of His own congregation:

> ***I will declare Your name to My brothers. Among the [congregation], I will praise You****. You who fear the* LORD*, praise Him! All you descendants of Jacob, glorify Him! Stand in awe of Him, all you descendants of Israel! For He has not despised nor abhorred the affliction of the afflicted, neither has He hidden His face from Him; but [in His salvation cry to Him], He heard.* ***Of You comes My praise in the great [congregation]****. I will pay My vows before those who fear Him. The [afflicted] shall eat and be satisfied. They shall praise the*

LORD who seek after Him. Let your hearts live forever.
(Psalm 22:22–26)

Who shall bear witness to the resurrected Christ? *His own congregation* shall bear witness to Him. And who is this congregation? First, it is the congregation of all of those who have been baptized, spiritually, into His death, and thus have become *sharers with Him in His afflictions*:

For He has not despised nor abhorred **the affliction of the afflicted**, *neither has He hidden His face from Him; but [in His salvation cry to Him], He heard.* (Psalm 22:24)

Christ was afflicted, and in the same manner those who have been baptized, spiritually, into His death, share with Him in His afflictions. This is what makes them His own congregation:

The [afflicted] shall eat and be satisfied. *They shall praise the LORD who seek after Him. Let your hearts live forever.*
(Psalm 22:26)

Second, Christ's own congregation, who shall bear witness to His glorious resurrection from the dead, *are those who fear the Lord*. By faith, they have died to sin, are living for righteousness, and thus are those who know and fear the Lord:

You who fear the LORD, *praise Him! All you descendants of Jacob, glorify Him! Stand in awe of Him, all you descendants of Israel!* (Psalm 22:23)

And,

Of You comes My praise in the great [congregation]. I will pay My vows **before those who fear Him**. (Psalm 22:25)

God's people, His elect, *the afflicted ones, who fear Him*, constitute the congregation of Christ. And the saints of this congregation shall be His witnesses to His resurrection. For, in the midst of this great congregation, the risen Christ shall praise the Father who raised Him from the dead:

Lord, how long will You look on? Rescue my soul from their destruction, my precious life from the lions. ***I will give You thanks in the great [congregation]****. I will praise You among many people.* (Psalm 35:17–18)

And,

Let them exalt Him also in the [congregation] of the people*, and praise Him in the seat of the elders.* (Psalm 107:32)

And again,

Praise the L*ORD**! Sing to the* L*ORD** a new song,* ***His praise in the [congregation] of the saints****.* (Psalm 149:1)

O how precious is the congregation of Christ! For, He purposed that His resurrected glory be revealed right in the midst of the congregation of His afflicted saints, who fear Him. In His perfect wisdom, He chose to reveal His resurrected glory first, and exclusively, to the congregation of the earliest Church. The wicked were not made privy to this initial, historical, resurrected glory. Only the faithful, the Apostles and the earliest saints, were allowed to witness it, since it is *for the Church* that Christ died, and *for the Church* that He shall return:

... to Him be the glory ***in the [Church]*** *and in Christ Jesus to all generations forever and ever. Amen.* (Ephesians 3:21)

Where does the resurrected Christ bear witness to the praises of God the Father? What venue does He choose for the revelation of His resurrected glory, such that He can praise the Father before many witnesses? Is this not the Church, which is the congregation of His brethren? And why are they called His brethren? Is this not because He assumed humanity, a full human nature, in order to reveal His resurrected glory to us in real, *human* flesh and blood?

> *For it became Him, for whom are all things, and through whom are all things, in bringing many children to glory, to make the author of their salvation perfect through sufferings. For both He who sanctifies and those who are sanctified are all from one, for which cause* **He is not ashamed to call them brothers**, *saying,* **"I will declare Your name to My brothers. Among the congregation I will sing Your praise."** (Hebrews 2:10–12)

Where—in what location—does He reveal His resurrected glory and praise His Father? He does this only in the midst of the congregation, His true Church. His holy, resurrected presence, made known in the Church by the sending of the Holy Spirit upon the Church, declares God's praises in the congregation of the saints. Therefore, *Christ Jesus*, and *not* some designated musician, is the true "Worship Leader" in the Church. He is the Firstborn from the dead, and the Head of the Church, and thus He alone, in His resurrected glory, as both fully God and fully Man, can serve as the one Mediator between God and man, and thus lead the Church in the kind of worship with which the Father is pleased.

Blessed, then, are those local churches whose Worship Leader is Christ Himself. They share in His afflictions, fear His holy name, and thus submit themselves to His headship by obeying His holy commandments. Casting out all false teachings and all unholy practices from their midst, these local churches are filled with Christ's Spirit of holiness, and thus inhabited, spiritually, by the resurrected glory of Christ. In their humble, repentant prayers and meek, suffering love for God the Father, they are allowed to praise the divine glory of the resurrected Christ in their midst, bearing witness to Him, even as He Himself declares the praises of the Father who raised Him from the dead.

But woe, woe, woe to those local churches whose worship is not governed by Christ Himself! For, they may sing their songs to God as loudly as they would like to sing them, and also play their organs and pianos, or else their guitars and drums, as passionately as they would like to play them, but if they do not fear Christ and are not willing to suffer disgrace for the sake of His name, then they are deprived of His resurrected glory in their midst. They may speak falsely and presumptuously of His presence amongst them, employing New Age, yoga-like, mystical language, but the real Christ, the King of glory, will not manifest His love and His glory to such local churches. They say that they are singing His praises, but at the Judgment it shall be revealed that the only praises that they were singing, to the pagan tunes of Romanticism and Existentialism, were their own.

ALL THE ENDS OF THE EARTH

Therefore, only in the true, universal Church, which is a spiritual Church, being the afflicted Church that truly fears His name, does Christ Jesus manifest His resurrected glory. Yet since the true, universal Church, being a spiritual Church, when calculated as the sum of the saints throughout history, and not just those who are alive at any one given time in history, is vast in number, having more members than the stars in the sky or the sands on the seashore, this constitutes a vast multitude of witnesses to the resurrection of Christ from the grave. And yet there is more, since Christ has ordained that the witnesses to His resurrected glory be not only of His *"congregation,"* but also of *"the nations."* That is to say, God has purposed that His congregation consist of His chosen saints from every tribe, tongue, and nation, all of whom bear witness to the glory of His resurrected Christ:

> ***All the ends of the earth*** *shall remember and turn to the* LORD. ***All the relatives of the nations*** *shall worship before You. For the Kingdom is the* LORD*'s. He is the ruler over* ***the nations***. *All the [choice] ones of the earth shall eat and worship. All those who go down to the dust shall bow before Him, even he who cannot keep his soul alive.* (Psalm 22:27–29)

It is a *congregational* witness to the glory of the risen Christ, and yet this witness is composed of *many nations*. His witnesses, to be sure, will be from the congregation. The saints of His Church shall bear witness to His resurrected glory. Yet His witnesses also will be a vast seed coming from all nations. The elect of God from every nation, tribe, tongue, and people on earth shall bear witness to the Gospel by coming to worship the resurrected Christ, who Himself declares the praises of the Father.

God raised the Lord Jesus Christ from the dead. His congregation bears witness to this, and this congregation is composed of peoples from all the ends of the earth. God has ordained that His elect from all nations bear witness to the resurrected glory of His Son. And this is in fulfillment of God's great promise to Abraham:

***All the nations of the earth** will be blessed by your offspring, because you have obeyed My voice.* (Genesis 22:18)

Who bears witness to Christ's resurrected glory? Who shall serve Christ, who was afflicted, but is afflicted no more? Is this not the elect from all nations? Shall not a remnant from all nations arise and bless the resurrected Lord?

His name endures forever. His name continues as long as the sun. Men shall be blessed by Him. ***All nations will call Him blessed****.* (Psalm 72:17)

And,

All nations You have made will come and worship before You, Lord*. They shall glorify Your name.* (Psalm 86:9)

The resurrection of Christ from the grave was a historical fact that Rome, at the time of the resurrection, virtually ignored. The wicked Roman rulers of the time thought that it was a sectarian Jewish myth, and nothing more. Yet in just a few centuries the Church's suffering witness to the resurrection of Jesus of Nazareth from the dead had spread to so many tribes, tongues, and nations, that even Rome itself was forced to acknowledge the power of the Gospel. Constantine declared himself a Christian emperor, partly because the Church's trans-national witness was so vast and transformative that it could no longer be ignored. And thus Heaven will be filled with saints from such a vast representation of peoples and nations that the multiethnic array of saints in Heaven will, in itself, be quite astounding, and all as a witness to the power of the Gospel of the crucified and risen Christ:

It shall happen in the latter days, that the mountain of the LORD's House shall be established on the top of the mountains, and shall be raised above the hills; **and all nations shall flow to it**. (Isaiah 2:2)

And, according to the prophecy of Jesus,

This [Gospel] of the Kingdom will be preached in the whole world for a testimony **to all the nations**, *and then the end will come.* (Matthew 24:14)

Jesus suffered for the sins of the nations, in obedience to the Father's will. Therefore, the Father has commanded that all nations must fear Him, the risen Christ, and thus, for those who do fear Him out of sincere love for Him, become the joyful posterity of Christ:

Who shall not fear You, O Lord, and glorify Your name? For You alone are holy. **For all nations shall come and worship before You**, *for Your judgments have been manifested.* (Revelation 15:4)

Who is it that bears witness to the resurrected Christ? It is His congregation, which is afflicted with His afflictions, and which fears His holy name, and this congregation is a remnant gathered from all of the nations of the earth. Jews and Arabs, Africans and Europeans, and Asians and South Americans alike shall come and worship Christ, the resurrected Lord. They shall bear witness to His resurrected glory.

Therefore, away with this unfounded argument against Christianity that it is a Western cultural norm that has been forced, imperialist style, upon the other regions and cultures of the world! To this empty argument, we reply with the question, "What about Christian evangelists such as Wang Mingdao?" For, Wang Mingdao was born in Beijing, not in London. He was fiercely independent, advocating for an indigenous Chinese Church that was free from the doctrinal corruptions that many Western missionaries had introduced into the churches in China. Yet being thoroughly Chinese, and thus opposed to much of Western culture, he nevertheless was willing to suffer for no less than twenty-two years in prison on account of his testimony to the supernatural nature of the Bible, and thus the supernatural nature of Christ's resurrection from the dead. Is, then, Christianity merely a Western phenomenon? Is it not, rather, founded on the historical fact of Christ's resurrection from the dead, a fact that is attested to not only by its original, *Jewish* Apostles, but also by multitudes of martyrs from *all of the nations of the earth*?

Yet Satan is crafty. He hates missions, for the end of missions is the Second Coming of Christ. Therefore, Satan, in his craftiness, seeks to redefine "missions" in the Church. He employs doctors in theology to write books about how the heart of missions is "social justice." Then, gullibly, the Church begins to follow those doctors in theology in redefining both the vision and the work of missions in the liberalized language of secularized economics, technological education, feminist ideology, population control, an overall improvement in a people's standards of living, and etc.

This is not missions. Giving food, clothing, and shelter to hungry and impoverished people, and also exercising justice on behalf of the persecuted poor (especially the Christian persecuted poor, many of whom are widows, orphans, and refugees) and the afflicted (not limited to, but necessarily including the preborn children in the womb) is most biblical, to be sure, and even demanded by God's holy commandments [see, for example, Matthew 25:35-36 and 1 John 3:17], but what is commonly termed "social justice," and especially the modern world's vision of it, *is not the heart of missions*. Rather, the heart of missions is the worship of God the Father through the worship of God the Son, all by the regenerating, illuminating, and sanctifying work of the Holy Spirit. It summons the nations to repent, to abhor their idols, and to worship God. It exposes the utter filthiness of the pride of man, and calls man to abhor his pride, and thus to repent of his sins, even in spiritual sackcloth and ashes. It involves much fear and trembling before the holiness of the resurrected Christ.

Therefore, the Church's vision of missions cannot be missions, rightly defined, unless it involves the proclamation of: the Triune nature of the eternal God; God's creation of the universe as being very good, free from all suffering and death; the miseries brought upon the world through Adam's sin; the wrath that God revealed against the wickedness of mankind through the global flood in the days of Noah; the calling of Abraham to be a blessing to all nations; the real, supernatural parting of the Red Sea under Moses; the history of redemption that God worked through His covenant with Israel, and especially through His covenant with David, the son of Jesse, His servant; the wondrous Old Testament prophecies about the Christ, all of which are fulfilled in Jesus, the Son of Man, born of a virgin, who is the Savior of the world; the miracles of Jesus; the betrayal of Jesus by Judas, one of His own, typifying His betrayal by the Jews; the hatred of Christ by the world, thus leading to His crucifixion under Pontius Pilate; the atonement of Christ as a necessary, sufficient, and substitutionary atonement for sinful man; the true-historical death, burial, and resurrection of Jesus; the ascension of Jesus Christ to the right hand of the Father, in glory; the sending of the Holy Spirit upon the Church at Pentecost; the inerrant authority of the teachings the New Testament Apostles; the absolute necessity of the new birth, which comes only by faith, apart from works, in order for sinners to be saved from their condemnation under sin; the call to holiness and separateness from the world as the evidence of saving faith; the surety of the Second Coming of Christ in real flesh and blood, on the clouds, with His holy angels, when He shall judge and make war against the wicked; and the ultimate state of the righteous in unspeakable, everlasting joys in Heaven, and of unbelievers in conscious, everlasting punishments in Hell. Unless this eternal Gospel is proclaimed to the nations, in full, in the fear of God, then no matter what acts of so-called "social justice" have been executed, no true missions have been performed.

THEY WILL DECLARE HIS RIGHTEOUSNESS

The elect from all nations, then, are those who compose this vast army of witnesses to Christ's resurrected glory. They are His faithful remnant, being the true members of His Church, and they come from every tribe, tongue, and people, since they are a seed composed of many nations. Yet what, exactly, does this vast army of witnesses declare? Surely, they bear witness to His resurrected glory. He who was afflicted is afflicted no more, but raised in glory. Yet once they have seen His resurrected glory, what does this great, global congregation declare? If they are His witnesses, then what is the declaration of their witness?

> *Posterity shall serve Him. Future generations shall be told about the Lord. They shall come and* **shall declare His righteousness** *to a people that shall be born, for He has done it.* (Psalm 22:30–31)

Since Christ Jesus has suffered, and since He has been raised from the dead, the declaration of the Church, as God's true witness in the world, is a declaration of *God's own righteousness*. That is, whenever the Church rises up in her worship to declare the resurrected glory of Christ Jesus, her song must be a bold declaration of *the righteousness of God*:

> *I have proclaimed* **glad news of righteousness** *in the great [congregation]. Behold, I will not seal my lips, O LORD, You know. I have not hidden* **Your righteousness** *within my heart. I have declared Your faithfulness and Your salvation. I have not concealed Your loving kindness and Your truth from the great [congregation].* (Psalm 40:9–10)

What is the Gospel of Christ? How does the congregation, the Church, bear witness to the resurrected glory of Christ? What message does the Church declare when she declares the Gospel of Christ? She declares, ever so boldly, *the righteousness of God* which is revealed in Christ:

> *For I am not ashamed of the Gospel of Christ, for it is the power of God for salvation for everyone who believes; for the Jew first, and also for the Greek.* **For in it is revealed [the righteousness of God]** *from faith to faith. As it is written, "But the righteous shall live by faith."* (Romans 1:16–17)

And also,

I Will Declare Your Name to My Brethren

*But now apart from the Law, **[the] righteousness of God has been revealed**, being testified by the Law and the Prophets; even **the righteousness of God through faith in Jesus Christ** to all and on all those who believe.* (Romans 3:21–22)

When our children ask us, "Why did Jesus suffer so, even feeling forsaken by His Father upon the cross?" we ought to answer our children by saying, "*God is righteous*. Thus He had to punish our sin, and yet in His great love for us He chose to punish our sin in the body of Jesus upon the cross."

Then, when our children ask us, "And how can we, filthy sinners, be permitted to enter into Heaven, since we, too, have spit in the face of God by our sins?" we should answer, solemnly, "*God is righteous*. Therefore, none who are unclean can enter into Heaven. But by repentance and faith in Him, we are granted Christ's own garments of righteousness to wear in the Kingdom of Heaven. For with the heart one believes unto righteousness."

Again, when our children ask us, "And why did Jesus rise from the dead in victory, proclaiming both His Lordship over death and His right to rule the nations with an iron scepter?" we should reply, "*God is righteous*. He would not suffer His Son to be mocked, but rather raised Him for the dead to give Him the name that is above every name, that at His name all of Heaven and earth should bow."

One last time, when our children ask us, "Why shall Jesus come in wrath and fury to judge the world?" we ought to answer, looking into their eyes with much seriousness of heart, "*God is righteous*. Therefore, Jesus must judge the world in righteousness, rendering eternal life to those who by patient continuance in doing good seek for glory, honor, and immortality; but to those who are self-seeking and do not obey the truth, but obey unrighteousness—indignation and wrath, tribulation and anguish, on every soul of man who does evil."

What does the resurrection of Christ from the grave declare? Certainly, it declares that Christ is victor! As it is written, *"O Death, where is your sting? O Hades, where is your victory?"* (1 Corinthians 15:55). Yet the resurrection of Jesus from the dead also declares, both in the Heavenly realms and to all of the nations of the earth, that *God is righteous*. Now that Christ is raised from the dead, the whole world is accountable to God. All men, everywhere, must repent before the resurrected majesty of this Lord and Christ. For, God has spoken to all nations in this manner:

> *"...because He has appointed a day in which **He will judge the world in righteousness** by the Man whom he has ordained; of which He has given assurance to all men* [how so? How has He assured it?] ***in that He has raised Him from the dead.***" (Acts 17:31)

Hallelujah! Christ is risen! Hallelujah! Our hope is founded upon the glory of His resurrection, and thus we affirm:

> *Posterity shall serve Him. Future generations shall be told about the Lord. They shall come and **shall declare His righteousness** to a people that shall be born, for He has done it.* (Psalm 22:30–31)

In the Heavenly congregation, full of the everlasting harmony of an unbreakable bond of peace amongst all of the saints, we shall declare the majesty of the righteousness of Christ Jesus our Lord, and thus shall sing forever of the eternal righteousness of God the Father, giving glory to the luminous righteousness of His blessed Holy Spirit, with praises unceasing, world without end. Amen.

Part Three:

THE CROSS
in Isaiah 53

9

GOD'S HIDDEN SERVANT
The Cross in Isaiah 52:13 – 53:4

Behold, My Servant will deal wisely. He will be [high] and lifted up, and will be very [exalted]. Just as many were astonished at You—His [visage] was marred more than any man, and His form more than the sons of men—so He will cleanse many nations. Kings will shut their mouths at Him: for they will see that which had not been told them; and they will understand that which they had not heard. Who has believed our message? To whom has the arm of the LORD been revealed? (Isaiah 52:13 – 53:1)

GOD, in ages past, from ancient times, purposefully kept His Servant hidden from the nations, but now, in these last days, has revealed Him to the nations. This hidden Servant was foreordained before the foundation of the world. However, He was not made manifest to the nations until these last times, namely, until the days of the Church. Now, in the times of the Gentiles, the hidden Servant of God is made manifest to an elect remnant—to all of those who believe upon the divine glory of the Servant's name—from every tribe, tongue, people, and nation.

He sprinkles many nations. Kings who have not been told about Him suddenly come to see Him and worship Him. Princes who have not heard about Him suddenly begin to understand the Gospel about Him. That is, just as the preaching of the Prophet Daniel brought several of Babylon's kings to their knees before the God of Israel, so too shall the preaching of the Church in the times of the Gentiles bring the princes of many nations to bow down in worship before God's hidden Servant.

Isaiah's great prophecy about many kings of distant nations bowing to the Gospel foretells many wonderful, future events. The Christian martyrs under the terrible Roman persecutions of the early fourth century shall die while bearing witness to "God's hidden Servant," and within a few decades Emperor Constantine, and all of the political powers of Rome with him, shall bow the knee—some in faith and some not in faith—to this hidden Servant. Shortly thereafter, Patrick of Britain shall preach to Ireland, casting out demons in the name of God's hidden Servant, and many princes of Ireland shall pay homage in worship to the Servant.

Much later in history, Henry Martyn will evangelize and produce hitherto unknown Bible translations in India and Persia, while David Brainerd will proclaim the Gospel of God's hidden Servant to the Native Americans in New Jersey, and, consequently, over time, many thousands in India and Persia, and also many Native Americans in America, will pledge themselves to obey God's hidden Servant as their own Lord.

Even in China, once so closed off to the outside world, Robert Morrison will begin distributing the Scriptures to the Chinese people, even the Scriptures which they have not before read. Within those Scriptures, the Chinese will read this prophecy of God's hidden Servant, about whom they have not before heard. And as a result of Morrison's labors, followed by the courageous, sacrificial labors of Hudson Taylor, over time, ten thousands upon ten thousands of Chinese people will worship the Servant.

He *has been hidden* from the nations. He *is now being revealed* to the nations. Who has believed our report? And to whom has the arm of the Lord been revealed? The Jews, by and large, have not believed. Rather, it is mostly to the Gentiles that He has been revealed. Thus Paul of Tarsus became the great Apostle *to the Gentiles*, since he knew that the hidden Servant was to be revealed to them:

> *Yes, making it my aim to preach the Gospel, not where Christ was already named, that I might not build on another's foundation. But, as it is written,* **"They will see, to whom no news of Him came. They who have not heard will understand."** (Romans 15:20–21)

God's Hidden Servant

The Hiddenness of the Servant

He is a *hidden* Servant. He indeed was foreordained from the foundation of the world, yet He also was kept *hidden* for so many ages. Who is He? Who is this hidden Servant? The Lord God calls Him *"My Servant"*:

*Behold, **My Servant** will deal wisely. He will be [high] and lifted up, and will be very [exalted]. (Isaiah 52:13)*

God calls Him *"My Servant,"* and this means that He is God's *hidden* Servant. For, in the middle chapters of the book of Isaiah, there is an enigmatic, hidden Servant, in whom God delights. We hear about Him, but His identity remains hidden from us in these chapters:

*Behold, **My Servant**, whom I uphold; My chosen, in whom My soul delights—I have put My Spirit on Him. He will bring justice **to the nations**. (Isaiah 42:1)*

Once again, then, God's enigmatic, hidden Servant, is to be a Savior for Israel, to be sure, but also a light to the Gentiles:

*Now the LORD says, He who formed **Me** from the womb to be **His Servant**, to bring Jacob again to Him, and to gather Israel to Him, for I am honorable in the LORD's eyes, and My God has become My strength. Indeed, He says, "It is too light a thing that You should be **My Servant** to raise up the tribes of Jacob, and to restore the preserved of Israel. I will also give You as **a light to the nations**, that You may be My salvation to the end of the earth." (Isaiah 49:5–6)*

Who is He? Who is God's hidden Servant? He reappears in the fiftieth chapter of Isaiah as One who must be *obeyed*:

*Who among you fears the LORD, **and obeys the voice of His Servant**? He who walks in darkness, and has no light, let him trust in the LORD's name, and rely on his God. (Isaiah 50:10)*

Also here, in the fiftieth chapter of Isaiah, we learn more about God's hidden Servant. In specific, we learn that He is not only a hidden Servant, but also a *suffering* Servant:

> ***I gave My back to those who beat Me, and My cheeks to those who plucked off the hair****. I did not hide My face from shame and spitting.* (Isaiah 50:6)

This is God's hidden Servant. Who, then, is He? Somehow, this hidden Servant of God is to be equated with God Himself. As a son is of the same nature as his father, so too is this hidden Servant of the same nature as God. It is as if God is the Father, and the Servant is the Son. Both are of the divine nature. Both are essentially God.

We know this because of the way in which the Prophet Isaiah describes this hidden Servant. He is described as being *"high"* and *"lifted up"*:

> *Behold, My Servant will deal wisely. He will be **[high] and lifted up**, and will be very [exalted].* (Isaiah 52:13)

This language is more than striking. It is heavens-shattering and earth-shaking language. For, to describe the hidden Servant as being *"high and lifted up"* is to use the exact same language of the Prophet Isaiah's *throne-room vision of God* back in the sixth chapter:

> *In the year that king Uzziah died, I saw the Lord sitting on a throne, **high and lifted up**; and His train filled the Temple. Above Him stood the seraphim. Each one had six wings. With two he covered his face. With two he covered his feet. With two he flew. One called to another, and said, "Holy, holy, holy, is the L*ORD *of Hosts! The whole earth is full of his glory!"* (Isaiah 6:1–3)

Who is *"high and lifted up"*? In the sixth chapter of Isaiah, the Lord Himself is *"high and lifted up,"* so much so that He causes the fierce, fiery, throne-room angels to quake with fear. But then in fifty-second chapter, God's hidden Servant is also described as being *"high and lifted up."* Therefore, the glory that Isaiah saw, sitting on the throne of Heaven, is the same glory that Isaiah now sees in the face of this hidden Servant. It is a terrifyingly transcendent glory. It is a thrice-holy, divine glory.

Why, then, is this divine glory hidden in the form of a *Servant*? Can the sublime, unapproachable light of the glory of God really be cloaked in the guise of a *Servant*? What are we to think, that God will come to us incognito, wrapping a towel around His waist and washing the feet of His disciples, much like a common house slave? Will the Almighty God wash our feet? Will He condescend not only to take up human flesh, but even human flesh in the form of a *Servant*?

> *Have this in your mind, which was also in Christ Jesus, who, **existing in the form of God**, did not consider equality with God a thing to be grasped, but emptied Himself, **taking the form of a servant**, being made in the likeness of men.*
> (Philippians 2:5–7)

Do you have eyes to see this? Can you see the One who shut in the oceans with doors, and who made clouds their garments; who alone has entered the springs of the seas, and walked in search of the depths; who alone has entered the treasury of snow, and has seen the treasury of hail [Job 38:8-9, 16, 22]? Can you see Him, the One who commands the lightning bolts and numbers the clouds, picking up a lowly carpenter's hammer and assuming a humble servant's attire? Can you see God, in the Person of the Son of God, becoming a Servant?

God hides His glory in Servanthood. He rebukes the *proud* by *hiding* His glory from them, but He gives grace to the *humble* by *revealing* His glory to them. He refuses to serve the wicked, in all of their haughty idolatry and unbelief. He hides Himself from those who love sin and refuse to repent of their sin. Yet He is pleased to serve, with His own sweat and blood, the God-fearers of the nations: the God-fearing poor, persecuted, sick, widowed, orphaned, and afflicted.

Is God the Son a hidden Servant, and will we not follow Him as His little servants? Should we chase the money and prestige of the world? Should we not rather lower ourselves to become servants? Does not Christ Jesus hide His glory today amongst His lowliest of servants? Is not the glory of the Gospel hidden even today amongst those who are rejected by the world? Is it not the lowly, frail, lonely, meek, persecuted, suffering, and quietly weeping saints whom God has chosen to be the vessels of the hidden treasure of the Gospel of His glory?

O precious Christian, if you deem yourself to be a failure, since you are, in truth, quite unimportant in the eyes of the world, perhaps this is because you are ever so important to God. You are His servant, His little, hidden servant living amongst this wicked and adulterous generation, and He has chosen *you* to be a fragile, earthen vessel in which to *hide* His glorious Gospel. Therefore, O valuable Christian, keep on serving, quietly, faithfully, with much godly suffering, and very much in secret. Your Father in Heaven sees your spiritual service that is done for Him in secret, and He, your blessed Father, shall reward you.

THE SERVANT'S HIDDEN MAJESTY

God's hidden Servant has His own hidden, divine glory. He comes to us incognito, in the form of a Servant. Yet beneath the humble frame of the Man, lies *a hidden majesty*. The majesty, however, is hard to see. It can only be seen by faith, not by sight. For, God has chosen to send His eternal Son to us with a most uncomely form and a most unassuming visage:

> *For He grew up before Him as a [nursing infant], and as a root out of dry ground. He has **no [form]** or majesty. When we see Him, there is **no [visage]** that we should desire Him.*
> (Isaiah 53:2)

Christ Jesus comes not as Joseph. In the book of Genesis, Joseph is handsome both in *"form"* and in *"visage"*:

> *Thus he left all that he had in Joseph's hand, and he did not know what he had except for the bread which he ate. Now*

*Joseph was handsome in **form** and [**visage**].*
(Genesis 39:6, NKJV)

So Christ is not handsome like Joseph. He is not ruddy and handsome like David. Also, in terms of a feminine counterpart, He is not desirable to look at, as Rachel was. More like Leah and less like Rachel, Christ has no form or visage:

*Leah's eyes were weak, but Rachel was beautiful in **form** and [**visage**].* (Genesis 29:17)

What, then? Shall people say of us that we think that our King is not handsome? Shall they say of us that we worship a God whom we find undesirable? Spiritually speaking, may it never be! Spiritually speaking, we, the Church, are His Bride, and we find Him, the Lord Jesus Christ, to be the handsomest of all kings and the loveliest of all husbands:

*My Beloved is white and ruddy. The best among ten thousand. His head is like the purest gold. His hair is bushy, black as a raven. His eyes are like doves beside the water brooks, washed with milk, mounted like jewels. His cheeks are like a bed of spices with towers of perfumes. His lips are like lilies, dropping liquid myrrh. His hands are like rings of gold set with beryl. His body is like ivory work overlaid with sapphires. His legs are like pillars of marble set on sockets of fine gold. **His [visage]** is like Lebanon, excellent as the cedars.*
(Song of Solomon 5:10–15)

Still, the majesty of Christ is a *hidden* majesty. In order to be foolishness to the Greeks and an offense to the Jews, He comes in the flesh with neither a handsome form nor a lovely visage. Instead, He is unwanted by the world. Like a young, nursing baby boy, Christ is considered quite unimportant by the covetous Pharisees of Judea and the pompous politicians of Rome. Or, like a root out of dry ground, He will indeed come from the root of Jesse, and yet no one will notice Him because of the unattractive, dry ground of His humble poverty.

Who is the King of kings? The world looks for billionaires in fancy suits. It turns its gaze upon proud warriors whose muscles bulge. It seeks highly educated men with cunning political savvy to sit upon the thrones of its various nations. Yet Christ Jesus is none of these. Outwardly, He is a root out of dry ground, with no form or visage that we should desire Him. Yet the Lord God always works this way. He judges not the outward appearance, but rather the inner heart:

> *But the* L<small>ORD</small> *said to Samuel* [concerning Eliab, David's oldest brother], ***"Do not look on his [visage]****, or on the height of his stature, because I have rejected him; for I do not see as man sees.* ***For man looks at the outward appearance, but the*** L<small>ORD</small> ***looks at the heart."*** (1 Samuel 16:7)

Yet why does God do this? Why does He reveal His *hidden* Servant to the world with such a *hidden* majesty? Why does the glory of Christ Jesus have to be cloaked in such poor, unattractive flesh and bones, such that He has no form or visage that we would desire Him?

To answer this question, we pay particular attention to the *"visage"* of Christ in its connection with the word *"desire"* in Isaiah 53:2:

> *For He grew up before Him as a [nursing infant], and as a root out of dry ground. He has no [form] or majesty. When we see Him, there is **no [visage]** that we should **desire** Him.*

It is illuminating to see that when the Lord God made the Garden of Eden, He made the good trees in the Garden very much *"desirable."* In fact, the book of Genesis says that the good trees in the Garden of Eden even were *"desirable"* to the *"visage"*:

> *Out of the ground the* L<small>ORD</small> *God made every tree to grow that is **[desirable] to the [visage]**, and good for food, including the tree of life in the middle of the Garden and the tree of the knowledge of good and evil.* (Genesis 2:9)

Yet something went very wrong in the Garden of Eden. Eve, the woman, chose to *"desire"* sin, rather than the good gifts of God. That is, instead of *"desiring"* the good trees that were *"desirable to the visage"*—the good trees in the Garden—she chose rather to *"desire"* the one bad tree in the Garden, which was the tree of the knowledge of good and evil:

> *When the woman saw that the tree was good for food, and that it was a delight to the eyes, and that the tree was **to be desired** to make one wise, she took some of its fruit, and ate; and she gave some to her husband with her, and he ate it, too.* (Genesis 3:6)

Why, then, does Christ come with *"**no visage** that we should **desire Him**"*? This is so that our hearts may be exposed. That is to say, for those who love sin, and thus *desire* sin, wanting to be their own gods, and thus wanting to make the determination between good and evil according to their own, self-defined lusts, and not according to the Law of Christ, He, the Lord Jesus Christ, makes Himself very *undesirable*. He will have no competing gods before Him. He will not allow men to worship both Him and Mammon. Therefore, for those whose unrepentant *desire* is selfish pride and idolatry, they will only see Christ as a root out of dry ground, and will never be made privy to His hidden majesty. This is a divine judgment against them.

However, there are those who have eyes to see Christ Jesus for who He really is. Gazing at the impoverished, stricken, afflicted Man from Nazareth, these God-fearing believers are enabled by the Holy Spirit to look into His eyes and see the majesty within them. They immediately tremble, for they realize that the unattractive garb of the Nazarene is merely a cloak. Beneath it is hidden an eternal glory and majesty that is so bright that it would blind all men, were it allowed to shine in its full brightness.

O Church of the risen Christ, how do you look upon Him? What kind of *form* and *visage* do you see when you look unto Jesus? This all-important matter depends upon your own heart. If, in your heart, you *desire sin more than God*, then you will never see God rightly. You will think that entertainment venues, luxury homes, academic prestige, the praises of men, bodily comforts, and man-centered visions for social utopia are much more desirable than your father or mother's old, page-worn Bible. You will trade the glory of the incorruptible God for an image of an ox that eats grass, or a Buddha that cannot talk, or the kind of Sodomite "equal sign" that has the power to cast your whole body into Hell.

Why, then, do the churches spend such wasteful amounts of time and money fretting over their own worldly "forms" and "visages"? Does it not vex and anger God when the churches spend thousands of tithe dollars on their logos and their "overall images," making sure that they are socially marketable amongst the church-growth race of new, trendy, and widely popular churches? For example, is it not an abomination in the Lord's sight for church musicians to take on both the "forms" and the "visages" of the idolatrous musicians of the world?

Where are the believers today who truly understand the *hidden* majesty of the meekness of Christ? Where can one go to find the true, Gospel power of the Holy Spirit that works through poverty, suffering, and meekness, and without having to use an expensive video production? Where today are the pastors who know how to wax mighty not in the leadership seminar, where they are seen by men, but rather in the hidden prayer closet, where they are considered of no reputation among men? Where, too, are the Christian fathers and mothers of today who know the hidden majesty of family-based discipleship, which is so scorned by the world, but so honorable in the Kingdom of God? Is not Christ's majesty a *hidden* majesty? Therefore, should not we, His disciples, be willing to be scorned and despised by the world with Him?

THE SUFFERING SERVANT

Jesus Christ is God's *hidden Servant*. He possesses infinite majesty, and yet He comes in the flesh with no form or visage, such that His is a *hidden majesty*. And then, He suffers. He suffers greatly not for His own sins, since He has none, but for our sins, which are so very vile. He carries our sorrows, our griefs, and our sicknesses in His own body. Therefore, He is *"not esteemed"*:

He was despised, and rejected by men; a Man of suffering, and acquainted with disease. He was despised as One from whom men hide their face; **and we did not [esteem] Him***. Surely He has borne our sickness, and carried our suffering;* **yet we [esteemed] Him plagued***, struck by God, and afflicted.* (Isaiah 53:3–4)

He possesses infinite majesty, but such majesty is hidden beneath an exterior of sorrows, sicknesses, and sharp pains. Therefore, how do men esteem Him? They esteem Him stricken, smitten by God, and afflicted. They count Him as cursed by God. Much like Job, that persevering man of old, they esteem Christ as an alien and a stranger, a plagued Man, struck with the painful boils of sinful men, who is to be avoided, lest the suffering prove to be contagious.

He suffers. He is God's *hidden* Servant because He is God's *suffering* Servant. It is His suffering, and that on our behalf, which causes Him to be so *"despised"* by the world:

He was ***despised****, and rejected by men; a Man of suffering, and acquainted with disease. He was* ***despised*** *as One from whom men hide their face; and we did not [esteem] Him.* (Isaiah 53:3)

Who is despised? In the Scriptures, it is the poor man, who is the suffering man, who is despised:

Then I said, "Wisdom is better than strength." ***Nevertheless the poor man's wisdom is despised****, and his words are not heard.* (Ecclesiastes 9:16)

Jesus Christ is God's hidden Servant, possessing a hidden majesty of eternal, Heavenly glory, and yet He is despised by men:

The LORD, the Redeemer of Israel, and his Holy One, says ***to Him whom man despises****, to Him whom the nation abhors,* ***to [the Servant] of rulers****: "Kings shall see and rise up; princes, and they shall worship; because of the LORD who is faithful, even the Holy One of Israel, who has chosen You."* (Isaiah 49:7)

And,

> *But I am a worm, and no man; a reproach of men, **and despised by the people**. All those who see Me mock me. They insult Me with their lips. They shake their heads, saying, "He trusts in the* LORD; *let Him deliver Him. Let Him rescue Him, since He delights in Him!"* (Psalm 22:6–8)

Why is He so despised? He is despised because He loves the Father and always speaks the Words that His Father gives to Him. The world hates Him because the world hates His Father also. He is hated without a cause. He is loathed by men only on account of His holy, divine nature, which tells men that their deeds are evil. This is why they devalue Him at a mere thirty pieces of silver. This is the very reason why they crucify Him. They falsely accuse and murder Christ because in their rebellion against God their ultimate aim is to assassinate God.

Here, then, at the cross of Golgotha, the glory of Christ is hidden in a most lamentable way. The Son of God's glory is hidden beneath streams of blood and torrents of tears. For, there is a cross-centered reason why He has no *form* or *visage* that we should desire Him. Namely, on the way to the cross His *form* and *visage* have been beaten and marred beyond recognition. The hatred of men towards God has bludgeoned Jesus' *form* and *visage* to the point of being unrecognizable:

> *Just as many were astonished at You—His **[visage]** was marred more than any man, and His **form** more than the sons of men.* (Isaiah 52:14)

What kind of hidden glory is this, that the King of kings and Lord of lords would suffer such things at the hands of sinful men? For our sins, will He really allow them to twist a crown of thorns upon His head? In order to absorb the wrath of God for our sins in His own body on the tree, will He really allow them to spit at Him, strike Him in the face, and pierce His hands and His feet?

Hear it again, O sin-soaked Mankind, and clasp your hand over your mouth when you hear it. Sinful man has hated God enough to beat His only-begotten Son beyond recognition. Sinful humanity has marred His form and His visage until it is unrecognizable:

*Just as many were astonished at You—**His [visage] was marred more than any man, and His form more than the sons of men**—so He will cleanse many nations.* (Isaiah 52:14-15a)

This is where God chooses to hide His glory. The glory of God is hidden in the mutilated body of Jesus Christ, on the cross. In Him are hidden all the treasures of wisdom and knowledge. And yet these treasures are now hidden in the pierced, crucified body of Jesus, as He cries out in anguish, commits His spirit into the Father's hands, breathes His last breath, and gives up His spirit.

Where, then, does God choose to hide His glory today? He hides His glory in the suffering men and women who are His chosen children. When we, as Christians, are esteemed as fools for Christ's sake—when we go hungry and thirsty, are poorly clothed, are beaten, and homeless, and when we are reviled, persecuted, and despised by men, being defamed, then God chooses to hide the glory of the Gospel in us. The hidden glory of Christ fills up in our flesh what is lacking in the afflictions of Christ.

Do you see it, then, O beloved Church? Do you see the *hidden* glory of God's *hidden* Servant? He comes with *hidden* majesty, since He wants us to desire Him, even in a state of His having no comeliness. He also comes suffering, as a despised and rejected Man of sorrows, so that the glory of God might be hidden from the eyes of wicked men, and only revealed to those little children who see the greatness of His love for us in the greatness of His suffering for us. They see a blasphemer. We see the eternal Son of God bleeding for us, as the sacrificial Lamb of God who takes away our sins. They see a cursed and dying Man, and so they despise Him. We see the Father when we see Him, and we come to the Father only through His wounds.

His glory is hidden in His sufferings, but we preach that His glory will be revealed to all nations on the Last Day. Concerning the reprobate, the unveiling of His once-hidden glory will mean everlasting wrath and torment. Yet concerning us, His saints, the full revelation of His once-hidden glory will bring with it our everlasting rest in Him, and evoke our everlasting praises unto Him. For, His hidden glory will be hidden from us no more, even as we will worship Him forever, and will glorify the Father forever, praises never ceasing, world without end. Amen.

10

HE WAS PIERCED
The Cross in Isaiah 53:5-9

But He was pierced for our transgressions. He was crushed for our iniquities. The punishment that brought our peace was on Him; and by His wounds we are healed. All we like sheep have gone astray. Everyone has turned to his own way; and the LORD has laid on Him the iniquity of us all. (Isaiah 53:5-6)

GOD'S hidden Servant is divine. In the fifty-third chapter of Isaiah, the Suffering Servant is the *Divine* Servant. He is to be seen as being *essentially God—in essence, God.* Yet throughout history *"those who say that they are Jews, and they are not, but lie"* (Revelation 3:9) are those who have *"stolen [the LORD's] Words"* (Jeremiah 23:30) from Him regarding the fifty-third chapter of Isaiah. In general, they have claimed, falsely, that the Hebrew Old Testament is their book, and not ours. Therefore, in specific, they have made the false claim that Isaiah 53 is a chapter that properly belongs to them, and not to us. Then, they have asserted, with words of utter blasphemy, that the Suffering Servant in Isaiah 53 refers not to an individual Messiah, but rather, metaphorically, to the nation of Israel, as a whole. This is a lie proceeding out of what our Lord calls *"the synagogue of Satan"* (Revelation 3:9, again).

Isaiah 53 is, indeed, about an individual Man, the individual Person of the Messiah. Much more than that, however, is the truth that this individual Person of the Messiah also is to be seen as *God Himself*. For, just as Isaiah, in the divine-throne-room vision of chapter 6, describes the Lord as being *"high"* and *"lifted up,"* so too is the Messiah, the Suffering Servant of chapter 53, now described as being *"high"* and *"lifted up."* That is, as the Lord God is glorified, so too is the Suffering Servant glorified. Therefore, as the Lord God ought to be worshipped, so too ought the Suffering Servant to be worshipped. God is exclusively God, and, at the same time, the Suffering Servant is exclusively God.

How, then, can He be pierced? If He is to be worshipped as God, how can the Prophet say that He is pierced? Can God be pierced? Will mortal man mortally wound the immortal God? The Prophet does, in fact, call Him pierced:

> *But **He was pierced** for our transgressions. He was crushed for our iniquities. The punishment that brought our peace was on Him; and by His wounds we are healed.* (Isaiah 53:5)

What does this mean, that He was pierced? It means that His *body* was pierced, as with a *sword*:

> *You therefore, son of man, prophesy, and strike your hands together; and let **the sword** be doubled the third time, **the sword of the [pierced]**: it is **the sword** of the great one **who is [pierced]**, which [penetrates deeply].* (Ezekiel 21:14)

Thus in Isaiah 53, we behold this Suffering Servant who is a *Pierced* Servant. Dogs have surrounded Him; the congregation of the wicked have enclosed Him. They have pierced His hands and His feet [Psalm 22:16]. Moreover, it is His own people, the Jews, who have pierced Him. Thus His *heart* is wounded; His *heart* is pierced within Him [Psalm 109:22]. The Romans pierced His heart with a spear, but the Jews pierced His heart with their hatred of their own God and King. He weeps for them. They gnash their teeth at Him and pierce Him. Therefore, they will not see Him again, until they say, *"Blessed is He who comes in the name of the Lord,"* and until they look upon Him whom they have pierced [Psalm 118:26; Luke 13:35; Zechariah 12:10; Revelation 1:7].

He Was Pierced

By His Wounds We Are Healed

We find ourselves, then, standing directly in front of the cross of Jesus Christ. The Prophet directs us to look, with tears, upon the Servant who has been pierced for our transgressions, and crushed for our iniquities. Yet vast multitudes of people around the world *cannot* see this. Their hearts are made dull, their ears are made heavy, and they have shut their eyes; thus they *cannot* see with their eyes, and hear with their ears, and understand with their heart, and turn and be healed [Isaiah 6:10]. Those that *cannot* see *cannot* be healed.

Yet by grace, through faith, we *can* see this. By the grace of the Gospel, our eyes have been enlightened to see the Servant who was pierced for our transgressions and, therefore, we *can* be healed. To put the accent upon the verb "to heal," then, we say: they, who cannot see Him rightly, cannot be **healed**; but we, who by the illumination of the Holy Spirit can see Him as the Pierced Servant, can be **healed**. If we see His pierced hands, feet, and side, and look upon them rightly, through repentant eyes, we can indeed be **healed**:

*But He was pierced for our transgressions. He was crushed for our iniquities. The punishment that brought our peace was on Him; and by His wounds we are **healed**.* (Isaiah 53:5)

Whom do we see when we look upon the cross? Upon *whom* do we gaze when we gaze upwards upon the cross? We ought to see the pierced Servant who has power to *heal* us. He is the God who *heals* His people:

[The LORD is He]...*who forgives all your sins;* **who heals all your diseases**. (Psalm 103:3)

Jesus came healing the sick, the blind, and the lame. Yet He also came to heal us, who were very sick in our sins. For, God is the One who strikes sinners with sickness. He wounds transgressors on account of their transgressions. At the same time, however, He also desires *to heal those whom He has struck*:

For He wounds, and binds up. He injures, **and His hands [heal]**. (Job 5:18)

Also,

The L*ORD* *will strike Egypt,* **striking and healing**. *They will return to the* L*ORD*, *and He will be entreated by them,* **and will heal them**. (Isaiah 19:22)

And again,

[Speaking of Israel:] *"I was angry because of the iniquity of his covetousness,* **and struck him**; *I hid Myself and was angry; and he went on backsliding in the way of his heart. I have seen his ways,* **and will heal him**: *I will lead him also, and restore comforts to him and to his mourners. I create the fruit of the lips: Peace, peace, to him who is far off and to him who is near,"* says the L*ORD*; **"and I will heal them."** (Isaiah 57:17–19)

Speaking on behalf of all of mankind, our sins are great, and so our sicknesses our great. In our rebellion against God, we have heaped up iniquity upon iniquity against Him. Therefore, our wounds and sicknesses are severe, so much so that they seem incurable. Yet for those who will be pierced to the heart with repentance, God is able to heal even the most seemingly incurable of wounds:

For the L*ORD* *says, "Your hurt is* **incurable**, *and your wound grievous....For I will restore health to you,* **and I will heal you of your wounds**.*"* (Jeremiah 30:12, 17a)

And also,

Come, and let us return to the L*ORD*; **for He has torn us to pieces, and He will heal us; He has injured us, and He will bind up our wounds**. (Hosea 6:1)

Thus God wounds, and heals. He makes sick, and He heals sickness. Due to our rebellious sins as a wicked humanity, He plagues us with disease. Yet due to His grace and compassion towards sinful men, He is willing to remove our plagues and heal our diseases.

Yet how is God able to do this? For, in the very opening chapter of the book of Isaiah, does not God describe Israel as being so sick with sin that she is unable to heal herself?

> *Why should you be beaten more, that you revolt more and more?* ***The whole head is sick, and the whole heart faint.*** *From the sole of the foot even to the head there is no soundness in it: wounds, welts, and open sores. They have not been closed, neither bandaged, neither soothed with oil.* (Isaiah 1:5–6)

How, then, can Israel be healed? Moreover, if I, as a sinner, look at the disgusting nature of my own sins, and see the sicknesses of body and soul that have resulted from them, how can I ever hope to be healed of them?

> *But He was pierced for our transgressions. He was crushed for our iniquities. The punishment that brought our peace was on Him; and* ***by His wounds we are healed***. (Isaiah 53:5)

Christ died on the tree of Calvary so that *His wounds* could be *our healing*. He suffered for our health. He was plagued with death in order to remove our plague and give us life:

> *... who His own self bore our sins in His body on the tree, that we, having died to sins, might live to righteousness;* ***by whose stripes you were healed***. (1 Peter 2:24)

O dear Reader, are you healthy, or are you sick? It is not the healthy who need a physician, but the sick. The problem with the world today is that the people of the world think that they are healthy, when in truth they are extremely sick. Ask a worldly man who is exercising his muscles vigorously at the neighborhood athletic club, "Are you healthy, or are you sick?" and he will despise you even for asking the question. Ask a worldly scholar at the local university, "Is your intellect healthy, or is it sick?" and he will delight in boasting of all of his mental powers in order to seek to convince you that his mind is extremely brawny and fit. Yet the truth is that both men are dangerously sick. They boast of their strong physical and intellectual health, but inside their souls are deathly ill with idolatrous sin.

Here is where all true Gospel proclamation begins. It begins with the proclamation God—that is, God as the Creator of the heavens and the earth, who is glorious, and who created the world to be very good—and then it moves to sinful man, who is desperately sick. The true Gospel does not flatter sinful man. Rather, it says to him, with all the threatening force of true love, "You are sick. You are so sick as to be on the verge of everlasting death. O proud Sinner, you are not a good person. Your soul is sick with sin. You are dead to God in your sins. Up until now, you have thought of yourself as a righteous person, but the truth is that you have been wicked. Your rebellion against God's holy commandments has been wicked, and it has made you so spiritually sick as to be on the verge not only of physical death, but of the Second Death, the death of eternal, conscious misery in Hell."

This is where true Gospel proclamation begins, and yet it is not what most Americans believe about the Gospel. For, most Americans have heard a false version of the Gospel. They have heard the Prosperity Preachers say that the Gospel has come to grant us *physical* health and *physical* prosperity in this mortal flesh. These false teachers preach a Positivity Gospel, which is a toothless Gospel, wherein the Lion of Judah has no bite, and the Lamb of God has no wrath. They prefer to speak of sin as a state of ignorance concerning the power of Positive Thinking, rather than the true, God-hating, Christ-cursing plague of guilty humanity that God Himself proclaims it to be.

Here, and here only, then, is the love of God that is revealed in the true Gospel. It is that love that comes to God's own wicked, seditious, rebellious enemies *through the wounds of Christ*. That is, *we* were God's enemies, assaulting God and seeking to dethrone God in our sinful pride. *We* joined the ranks of God's enemies in seeking to assassinate God, so that we could become our own gods. Therefore, God, in His justice, struck *us* with the sicknesses and wounds of *our* sins.

Yet while we were still sinners, *Christ* died for us. *He* healed us *by His wounds*. This is true, Gospel power. This is divine power. For, does not blood stain white clothing? How, then, can the blood of Christ actually *wash* stained clothing, and make it white again? What kind of blood washes, without staining? Also, do not wounds make a man sick? Do not infections come from wounds? How, then, can these wounds of Christ actually *heal* a sick person? What kind of wounds heal, instead of making sick?

We come, then, by faith alone. We look upon His wounds, and by His wounds we are healed. We see our sin-produced sicknesses *in His wounds*. We watch His wounds absorb our guilt. And so we weep. We weep tears of repentance. For, this is what it costs God in order to forgive our sins. This is what is required of Christ in order to heal our sicknesses. The spotless, sinless Lamb of God must be pierced for our transgressions, and crushed for our iniquities, *and by His wounds we are healed*. Therefore, we repent of our sins, and we weep at the sight of His wounds.

THE SUBSTITUTIONARY LAMB

What is the true Gospel? When we look upon the cross, what should we see? First, we should see *the wounds that heal*. In this life, Christ's *physical* wounds heal our *spiritual* sicknesses.[1] In the life to come, Christ's wounds shall heal our physical bodies, too, through resurrection, unto immortality.

Then, second, when we stand before the cross, we should also see *the substitutionary Lamb*. For, Christ is not only a Lamb, but even more a *substitutionary* Lamb, given for wayward sheep:

---

[1] Sometimes, Christ chooses to heal our *physical* sicknesses in this life, too, even in supernatural ways. Yet it is the norm of the Christian in this present life to bear many sicknesses, even carrying around in our bodies *"[thorns] in the flesh"* (2 Corinthians 12:7), and *"fill[ing] up on [our] part that which is lacking of the afflictions of Christ in our flesh for His body's sake"* (Colossians 1:24).

All we like sheep have gone astray. *Everyone has turned to his own way; and the* LORD *has laid on Him the iniquity of us all.* (Isaiah 53:6)

In the true Gospel, we all are like sheep. We have gone astray from God's holy paths; we have wandered away from righteousness, and into the filth of our own sins. And this is deadly. We are not talking here about silly sheep that accidentally get lost. We are, rather, talking about rebellious sheep who deliberately disobey their Shepherd, wickedly leave His fold, and foolishly wander astray into the den of ravenous wolves:

*The man who **wanders out of the way of understanding** shall rest in **the assembly of the [dead]**.* (Proverbs 21:16)

Why do the sheep go astray? They love sin, and so they choose leaders who will lead them astray in the paths of sin:

*For those who lead this people **lead them astray**; and those who **are led by them** are destroyed.* (Isaiah 9:16)

Again, why do the sheep go astray? It is not because they are naïve, innocent sheep who simply lack greater educational opportunities. To the contrary, they love the voice of the false prophets who lead them astray, the ones who chant "Peace! Peace!" when there is no peace. They love lies, instead of truth, and so those lies lead them astray. They consult idols rather than God, for the spirit of harlotry leads them astray as they commit spiritual harlotry against their God.

Sinners are like lost sheep. They are deeply guilty in their sins. And we all like sheep have gone astray, each one to his own way:

I have gone astray like a lost sheep. *Seek Your servant, for I do not forget Your commandments.* (Psalm 119:176)

Remember that this is a deadly straying. This is not innocent sheep play. Rather, this is the kind of wretched rebellion against the Shepherd that lands the lost sheep in the hunting grounds of hungry lions. The wages of sin is death, for God said to Adam, *"For in the day that you eat of it, you will surely die!"* (Genesis 2:17).

Someone, then, *must die*. A lamb must be put to death. The jealous wrath of the Shepherd demands the death of the rebellious sheep. Yet He also loves the sheep with a gracious and compassionate love. What, then, does the righteous Shepherd do? He provides a *substitutionary* sacrifice. He allows a blameless, spotless *lamb* to die in the stead of His rebellious *sheep*.

Thus we have the Gospel typified in the substitutionary lambs of the Law of Moses. We have, for example, Abraham preparing to offer Isaac, his only-begotten son, as a sacrifice to God, while Isaac says to his father, *"Here is the fire and the wood, but where is the lamb for a burnt offering?"* And Abraham, believing the Gospel, replies to his son and says, **"God will provide Himself the lamb** *for a burnt offering, my son"* (Genesis 22:7-8).

We also have the Passover lamb, which was a substitutionary lamb. During the Exodus, it was the blood of the Passover lamb that kept the angel of death from striking down Israel's firstborn sons. The lamb was a sacrificial *substitute* for their own sons.

The Prophet says, *"All we like sheep have gone astray"* (Isaiah 53:6), thus deserving death. Yet God is the Good Shepherd, who Himself is willing to suffer on behalf of His wayward sheep. What, then, does God do? He provides a lamb, the Lamb of God, to die in our place:

The next day, he saw Jesus coming to him, and said, **"Behold, the Lamb of God, who takes away the sin of the world!"** (John 1:29)

All we like sheep have gone astray. How, then, can we be saved? We can be saved *"with precious blood,* **as of a faultless and pure Lamb,** *the blood of Christ"* (1 Peter 1:19). Therefore, when we look upon the cross, we, as sheep, should see the substitutionary Lamb who died for our sins:

All we **like sheep** *have gone astray. Everyone has turned to his own way; and the* LORD *has laid on Him the iniquity of us all.*

*He was oppressed, yet when He was afflicted He did not open His mouth. As **a lamb** that is led to the slaughter, and as **a sheep** that before its shearers is silent, so He did not open His mouth.* (Isaiah 53:6–7)

Only a sheep can die in place of other sheep. Only a spotless, unblemished lamb can substitute for other, rebellious lambs. In the same way, only a sinless Human—the very Son of Man—can die a substitutionary death in the place of other humans. Therefore, Jesus became flesh and made His dwelling among us.

The doctrine of Christ is no trifling matter. Our very salvation depends upon it. For, if Christ is not truly God, and thus uncreated and eternal in His sinless Person, then His blood lacks the worth or value to pay for the sins of the world. At the same time, if Christ is not truly Man, then He cannot properly substitute for sinful men. For, only a true, incarnate sheep can die in the stead of other sheep. Therefore, Christ must be fully God and fully Man, or else none can be saved.

Think, then, upon the goodness of God, our Shepherd. Jesus Christ, our Shepherd, became a sheep for us. He offered Himself as an innocent, spotless Lamb, as the *substitutionary* sacrifice for our sins. He was pierced *for our transgressions*, and He was crushed *for our iniquities*. The sinless Shepherd condescended to suffer the immeasurable pains of the cross for the sake of His rebellious, wayward sheep. How worthy, then, is the blood of Christ! As a Lamb, He was slaughtered for us. Therefore, as the Lamb who was slain, He shall be worshipped by us, who believe, for all of the days of eternity. And to the degree that His substitutionary slaughter for us was excruciatingly and unfathomably painful, to that same degree will His eternal glory be praised at the great wedding feast of the Lamb [Revelation 19:7-9]!

HE DID NOT OPEN HIS MOUTH

The Suffering Servant is the Pierced Servant. We are kneeling, therefore, right in front of the cross. What, then, should we *hear*? When we humble ourselves before the cross, crying silent, mournful tears of repentance and love before our crucified Lord, what is it that we should *hear*? Certainly, we should *see* Christ's wounds that heal, since He is the substitutionary Lamb, slain for unworthy sinners. Yet when we kneel before the cross of Christ—removing our shoes as we do so, since we are kneeling upon such holy ground—we also should *hear* something. We not only should *see* the wounds that heal, and thus *see* the substitutionary Lamb, but also should *hear* something. Namely, we should *hear* the innocent *silence* of the Lamb. Unlike the violent, deceitful mouths of the wicked, which boast and scoff loudly, the mouth of Christ is both innocent, and *"silent"*:

> *He was oppressed, yet when He was afflicted* **He did not open His mouth**. *As a lamb that is led to the slaughter, and as a sheep that before its shearers* **is silent**, *so* **He did not open His mouth**. *He was taken away by oppression and judgment; and as for His generation, who considered that He was cut off out of the land of the living and stricken for the disobedience of My people? They made His grave with the wicked, and with [the] rich in His death; although He had done no violence, nor was any deceit in His mouth.* (Isaiah 53:7-9)

There is, here, a great moral contrast between Christ and the rich. In Christ's *"mouth,"* there is neither *"violence"* nor *"deceit."* Yet in the *"mouth"* of *"the wicked,"* whom the Prophet Isaiah identifies with *"the rich,"* there is both *"violence"* and *"deceit."* This *"violence"* and *"deceit"* of Israel's *"rich men"* is also affirmed by the Prophet Micah:

> *Her* **rich men** *are full of* **violence**, *her inhabitants* **speak lies**, *and their tongue is* **deceitful** *in their speech.* (Micah 6:12)

Not all rich people are wicked. William Wilberforce was rich, and yet he gave his riches as offerings towards many great causes of the Kingdom of Heaven. Still, *most* rich people *are* wicked, which is why the Prophet identifies the wicked with the rich. As

John Calvin says of Isaiah's poetry here, "By the terms 'wicked men' and 'rich men' the same thing, in my opinion, is denoted."[2]

This is why Jesus says, *"But woe to you who are rich!"* (Luke 6:24). This is also why James says, *"Come now, you rich, weep and howl for your miseries that are coming on you!"* (James 5:1). It is typically the rich who murder the righteous. It is most often the rich in whose mouths are found violence and deceit.

What, then, does this say about rich, gluttonous America? In the latter half of the twentieth century, did not America become *filthy* rich, even gaining her riches by way of the unjust practices of usury, unfair trade, and the employment of cheap international laborers through sweat shops? Moreover, did not much of her wealth come from the filth of her fornications, as she exported her violent and seductive movies, her immodest clothing lines, her idolatrous sports, her secularized educational systems, her covetous commercialism, and her computer technologies, derived from her craft as a warmonger, to all of the nations of the earth? Yet even more monstrously, did not America rise to riches through her mass population control, complete, at first, with forced sterilizations? Did she not grow rich on the monstrous practice of birth control, and even richer on the blood of millions upon millions of preborn children, the very helpless babies who were handed over, oftentimes in the name of economic pragmatism and individual prosperity, to the murderous houses of legally sanctioned abortion clinics? Does not the blood of the Abortion Holocaust, which is the blood of child sacrifice, betray the violence of the rich?

When we look upon the cross, we must *see* the wounds that heal us, even as we *see* the spattered blood of atonement for our sins, the blood of Christ our Lord, who is our substitutionary Lamb. Yet we must also *hear* something. We must *hear* the innocent *"silence"* of the Lamb of God:

He was oppressed, yet when He was afflicted **He did not open His mouth**. *As a lamb that is led to the slaughter, and as a*

---

[2] John Calvin, *Commentary on the Prophet Isaiah* (trans. William Pringle; Edinburgh: The Calvin Translation Society, 1850-1853), 4:122.

*sheep that before its shearers **is silent**, so **He did not open His mouth**.* (Isaiah 53:7)

Jesus is not like Job in this respect: Job opened his mouth to defend his own innocence, but Jesus did not open His mouth. Instead, Jesus is the Suffering Servant, and in His suffering, He does not open His mouth:

*My [loved ones] and My friends stand aloof from My plague. My kinsmen stand far away. They also who seek after My life lay snares. Those who seek My hurt speak mischievous things, and meditate deceits all day long. But I, as a deaf Man, do not hear. **I am as a mute Man who does not open His mouth**.* (Psalm 38:11–13)

And,

*I was mute. **I did not open My mouth**, because You did it.* (Psalm 39:9)

Jesus is completely innocent. He is spotless and without sin of any kind. Yet we, kneeling before the cross, *hear* the innocent *silence* of the Lamb. Just prior to the cross, Pilate asks Jesus for His defense, but Jesus answers him not one word, such that the governor marvels greatly. Jesus, our Lord, suffers *silently* for us. Like a lamb led to the slaughter, He does not open His mouth:

*For to this you were called, because Christ also suffered for us, leaving you an example, that you should follow His steps, who did not sin, **"neither was deceit found in His mouth."** Who, when He was cursed, **did not curse back**. When He suffered, **did not threaten**, but committed Himself to Him who judges righteously.* (1 Peter 2:21–23)

Behold the sinless innocence of Christ being like that of a lamb. A little girl is given by her father a newborn lamb as a gift. She holds the lamb while the lamb nuzzles her face. She feeds the lamb from a bottle. The little girl delights to watch the tiny lamb sleep. She loves the lamb, though the lamb, with its soft bleating, oftentimes remains silent. The lamb's silence marks its innocence.

In the same way, behold the *relative* innocence—for all babies other than Christ are born with a sin nature—of a human baby boy. The tiny baby boy cannot talk. He watches his siblings play, and smiles and laughs with joy when his mother enters the room to pick him up after his morning nap. Yet for the most part, he is silent. His silence speaks of his relative innocence.

How much more, then, shall we praise the innocence of the Man, Christ Jesus! He who *spoke* and the heavens and the earth came into being now chooses to be *silent* at the cross. He is wholly innocent, without the slightest spot or blemish of sin in His heart. He loves us, all the way to the cross, in silent suffering and in silent innocence. He entrusts Himself to the Father's judgment.

What, then, shall the Father do when He sends the Son to judge the living and the dead? Shall he not *silence the wicked*—the rich scoffers who scoffed at Jesus while He was on the cross, and all of the mockers who mock God's Son even to this very day—with *the roar* of His fury and *the deafening sounds* of the torrential rains of the fire of His wrath?

Yet we extol the glory of His silent sinless-ness. The Lamb of Heaven need not speak. He simply stands, silently, in the midst of the throne and of the four living creatures, and in the midst of the elders, and immediately all of Heaven erupts with a most thunderous shout of praise:

> *I saw, and I heard something like a voice of many angels around the throne, the living creatures, and the elders; and the number of them was ten thousands of ten thousands, and thousands of thousands; saying* **with a loud voice***, "Worthy is the Lamb who has been [slain] to receive the power, wealth, wisdom, strength, honor, glory, and blessing!"*
> (Revelation 5:11–12)

Thus Heaven will not be silent, but rather very loud and even roaring with the praises of Jesus Christ! And thus we shall spend our everlasting days extolling the worthiness of Him who was pierced for our transgressions, and crushed for our iniquities, even as we shall extol the Father who gave Him as the substitutionary sacrifice for our sins, forever and ever, world without end. Amen.

Prophecies of the Cross

11

IT PLEASED THE LORD TO CRUSH HIM
The Cross in Isaiah 53:10

*Yet it **pleased** the LORD to [crush] Him. He has [put] Him to [sickness]. When You make His soul an offering for sin, He will see His [seed]. He will prolong His days, and the LORD's **pleasure** will prosper in His hand.* (Isaiah 53:10)

GOD is King, both of Heaven and earth, and so He does whatever *pleases* Him. Since He sits enthroned in Heaven, He is able to do whatever pleases Him. There is no roaring wind that will not submit to His every command, and there is no blinding blizzard that will not cease at the very moment that He utters His voice and orders it to flee away.

Also, He governs the nations according to His own good pleasure. The Lord does not have to keep time with Swiss trains and international business deadlines. The nations of the earth may rage against Him, but He will rule them with an iron scepter, and dash them to pieces like pottery. The United Nations may vote to strike down His holy commandments, but He shall accomplish whatever *pleases* Him on the earth.

What is it, then, that pleases the Lord? Surely, what pleases Him is not what pleases sinful man. He takes no pleasure in the idolatry of the belly. God is pleased neither with the gluttonies of ancient Rome, nor with the rich delicacies of today's global Babylon.

He also takes no pleasure in the various idolatries of the human heart. The lusts of the flesh, the lusts of the eyes, and the pride of life are all detestable to God. The human eye is enamored by the seductive luster of the abundant idols of the world, but to God all such images are abominable.

Rather, the Lord delights in executing justice and righteousness on the earth. His holy nature is *pleased* to bring wrathful judgments against unrepentant, wicked men. Thus when Hophni and Phinehas, the two sons of Eli, refused to heed their father's voice and cease their lustful desecrations of the Lord's Tabernacle, the Lord was *pleased* to slay them. He struck them dead, and this *pleased* Him, since His offended glory required their death, for the sake of the righteousness of His name.

The Lord is pleased only to act for the sake of His own righteousness. To this end, He will exalt His holy Law and make it majestic. It is the exercising of justice and righteousness in which He is pleased. Thus only those who know and love His ways of righteousness, and so walk in His paths of righteousness, are able to please Him.

Therefore, is it not terrifyingly true that the wrath of God is being revealed from Heaven, even now, against all the ungodliness and unrighteousness of men? Since men have seen His glory in the created order, have refused to honor Him as God and to give thanks to Him as their Creator, and have, instead, exchanged His glory for images of perishable man, and beasts, and birds, and creeping creatures, does it not *please* God to execute His wrath upon the earth [Romans 1:18-23]? When He sends His earthquakes, famines, pestilences, and wars upon the earth, and when He judges wicked men for their foolish myths and grotesque practices—on account of which they make apes their imagined forefathers and perverse, homosexual unions their wedding feasts—does this not *please* Him? Shall not the righteous Judge be *pleased* to execute His righteous judgments against all of those who murder His elect and who destroy His good creation?

HE IS PLEASED TO BE MERCIFUL

Yet God is also rich in mercy. Being merciful, He is not pleased to watch the wicked perish. He asks, rhetorically, **"Have I any pleasure in the death of the wicked***…and not rather that he should return from his way, and live?"* (Ezekiel 18:23). Surely, the

Lord is pleased to punish sin, even with everlasting wrath. Yet when the wicked cast themselves into Hell, through their own hard-hearted unbelief, He is *not pleased* to witness it. Rather, God is longsuffering towards all men, not being pleased that any should perish, but rather wanting all to come to repentance [2 Peter 3:9].

The Lord of mercy is pleased to show mercy to repentant sinners. He is pleased with mercy, and not sacrifice, and with the knowledge of Him more than with burnt offerings [Hosea 6:6]. What pleases Him is the redemption of enslaved sinners into spiritual freedom. He is pleased to bestow mercy upon His former enemies, once they have repented of their crimes against Him. He is *not pleased* with proud, wicked works of the Law, as if an already condemned man could work his way out of condemnation. Instead, He is pleased with those who have faith in Him, since without faith it is impossible to please Him [Hebrews 11:6].

This is what pleases God, namely, to show mercy to naked, poor, and desperate sinners. Thus the Prophet Micah says of God:

> *Who is a God like You, who pardons iniquity, and passes over the disobedience of the remnant of His heritage? He does not retain His anger forever,* **because He [is pleased] in loving kindness**. (Micah 7:18)

Yet not all have faith. Multitudes upon multitudes of people hate this holy God of mercy. In order to flatter Him, they utter prayers from their lips in order to bring their sacrifices of praise to Him, yet their hearts are far from Him [Isaiah 29:13]. In their hearts, they neither love Him nor fear Him. Thus the Muslims bring their Muslim sacrifices, the Hindus bring their Hindu sacrifices, the unbelieving Jews bring their unbelieving-Jewish sacrifices, and the charlatan Christians bring their charlatan-Christian sacrifices. Yet with none of these sacrifices is the Lord actually pleased:

> *"What are the multitude of your sacrifices to Me?" says the* LORD. *"I have had enough of the burnt offerings of rams, and the fat of fed animals.* **I [am not pleased with]** *the blood of bulls, or of lambs, or of male goats."* (Isaiah 1:11)

What is it, then, that can please God? If all of our sins are like scarlet, and if even our righteous acts, so stained by sin, have become like filthy rags, with what shall we please God? The terrifying truth is that our sins already have condemned us. The uncompromising truth is that all who are not born of the Holy Spirit are entirely unable to please God in any way. For, their refusal to glorify Him turns even their greatest acts of kindness into treasonous offenses against Him. Rebellious sinners can do no works of their own—absolutely none—to please God [Isaiah 64:6; Romans 8:8].

Yet there is something outside of us, a foreign righteousness, which pleases God. His eternal Son's willingness to condescend, to take on human flesh, and to die as a substitutionary sacrifice for our sins, *pleases Him very much*. The Lord is pleased to punish sin. Yet in His mercy, He is pleased to punish our sin in the body of His only-begotten Son:

> *But He was pierced for our transgressions.* **He was crushed** *for our iniquities. The punishment that brought our peace was on Him; and by His wounds we are healed.* (Isaiah 53:5)

Can it really please the Father to *"crush"* His beloved Son?

> *Yet it* **pleased** *the* LORD **to [crush] Him**.... (Isaiah 53:10)

How can this be? How can the Father, who has shared His eternal glory with His Son in eternity past, an eternal span before the world began, be pleased to crush His Son?

Surely, even as the mockers mock Jesus on the cross, they speak the truth about the Father being very pleased with Him:

> *"He trusts in the* LORD*; let Him deliver Him. Let Him rescue Him, since* **He [is pleased with] Him***."* (Psalm 22:8)

This is the Father's beloved Son, with whom He is well pleased [Mark 1:11]. And the love within the Godhead is reciprocal. Just as the Father is pleased with the Son, so too is the Son pleased to do the Father's will:

IT PLEASED THE LORD TO CRUSH HIM

*With sacrifice and offering **[You were not pleased]**; but a body You have prepared for Me. Burnt offering and sin offering You did not require. Then I said, "Behold, I come; in the scroll of the book it is written of Me. **I [am pleased] to do Your will**, O my God, and Your Law is within My heart."* (Psalm 40:6–8, NKJV)

The Son is very pleased to obey the Father, even if obeying the Father means going to Golgotha. Whatever it is that pleases the Father, this the Son desires to do:

*He was withdrawn from them about a stone's throw, and He knelt down and prayed, saying, "Father, **if [it pleases You]**, remove this cup from Me. Nevertheless, **not My will, but Yours, be done**."* (Luke 22:41–42)

The Father, then, is not pleased to crush His Son, in the sense of gaining any pleasure from watching His Son suffer and die. The Son's tears and cries of torment only serve to pierce the Father's heart with pain. Since He cannot bear to watch His beloved Son suffer so infinitely upon the cross, He must look away. The sky must become dark with Heaven's grief.

Why, then, does the Prophet say that it *pleased* the Father to crush Him? It only *pleased* Him in the sense that His Son's obedience brought about His *pleasure of redemption for sinful man*:

*Yet it **pleased** the LORD to [crush] Him. He has [put] Him to [sickness]. When You make His soul an offering for sin, He will see His [seed]. He will prolong His days, and the LORD's **pleasure** will prosper in His hand.* (Isaiah 53:10)

Is God pleased to bring suffering and death upon His Son? In the sense of Christ's agony, may it never be! Yet He is pleased to crush His Son in this sense only, namely, that the crushing of His Son worked the pleasure of the salvation of man. Since He was made to be sin for us, the Father was pleased to crush our sin on the cross by crushing Him on the cross. Yet this was only for our salvation, which, in turn, is proved by the resurrection of Christ from the grave. Thus God's *merciful redemption*, which is *the Lord's pleasure*, prospers in the powerful, resurrected hand of Christ Jesus.

The Father, then, is pleased to save us, desperate sinners, by crushing His Son. It is the Father's pleasure to cause salvation to prosper in the hand of His Son. Yet once His Son has been crushed for our sins, such that the eternal justice of God against our sins has been satisfied, fully, by the death of Christ on the cross, then how shall the Father honor the Son? Is it not the Father's *good pleasure* to show the whole world just how much He is *pleased with His Son*? Is not the Father *pleased to glorify the Son*, and to reward Him with an exaltation to the highest of the Heavenly heights?

> *Behold, My Servant will deal wisely.* **He will be [high] and lifted up, and will be very [exalted]**. (Isaiah 52:13)

This is how the Father is pleased. Having brought about our salvation through the crushing of Christ on the cross, the Father is now pleased to turn our salvation into the everlasting praise of the righteousness of His beloved Son. The Father is pleased to exalt His Only-begotten to the highest place, that at His name every knee should bow, of those in Heaven, and of those on earth, and of those under the earth, and every tongue confess His glorious Lordship [Philippians 2:9-11]. Jesus Christ was *crushed* for our sins at Calvary, according to *the pleasure of the Father's eternal plan*. Therefore, Jesus, our Lord, shall be exalted above the heavens, and the Father shall be *pleased* to honor His name over every name that is named, and over every throne and principality and power and dominion:

> *...which He worked in Christ, when He raised Him from the dead, and made Him to sit at His right hand in the Heavenly places,* **far above all rule, and authority, and power, and dominion, and every name that is named, not only in this age, but also in that which is to come**. *He put all things in subjection under His feet, and gave Him to be head over all things for the [Church].* (Ephesians 1:20–22)

It Pleased the Lord to Crush Him

If the Father was *pleased* to crush Him, it was only for our redemption. Since, then, the Son has been *pleased* to obey the Father, even to the point of immeasurable torment upon the cross, the Father is now *pleased* to exalt Him to His great, eternal throne, even seating Him at His right hand of majesty. For, it is *the pleasure of the Lord* that now prospers in His hand. And thus we shall please the Father in Heaven by bowing down and worshipping the Son in Heaven, whom He crushed for our redemption, who now is risen and glorified—and by giving thanks, through His eternal Spirit, unto the Father and unto the Son, with trembling joy before Him, forever and ever, time unceasing, world without end. Amen.

12

HE SHALL SEE LIGHT
The RESURRECTION in Isaiah 53:11-12

Yet it pleased the LORD to [crush] Him. He has [put] Him to [sickness]. When You make His soul an offering for sin, He will see His [seed]. He will prolong His days, and the LORD's pleasure will prosper in His hand. After the suffering of His soul, **He [shall see light]** *and be satisfied. My righteous Servant will justify many by the knowledge of Himself; and He will bear their iniquities. Therefore will I give Him a portion with the great, and He will divide the plunder with the strong; because He poured out His soul to death, and was numbered with the transgressors; yet He bore the sin of many, and made intercession for the transgressors.* (Isaiah 53:10-12)

GOD'S holy Servant shall *"see light"* (v. 11a). Many English translations of the Bible miss this in verse 11. They typically read, *"He shall see and be satisfied"* (v. 11a, ESV), but they lack the word *"light."* Yet the witness from antiquity says that the right reading of verse 11, a reading which is found in the translation footnotes of most Bibles, actually includes the word *"light"* in this precious verse: *"After the suffering of His soul,* ***He [shall see light]*** *and be satisfied."*[1]

Again, then, the Suffering Servant of Isaiah 53 shall *"see light"* (v. 11a). This is *resurrection*. First, He shall pour out His

---

[1] This reading follows the reading of the Dead Sea Scrolls and Septuagint, as opposed to the Masoretic Text. If this is correct, then the World English Bible (WEB), with its bold willingness to critique hegemonic, academic textual-critical assumptions, proves superior to other modern translations on this point.

soul unto death, but then, afterwards, He shall see light. That is, the Servant, at first, shall be placed in a dark, sealed tomb, but then, subsequently, shall be raised into the blazing daylight of resurrection. First comes the dark night of death on a cross, and also of burial within the tomb. Yet afterwards comes the victorious light of bodily resurrection from the grave.

This is why the Prophet says that He shall *"prolong His days"*:

Yet it pleased the LORD to [crush] Him. He has [put] Him to [sickness]. When You make His soul an offering for sin, He will see His [seed]. **He will prolong His days**, *and the LORD's pleasure will prosper in His hand.* (Isaiah 53:10)

Jesus died while being still relatively young of age. His days were cut short. Even though the Law says that those who obey God's commandments shall *prolong their days* [Deuteronomy 4:40; 5:33; 6:2; 11:9; 32:47]—and He obeyed the commandments flawlessly and sinlessly—His own days were cut short. At a relatively young age, He was cut off from the land of the living. Yet the Prophet Isaiah, speaking of His resurrection, says that *He shall prolong His days*. This is God's glorious gift to His beloved Christ, namely, a resurrection unto an eternal length of days. As it says in the Psalms:

For You meet Him with the blessings of goodness. You set a crown of fine gold on His head. He asked life of You, You gave it to Him, **even length of days forever and ever.** (Psalm 21:3–4)

Therefore, dear Brethren, we do not grieve in the same manner as unbelievers do. For, Christ is risen from the dead, and thus has prolonged His days. In turn, He, the firstfruits, shall raise all who have fallen asleep in Him. In specific, we hurt deeply over our loved ones in Christ who have fallen asleep. Their days have been cut short, and we have wept and wept over them. Yet on the great Day of Christ Jesus, they shall be raised, and our Lord shall prolong their days. The current separation from them is excruciating, but very soon we shall see their glad faces, and our days with them in the Kingdom of Heaven shall be prolonged, even everlastingly.

HE WILL SEE HIS SEED

God's Servant, the Christ, shall see light. He shall see the light of resurrection. In that light, then, what shall He see? Once He sees the light of resurrection, what shall He see in that light?

Yet it pleased the LORD *to [crush] Him. He has [put] Him to [sickness]. When You make His soul an offering for sin,* **He will see His [seed]**. *He will prolong His days, and the* LORD*'s pleasure will prosper in His hand.* (Isaiah 53:10)

Once Christ sees the light of resurrection, then He also shall see *His seed*. He died relatively young. Who, then, can speak of His descendants? Since He was cut off from the land of the living, how can we speak of Him as having any children? Yet this is exactly why He died, that in the light of resurrection, He might see His seed:

Their [seed] will be known among the nations, and their offspring among the peoples. All who see them will acknowledge them, that they are the [seed] which the LORD *has blessed.* (Isaiah 61:9)

Christ Jesus is the *"seed,"* singular, of Abraham:

The LORD *appeared to Abram and said, "I will give this land* **to your [seed]**.*" He built an altar there to the* LORD, *who had appeared to him.* (Genesis 12:7)

Yet Christ Jesus, the *"seed"* of Abraham, shall see His own *"seed."* He shall have His spiritual offspring. In the light of His resurrection, He shall see them.

This was the joy of Jacob upon seeing his own grandsons. Having been deceived by his other sons into thinking that his son Joseph had been slain by a wild beast, Jacob gave up all hope of ever seeing Joseph's face again in his mortal, earthly life. Yet near the end of his life, Jacob not only saw Joseph, face to face, but also was allowed *to see* Joseph's two sons. He *saw* the promised *seed of Israel* in the faces of his two grandsons:

> *Israel said to Joseph, "I did not think I would **see** your face, and behold, God has let me **see your [seed] also**."*
> (Genesis 48:11)

Moses saw the land that the Lord had sworn to give to Abraham, Isaac, and Jacob, saying, *"I will give it to **your seed**,"* (Exodus 33:1), but Moses was not allowed to witness the seed of Israel actually entering into that Promised Land. Yet Christ Jesus, in the light of resurrection, shall see His seed. He shall see His seed inherit the Promised Land of the Kingdom of Heaven.

How is this possible? If Christ is cut off from the land of the living at a relatively young age, how can we speak of His seed? The seed of Christ is a seed of a *spiritual generation*. We are not speaking here of the physical offspring of Christ. Rather, we are saying that Christ, who is God's *righteous* Servant, has carried the iniquities of His elect, such that *His righteousness* has made *them* to be *righteous*. The *just* Servant of God has *justified* a people for Himself, by bearing their iniquities:

> *After the suffering of His soul, He [shall see light] and be satisfied. **My righteous Servant will justify many** by the knowledge of Himself; and He will bear their iniquities.*
> (Isaiah 53:11)

Who are the true seed of Christ? They are those who have been *made righteous* through faith in *Christ's own righteousness*:

> *For as through the one man's disobedience many were made sinners, even so through the obedience of the One, **many will be made righteous**.* (Romans 5:19)

This is the seed of Christ. It is not the seed of charlatan, hypocritical Israel. The hypocrites of Israel, who profess God with their lips, while their hearts are far from Him, are a fake seed, an evil seed, and thus very much a spiritually dead seed:

Ah sinful nation, a people loaded with iniquity, ***[a seed] of evildoers,*** *children who deal corruptly! They have forsaken the LORD. They have despised the Holy One of Israel. They are estranged and backward.* (Isaiah 1:4)

Rather, the true seed of Christ is a *holy* seed. The true children of Christ have been made righteous through the righteousness of Christ:

If there is a tenth left in it, that also will in turn be consumed: as a terebinth, and as an oak, whose stock remains when they are felled; so ***the holy seed*** *is its stock.* (Isaiah 6:13)

Yet death must come first. The cross must come first. Jesus says, *"Most certainly I tell you, unless a grain of wheat falls into the earth and dies, it remains by itself alone. But if it dies, it bears much fruit"* (John 12:24). Thus the cross must come first. He must be pierced for our transgressions, and crushed for our iniquities. We who seek to be justified before God and yet cannot be so justified, due to the condemning nature of our sins, must be justified only by faith in Jesus, the Just, crucified for our sins. Then, only after His death, which brings life to us, and His condemnation, which is our justification, will He see His seed:

[A seed] shall serve Him. *Future generations shall be told about the Lord.* (Psalm 22:30)

And,

That is, it is not the children of the flesh who are children of God, but the children of the promise are counted as ***[the seed]****.* (Romans 9:8)

Do you see it, dear Christian? Does the illumination of the Holy Spirit now reveal to you how it is that the Christ of God, the Seed of Promise, had to die before He could see the light of resurrection, and, in that light, see *His seed*? First, the Seed itself must die. It must be sown into the ground, and thus before bearing fruit, it first must die. Only then can the fruitful plant rise up and spread its seed.

If, then, *we* are the seed of Christ, shall He not also sow *us* in the same manner? Shall we not continually be sown as the seed that dies? Shall we not carry in our bodies the death of Christ? Shall we not die daily? And in our dying, shall not Christ raise up more fruitful plants that are able to sow more fruitful seed, and all for His glory alone, so that when He sees His offspring at the final harvest, He shall see a countless multitude of godly seed?

Also, should we not be a *holy* seed? If He died in order to rise and see the light of resurrection, and in that light see His seed, what kind of seed ought we to be? Should we be a mixed seed, such that our sons and daughters intermarry with the sons and daughters of the world? Is this not detestable to Christ, who desires a pure and godly seed for Himself? And if Christ is raised to see light, and in that light to see His seed, should we not grant Him the satisfaction of seeing godly offspring and a most holy seed [Deuteronomy 7:3-6; Malachi 2:15]?

Dear Christian, the resurrection of our Lord is not freedom to sin. It is, rather, freedom *not to sin*. Let Christ, then, being risen, look upon His Church and see a *holy* seed. Let the Church come out of the darkness, forsaking all of the unfruitful deeds of darkness, and live in the resurrection light of holiness, so that Christ may find us to be a holy seed.

HE SHALL BE SATISFIED

In His resurrection, He shall see light. In that light, then, what shall He see? The Prophet says that He shall see His seed. And then, once He has seen His seed, the Prophet says that He shall *"be satisfied"*:

> *After the suffering of His soul, He [shall see light]* **and be satisfied**. *My righteous Servant will justify many by the knowledge of Himself; and He will bear their iniquities.* (Isaiah 53:11)

This is covenantal language, namely, that when Christ rises from the dead and sees light, He shall *be satisfied*. For, according to the covenant that God made with Israel, her obedience to His holy commandments, through her loving the Lord her God and serving Him with all of her heart, would prompt God to give to her the rain for her land in its season, such that her grain, her new wine, and her oil could be gathered in. The blessings of the early rain and the latter rain would send grass in her fields for her livestock. And in these covenantal blessings, Israel would eat *and be satisfied* [Leviticus 26:3-5].

Christ Jesus, then, fulfills the Law of the Covenant, the Law which Israel broke, and thus Christ is the King of the true Israel of God. He receives the covenant blessings, in perfection, since He obeyed the Covenant with sinless perfection. He shall see light *and be satisfied*. Yet this satisfaction does not come until *after His death*. As it goes, then, it is the wicked who are oftentimes satisfied in this mortal life, while the righteous have to wait until *after death* in order to be satisfied:

Arise, O LORD, confront him, cast him down; deliver my life from the wicked with Your sword, with Your hand from men, O LORD, from men of the world who have their portion in this life, and whose belly You fill with Your hidden treasure. They [the wicked] **are satisfied** *with children, and leave the rest of their possession for their babes. As for me, I will see Your face in righteousness;* **I shall be satisfied** *[when? Only after death:]* **when I awake in Your likeness**. (Psalm 17:13–15, NKJV)

Up until the empty tomb, all is suffering for Christ Jesus. In this mortal life, there is much trouble and hardship for the righteous. Yet in the midst of the trouble and hardship, our souls are taught by God's Spirit to yearn for the coming, future Day of Christ Jesus, on which Day we *shall be satisfied*:

[Prayed in the midst of intense suffering:] *My soul* **shall be satisfied** *as with the richest food. My mouth shall praise You with joyful lips.* (Psalm 63:5)

In the midst of our troubles, the Lord gives to us the great promise that if we persevere, by faith, through the tribulations, He will, in the future, *satisfy* our longing souls, and fill our hungry souls with goodness. Thus God promises the righteous man that after his troubles are finally over, a great satisfaction of soul awaits him:

*I will **satisfy him with long life**, and show him My salvation.* (Psalm 91:16)

First come the temporal days of trouble, and only afterwards the eternal days of satisfaction. First, Christ must suffer the terrible, unutterable darkness of the cross. Then, once He has finished His atoning work on the cross, He shall see light and be satisfied:

[The trouble of the cross, which must come first:] *For dogs have surrounded Me. A company of evildoers have enclosed Me.* ***They have pierced My hands and feet.*** (Psalm 22:16)

But then,

[The satisfaction that comes after the trouble is past:] *Of You comes My praise in the great assembly. I will pay My vows before those who fear Him.* ***The [afflicted] shall eat and be satisfied.*** *They shall praise the* LORD *who seek after Him. Let your hearts live forever.* (Psalm 22:25–26)

How, then, is Christ able to endure the incalculable torment of the cross? He knows His Father's promises. He clings to the promises of Scripture that say that after the great trouble is past, an even greater satisfaction will follow it. That is, after being engulfed by the darkness of the cross, He shall see light, and in that light He shall see His seed. And in seeing this seed, He shall *be satisfied*. It is, therefore, this promise from the Father—that of His coming, future satisfaction—which enables Him to endure the drinking of the bitter cup, the cup of the fury of the wrath of the Lord against all human sin, at Golgotha:

He Shall See Light

> *...looking unto Jesus, the [beginner] and finisher of our faith, who **for the joy that was set before Him** endured the cross, despising the shame, and has sat down at the right hand of the throne of God.* (Hebrews 12:2, NKJV)

What would have happened if John Bunyan (1628–1688), upon becoming a Christian—since Bunyan was not converted until after the birth of his first child—had been warned far in advance about the troubles he would have to face in order to follow Christ faithfully? If the Lord Himself had warned Bunyan that, in the future, he would have to watch his beloved, first wife die, and then face horrible slanders and false charges from those who hated his evangelistic preaching, and then be cast into a dark, unsanitary prison for twelve long years, such that the horrific prison conditions would destroy his health and shorten his lifespan, and then lose a baby through his second's wife miscarriage as a result of the trauma of his imprisonment, and then, worst of all, hear, while in prison, the news of the death of his precious, blind daughter, Mary, what would Bunyan have said in response to all of these warnings about his future? In the face of such foreboding trouble and anguish, would Bunyan have renounced his newly gained faith? Would he have promised never to become a preacher, if such a promise could release him from such future sufferings?

Not at all. In no way could any warning from the Lord about future events have persuaded Bunyan not to travel the pilgrim road that he chose to travel. For, Bunyan knew, by way of prayer in the Spirit and by way of searching the Holy Scriptures, that many troubles must come first. He was braced for them by his strong love for the Holy Scriptures. At the same time, he also knew the secret that would sustain him and give him endurance in all of his coming tribulations. That is, on the other side of the greatest of troubles, the faithful pilgrim is promised an even greater satisfaction. To be sure, the road to the Celestial City is stained with blood, and soaked with tears. However, Bunyan, who wrote *The Pilgrim's Progress* from prison, and thus from his prison cell taught the Church wondrous truths about the Celestial City, knew that his own future entrance into the gates of that City would cause his weary, battered soul to be completely satisfied.

O Faithful Pilgrims of the Church, remember that Christ's troubles preceded His satisfaction. First, He had to be troubled of soul, even to the point of sweating drops of blood from His brow, and only afterwards did He see light and become satisfied.

What shall we say, then, about those who think that they can have the satisfactions of the resurrection without first having the sufferings of the cross? Shall the soldier divide the plunder without first bleeding on the battlefield? Shall the athlete wear the gold medal without first wincing in pain in the contest? Shall the farmer eat of the crops without first sweating from his brow in the planting fields?

In this life, dear Christian, there will be much trouble and anguish of soul. The cross will pinch down upon the shoulder each and every day. The persecutions will come, for they are appointed to come. Rachel will weep for her children. Job will lament the day of his birth. The tears shall be many, and the bitter loneliness of being hated by the world shall be great. The sorrows of this life shall, at times, feel so overwhelming that you will wonder whether or not God has forgotten to be gracious towards you.

Yet this precious promise, dear Christian, will carry you through the worst of afflictions. After Christ's troubles, He was satisfied. In the same way, after your lesser troubles—for, however great they are, they are certainly less than His—have come to an end, you, too, shall be satisfied. When you awake from your troubles, and find yourself in the presence of Christ, and within the gates of the Celestial City, you shall be satisfied with the sight of His radiant countenance, as it shines upon you.

HE SHALL HAVE HIS REWARD

There shall be trouble for Christ. There shall be a cross on which to die. Yet on account of the trouble of His soul, He shall see light and be satisfied. What is the reward that awaits, then, such a glorious Christ? If He has obeyed His righteous Father with such perfect obedience, out of such perfect love for the Father, how shall the Father reward Him? Will not the reward of the Father for His Son be infinitely great?

***Therefore will I give Him a portion with the great**, and He will divide the plunder with the strong; because He poured out His soul to death, and was numbered with the transgressors; yet He bore the sin of many, and made intercession for the transgressors.* (Isaiah 53:12)

When Asa, king of Judah, trusted in the Lord in battle, even though his army was so greatly outnumbered by their Ethiopian attackers, the Ethiopians were overthrown, and could not recover, for they were broken before the Lord and His army, and Asa and his men carried away *"very much spoil"* (2 Chronicles 14:13). The reward was exceedingly great. And yet this is nothing in comparison with the reward of Christ, which the Father will give to Him:

*Behold, the Lord GOD will come as a mighty one, and His arm will rule for Him. Behold, **His reward is with Him**, and His recompense before Him.* (Isaiah 40:10)

And,

*Behold, the LORD has proclaimed to the end of the earth, "Say to the daughter of Zion, 'Behold, your salvation comes. Behold, **His reward is with Him**, and His recompense before Him.'"* (Isaiah 62:11)

He is, according to the prophecy, the Suffering Servant. By God's eternal decree, He must enter into the darkness of the grave. Yet once He sees the light of resurrection, He shall see His seed and be satisfied. He shall divide the spoil with the strong. He shall have the *pleasures* of His *eternal reward*:

*For You will not leave My soul in Sheol, neither will You allow Your Holy One to see corruption. You will show Me the path of life. In Your presence is fullness of joy. At Your right hand there are **pleasures forever more**.* (Psalm 16:10–11)

The Prophets, then, did not prophesy about the sufferings of Christ only. They also prophesied about the glories of *Christ's reward* that would follow His sufferings:

> [The Prophets were constantly]...*searching for who or what kind of time the Spirit of Christ, which was in them, pointed to, when He predicted the sufferings of Christ,* **and the glories that would follow them**. (1 Peter 1:11)

How richly magnificent and exceedingly graceful, then, is the Gospel that has been entrusted to us, since in the Gospel, Christ not only has His reward, but ever so generously and mercifully shares His reward with us. We formerly were His enemies. We previously were the ones who denied Him and abandoned Him in His time of shameful reproach and bitter torment. He bore the multitude of our sins on His own shoulders, and He made intercession on the cross for us, who formerly were great transgressors.

Yet being ever so rich in mercy, Christ Jesus not only obtained His reward, but chose to divide the spoil of His victory with us who believe in His name. We deserved death, and an everlasting debtor's prison in Hell. Yet He gave us light and immortality through the Gospel, and also the rich spoils of His own Heavenly reward:

> *Behold, I come quickly.* **My reward is with Me**, *to repay to each man according to his work.* (Revelation 22:12)

And,

> *He who did not spare His own Son, but delivered Him up for us all,* **how would He not also with Him freely give us all things**? (Romans 8:32)

As the old hymn goes, "What wondrous love is this, O my soul, O my soul?" Can the scorned and cheated Bridegroom really be this generous towards His once adulterous, but now repentant, cleansed, and sanctified Bride? Can the once hated Father truly be so lavishly loving towards His once defiant, yet now broken, contrite, and returned prodigal son? Surely, Christ must have His reward. His sacrifice was infinitely glorious, and thus His reward must needs be infinitely glorious. Yet must I somehow be obliged, by faith, to find the boldness to say that He, the resurrected Christ, has predestined even me, the chief of sinners, to be holy and blameless in His sight in Heaven, and thus to be a sharer in His own Heavenly reward?

O dear Brethren, will the very Son of God, whom we previously scorned, not only condescend to wash our feet with water, but also love us to the point of washing our sins away with His own blood? Will He not only forgive our sins, but clothe us in His own robes of righteousness? Will He not only clothe us in white, but also give us white stones, with new names written on the stones? Will the Father not only crush His Son for our redemption, but also be pleased to make us heirs of His Kingdom and joint-heirs with Christ?

O how wide and long and deep and high is the love of Christ, which surpasses knowledge! He who saw the darkness of the tomb was raised from the dead. He saw light, and in that light He saw us, His seed. We are His inheritance. And so the Father has been pleased to give Him the reward of all of the riches of all of the majesty of the glory of His eternal Kingdom. And He, in turn, has decided, in love, to share His reward, to divide the spoil amongst His offspring. Therefore, we shall render thanksgiving to Him forever and ever, and His prolonged days shall be eternal days of receiving the everlasting praise of His saints, and in this everlasting praise He, our Lord and our God, shall be satisfied, to the everlasting glory of God the Father, days unto days, ages unto ages, forever unto forever, world without end. Amen.

Part Four:

THE CROSS
in the Book of Zechariah

13

ME, WHOM THEY HAVE PIERCED
The Cross in Zechariah 12:1-14

[The burden of] the Word of the LORD concerning Israel. The LORD, who stretches out the heavens, and lays the foundation of the earth, and forms the spirit of man within him says: "Behold, I will make Jerusalem a cup of reeling to all the surrounding peoples, and it will also be on Judah in the siege against Jerusalem. It will happen in that day, that I will make Jerusalem a burdensome stone for all the peoples. All who burden themselves with it will be severely wounded, and all the nations of the earth will be gathered together against it. In that day," says the LORD, "I will strike every horse with terror, and his rider with madness; and I will open my eyes on the house of Judah, and will strike every horse of the peoples with blindness. The chieftains of Judah will say in their heart, 'The inhabitants of Jerusalem are my strength in the LORD of Hosts their God.' In that day I will make the chieftains of Judah like a pan of fire among wood, and like a flaming torch among sheaves; and they will devour all the surrounding peoples, on the right hand and on the left; and Jerusalem will yet again dwell in their own place, even in Jerusalem." (Zechariah 12:1-6)

GOD, the Creator, sovereignly has ordained a future for Jerusalem. He is the Creator of all things, and, therefore, has the power to accomplish His future purposes for Israel. Though Jerusalem may feel forgotten and forsaken by God, on account of her many sins, still the Lord has not forgotten her, but instead His plans for her restoration and glorification shall be accomplished. This is sure, since God is the Creator of all things, and all life:

> *[The burden of] the Word of the LORD concerning Israel.* ***The LORD, who stretches out the heavens, and lays the foundation of the earth, and forms the spirit of man within him****....* (Zechariah 12:1)

The Lord is He who sets spiral galaxies in their cosmic places. He is also the One who measures the distance from the earth to the farthest stars in the heavens not with a cosmic telescope, but with His own handbreadth. It is God, the Creator, who brings forth dry land from the midst of the raging sea, and it is the Lord, our Creator, who gives life and breath to all men. He alone is the omnipotent Creator, and thus He possesses in His own being the sovereign power to redeem Jerusalem from her sins, and to restore her to glory:

> *Why do you say,* ***O Jacob****, and speak,* ***O Israel****, "My way is hidden from the LORD, and the justice due me is disregarded by my God?" Have you not known? Have you not heard?* ***The everlasting God, the LORD, the Creator of the ends of the earth****, does not faint. He is not weary. His understanding is unsearchable.* (Isaiah 40:27–28)

If God, the Creator, who stretches out the heavens and lays the foundation of the earth, has purposed and designed a future for Jerusalem, then it shall come to pass. Nothing can stop it. Heaven and earth shall pass away, but the Word of the Lord shall never pass away.

O precious Christian, beloved of the Father on account of the Son's blood, in which you have been washed, and on account of your obedience of faith, do not lose hope in the promises of God. For, the same promises which you once saw so clearly from the distant, yet unblocked vantage point of your first love, when you only several months or years before had been born anew in Christ, are still fixed and immovable upon Mount Zion. Though they are difficult to see now that you have been ascending towards the

Mount, through dark woods and up a difficult, narrow path, for decades, and especially now that you find yourself in the blinding storms of persecutions or in the thick fog of tribulations, their permanence remains. Their beauty remains unchanged, enduring forever in the heavens. So then, cling to God, your Creator, who carries you when you are too weak and wounded to press onwards, and who, by His own power, shall see you safely to the glorious Summit of these great and precious promises.

JERUSALEM, A CUP OF REELING

Why, then, do doubts concerning God's Word to Jerusalem rise in our minds when we think of today's Jerusalem? Are the Jews so hardened as to be beyond the reach of repentance? Are the Muslim nations surrounding Jerusalem so strong as to preclude the rise of Jerusalem's throne over the nations? Has Islam made the peace of Jerusalem an impossibility? And have the heinous crimes of the nations against both Jewish and Gentile Christians gone unpunished for so long that we have all but lost hope in the coming justice of Jesus Christ? The Prophet is clear, and we dare not doubt the accuracy or divine authority of the Spirit's revelation to him. That is, *"the burden of the Word of the Lord"* will go neither unheard, nor unfulfilled:

> ***[The burden of] the Word of the LORD*** *concerning Israel. The LORD, who stretches out the heavens, and lays the foundation of the earth, and forms the spirit of man within him says:* ***"Behold, I will make Jerusalem a cup of reeling to all the surrounding peoples****, and it will also be on Judah in the siege against Jerusalem."* (Zechariah 12:1–2)

This is a great reversal of things. For the Lord to take the cup of drunkenness, which is a cup of judgment, out of Israel's hands, and to place it into the hands of the surrounding peoples, is a great reversal of things. For, it was Israel, under her sinful guilt, who first was made to drink from this cup of judgment:

> *You have shown Your people hard things.* ***You have made us drink the wine that makes us stagger****.* (Psalm 60:3)

Yet now, according to the Prophet Zechariah, Israel's time of judgment is coming to an end. Judgment begins with the Household of the Lord, but then it passes on to the pagans. First, Jerusalem was forced to drink of the cup of judgment. Yet now her tormentors, the surrounding peoples, will be forced to drink it to the dregs:

> *Awake, awake! Stand up,* ***O Jerusalem, you who have drunk from the LORD's hand the cup of His wrath****. You have drunk the bowl of the cup of staggering, and drained it…. Therefore now hear this, you afflicted, and drunk, but not with wine: Thus says your Lord GOD, your God who pleads the cause of His people,* ***"Behold, I have taken out of your hand the cup of staggering, even the bowl of the cup of My wrath****. You will not drink it any more:* ***and I will put it into the hand of those who afflict you****, who have said to your soul, 'Bow down, that we may walk over you;' and you have laid your back as the ground, like a street to those who walk over."*
> (Isaiah 51:17, 21–23)

Jerusalem, then, shall be restored to God's favor. In His hands, she shall become a goblet of reeling, a cup of drunkenness for the nations. He employed the nations to judge her, with severity. Now, He shall employ her to judge the nations, with finality. For, she is not only *a cup of judgment* for the nations. She is also *a heavy stone of judgment* for the peoples:

> *"It will happen in that day, that* ***I will make Jerusalem a burdensome stone for all the peoples****. All who burden themselves with it will be severely wounded,* ***and all the nations of the earth will be gathered together against it.****"*
> (Zechariah 12:3)

Jerusalem shall be a cup of drunkenness for the nations. She also shall be a heavy stone for all peoples. When they attack her, they only will cut themselves. When they try to lift her out of her place, they only will break their own backs. As Jesus warns all peoples:

***"He who falls on this stone** will be **broken to pieces**, but **on whomever it will fall**, it will **scatter him as dust.**"* (Matthew 21:44)

Jerusalem, then, shall be God's instrument of judgment upon the nations. She shall be, first, a cup of reeling in their hands, and, second, a heavy stone that will cut them in pieces. Then, third, the Prophet says that Jerusalem shall be *"like a pan of fire among wood"*:

*"In that day I will make the chieftains of Judah **like a pan of fire among wood**, and **like a flaming torch among sheaves**; and they will devour all the surrounding peoples, on the right hand and on the left; and Jerusalem will yet again dwell in their own place, even in Jerusalem."* (Zechariah 12:6)

God loves Jerusalem. For a time, He gives her over to judgment, on account of her idolatrous sins against Him. Yet in love, He redeems her, and then avenges Himself on her enemies. He makes Jerusalem His weapon, His instrument of judgment against the nations. They surround her like thick forests. Yet she shall be *"like a pan of fire among wood, and like a flaming torch among sheaves."* When the Lord comes to vindicate His people in Jerusalem, and to judge her oppressors, she shall be like a match thrown into the kindling, and like a blowtorch blazing amongst dry, autumn leaves:

*"**The house of Jacob will be a fire, the house of Joseph a flame, and the house of Esau for stubble**. They will burn among them, and devour them. There will not be any remaining to the house of Esau."* Indeed, the LORD has spoken. (Obadiah 18)

Also,

*"For, behold, the day comes, **it burns as a furnace; and all the proud, and all who work wickedness, will be stubble; and the day that comes will burn them up**,"* says the LORD of Hosts,

"that it shall leave them neither root nor branch."
(Malachi 4:1)

    God is not indifferent to the persecution of His beloved children. When Cain pierced Abel with the deathblow of his cruel hatred, the Lord God, whom Cain despised, was neither lenient, nor willing to negotiate in His sentencing of Cain. When the nations harassed and cruelly attacked Jerusalem both prior to, and during the days of the Prophet Zechariah, the Lord turned no blind eye to it. When the cunning Jews and calloused Romans crucified Jesus of Nazareth, piercing Him through, God did not pardon them, universally. *Those who did not repent* before the revealed glory of the crucified and risen Christ *were not pardoned*, and their high crimes against the Son of God were not forgotten by God, not even a single one of them. They died in their sins, and the vengeance of God against them for these crimes both has come upon them, in part, already, and shall come upon them, in full, at the final judgment. God will not be mocked. The burning fire of the fierceness of His furious anger shall scorch and consume all those who have trampled upon the blood of the Son of God.
    So, too, when the Romans crucified the Apostle Peter, beheaded the Apostle Paul, and cast the beloved Apostle John, in his old age, into the prison colony at Patmos, the Lord God was not indifferent to these things. Again, in AD 356, when the wicked Alexandrian imposter bishop, George, friend of the Arian heresy, intruded upon the God-fearing congregation of the noble bishop Athanasius, threatened the church's virgins with fire, and subsequently had them beaten until they were unrecognizable, such atrocities did not go unrecorded by the Lord of Israel.[1] Yet again, in the year 1730, when the wicked French Catholics arrested the newlywed, nineteen-year-old Marie Durand for her participation in the underground (Huguenot) church, and then *kept her in a miserable prison tower for the next thirty-eight years of her life,* our God was not uninformed of the atrocities of the French Catholics committed against Marie Durand and her family. Even at the present time, as is happening in the present day, when North Korean prison guards torture and execute Christians, even to the

---

[1] Athanasius, *Defense of His Flight* 6 (*NPNF*² 4:257).

third generation, on account of the sole charge of possessing a Bible, the Lord God is not unprepared to give a divine-judicial answer to the perpetrators of such unthinkable crimes.

O beloved Children, despair not over the persecution of the righteous. Now is the hour of suffering. Today is the day of weeping, and bleeding, and evangelistic dying for God's chosen ones. The world hates us, as it has hated our Lord. The world crucifies us, just as it once crucified our Lord.

Yet there will be a day of vengeance. Jerusalem, God's holy City, shall become the City of His holy people, once again. The City of God shall become the City of Christ. And on that day, Jerusalem shall be an instrument of God's vengeance: a cup of reeling for the nations, a heavy stone that will cut the nations in pieces, and a firepan that will scorch and consume the woodpile of the nations. Therefore, O Children of the Most High, wait patiently for God to avenge. He, the Lord, shall bring your righteousness to light, and shall cause your justice to shine like the noonday. As it is written in the Second Epistle to the Thessalonians:

> *Since it is a righteous thing with God* **to repay affliction to those who afflict you***, and to give relief to you who are afflicted with us, when the Lord Jesus is revealed from Heaven with His mighty angels* **in flaming fire, giving vengeance to those who do not know God, and to those who do not obey the Gospel of our Lord Jesus***, who will pay the penalty: eternal destruction from the face of the Lord and from the glory of His might....* (2 Thessalonians 1:6–9)

DAVID'S HOUSE WILL BE LIKE GOD

There is much hope for Jerusalem. The Lord shall again visit His people of Judah, and shall restore Jerusalem to glory. Yet He will come, first, to the meek. When He restores the land of Judah, He first shall visit *the meek, outlying villages of Judah* before He ever visits the strong, ruling residents of Jerusalem:

> *"***The LORD also will save the tents of Judah first***, that the glory of David's house and the glory of the inhabitants of Jerusalem not be magnified above Judah."* (Zechariah 12:7)

Upon whom does the favor of the Lord rest first? God first visits the outlying peasant peoples of Judah. He chooses to visit the rural craftsmen, the impoverished farmers, the struggling fishermen, and the lowly shepherds before He ever chooses to visit the urban rulers and scholars. The tents of Judah must be saved first, since God comes to save the meek. And so it was that Jesus was not "Jesus of Jerusalem," but rather *Jesus of Nazareth*:

Nathanael said to [Philip], **"Can any good thing come out of Nazareth?"** *Philip said to him, "Come and see."* (John 1:46)

Also,

*...***but God chose the foolish things of the world** *that He might put to shame those who are wise.* **God chose the weak things of the world***, that He might put to shame the things that are strong.* (1 Corinthians 1:27)

Yet after God saves the tents of Judah first, He shall go on to restore glory to the house of David and glory to the inhabitants of Jerusalem. The old, dilapidated hut of David shall be rebuilt in glory. The weak, impoverished armies of David shall be made strong and mighty:

"In that day the LORD *will defend the inhabitants of Jerusalem. He who is feeble among them at that day will be like David,* **and David's house will be like God***, like the Angel of the* LORD *before them. It will happen in that day, that I will seek to destroy all the nations that come against Jerusalem."* (Zechariah 12:8–9)

There is hope for Jerusalem, indeed, since the house of David shall become like the Angel of the LORD. And if the Angel of the LORD visits the house of David, in order to fight on behalf of Jerusalem, then the defense of the city is sure. For, the Angel of the LORD encamps around those who fear God, fighting for them and protecting them [Psalm 34:7]. It was He, the Angel of the LORD, who fought the great war against Pharaoh king of Egypt, slaying the firstborn amongst all of the Egyptians, and bringing the Israelites out of Egypt with a mighty hand and an outstretched arm [Numbers 20:16]. It was none other than the Angel of the LORD who came to Jerusalem's defense when Sennacherib king of Assyria had surrounded the city with his vast army of Assyrians. The Angel of the LORD went out at night and killed in the camp of the Assyrians one hundred and eighty-five thousand, so that the city of Jerusalem was never taken over by the Assyrians [2 Kings 19:35]. And it is He, the Angel of the LORD, who now shall arise and fight against those who attack Jerusalem. He, the Angel of the LORD, shall fight on her behalf:

Let them be as chaff before the wind, **the Angel of the LORD driving them on***. Let their way be dark and slippery,* **the Angel of the LORD pursuing them***.* (Psalm 35:5–6)

Yet how shall this come about? How can the worn-out hut of David ever be rebuilt in glory, and how can the tattered armies of the house of David ever be made this strong and mighty? The prophecy is that a divine Warrior shall arise, even One very much like the Angel of the LORD, from the House of David. The Messiah, the Christ, who has the key to the house of David, shall arise. He, the Christ, shall fight for David, and thus Jerusalem shall be saved:

To the angel of the Church in Philadelphia write: "He who is holy, He who is true, **He who has the key of David***, He who opens and no one can shut, and who shuts and no one opens, says these things...."* (Revelation 3:7)

Jesus Christ, risen from the dead, is *descended from David, literally*. Therefore, there is much hope for *literal* Jerusalem. We need not spiritualize Jerusalem away into a metaphorical oblivion. Instead, we believe the sacred Words of the Prophet Zechariah, and so we believe that the House of David will be made mighty in battle once again. Jerusalem's King, her Christ, shall come to her and fight for her, the same way in which the Angel of the LORD, of old, fought for Israel.

Accordingly, let those who attack Jerusalem, even today, beware. Let the princes of Islam beware. Let the liberal politicians who ignore the plight of Jewish Christians and Palestinian Christians, alike, in the Middle East, beware. For, the Lord is zealous for Jerusalem with a divine zeal. There will be a day when the nations gather together to come against Jerusalem. On that day, the Lord of the Heavenly Hosts shall fight for Jerusalem. Thus He shall route her enemies, and shall destroy all of those who come against her, even burning them with an unquenchable fire.

Literal Jerusalem matters much to the Lord Jesus Christ. Therefore, it is dangerously unwise to neglect or deny the historic Christian doctrine of *the Millennial Kingdom of Christ*. That is to say, there are some Christian pastors—and many of these are nevertheless very godly men—who recklessly follow Augustine of Hippo (354–430) and John Calvin (1509–1564) in denying the *literal* fulfillment of Christ's thousand-year reign on the earth. Yet these men act unwisely, and even dangerously so, on this point of doctrine. For, the sacred Words of the Prophet Zechariah speak of the *literal* house of David, and of the *literal* Jerusalem.[2]

God, the Creator of all things, still has a restorative plan for David's *literal* house and for Jerusalem's *literal* city gates. The Prophet Zechariah is not merely speaking here of God's spiritual protection of the Church from the persecutions of the nations. He is speaking, in literal fashion, of a time when Christ Himself shall return to defend Jerusalem, to slay her enemies, and, afterwards, to set up His throne within her gates, and all of this in order to reign in Jerusalem for a thousand years. There shall be a *literal* battle

---

[2] For the unwavering Pre-millennial doctrine of the earliest church fathers, consider, for example, Justin Martyr's unflinching defense of Pre-millennialism in his *Dialogue with Trypho* 81, 82 (*ANF* 1:239, 240): "But I and others, who are right-minded Christians on all points, are assured that there will be a resurrection of the dead, *and a thousand years in Jerusalem, which will then be built, adorned, and enlarged, [as] the prophets Ezekiel and Isaiah and others declare*....And further, there was a certain man with us, whose name was John, one of the Apostles of Christ, who prophesied, by a revelation that was made to him, *that those who believed in our Christ would dwell a thousand years in Jerusalem; and that thereafter the general, and, in short, the eternal resurrection and judgment of all men would likewise take place*" (emphases added).

between Christ and Antichrist. There shall be a *literal* victory over Antichrist. And, therefore, Christ shall return to Jerusalem, literally, in order to establish His glorious Millennial Kingdom.

AND THEY SHALL MOURN FOR HIM

Again, there is much hope for Jerusalem. The Sovereign Lord has ordained a glorious future for Jerusalem. Yet this means that there must be much hope for the Jews. If there is hope for Jerusalem, then there must be hope for the Jews. And there is:

> "***I will pour on David's house, and on the inhabitants of Jerusalem, the Spirit of grace and of supplication***; *and they will look on Me whom they have pierced; and they shall mourn for Him, as one mourns for his only son, and will grieve bitterly for Him, as one grieves for his firstborn. In that day there will be a great mourning in Jerusalem, like the mourning of Hadad Rimmon in the valley of Megiddo. The land will mourn, every family apart;* ***the family of David's house apart****, and their wives apart;* ***the family of the house of Nathan apart****, and their wives apart;* ***the family of the house of Levi apart****, and their wives apart;* ***the family of Shimei apart****, and their wives apart; all the families who remain, every family apart, and their wives apart."* (Zechariah 12:10–14)

This hope for the Jews comes in pairs: the house of David paired with the house of Nathan, and the house of Levi paired with the house of Shimei. Most likely, these pairs represent *the nobility* and *the priesthood* of the Jews, respectively. For, Nathan, one of David's sons, is one of the forefathers of Zerubbabel—Zerubbabel being the great governor of Jerusalem in the Prophet Zechariah's own day. Thus Nathan is a kingly figure, as is David. Shimei, on the other hand, is a priestly line, descended from Levi. Thus David and Nathan are kings, while Levi and Shimei are priests. Both *the kings* of Israel and *the priests* of Israel shall mourn over the One whom they have pierced.

There is yet much hope for the Jews. For, both the kingly line of the Jews and the priestly line of the Jews shall receive *the Spirit of grace* in the final days of human history. And this Spirit of grace shall call the Jews to lament, to *mourn* over the One whom they pierced by their own wickedness, and with their own hands:

> *"I will pour on David's house, and on the inhabitants of Jerusalem, **the Spirit of grace** and of supplication; and they will look on Me whom they have pierced; and **they shall mourn for Him**, as one mourns for his only son, and will grieve bitterly for Him, as one grieves for his firstborn. In that day there will be **a great mourning** in Jerusalem, like the **mourning** of Hadad Rimmon in the valley of Megiddo. The land will **mourn**, every family apart."* (Zechariah 12:10-12a)

They shall *mourn* for Him whom they *pierced*. After David heard that Saul and Jonathan had been *pierced through* in battle, he led Israel in lamenting and *mourning* over them. Even greater, however, was the *mourning* of Israel after King Josiah, one of the greatest of the kings of Judah, had been *pierced* by the Egyptians. Josiah was *pierced* near *Hadad Rimmon in the valley of Megiddo*, and all of Israel *mourned* for him deeply. In the same way, there will come a time when the Jews, first having experienced an extended hardening towards the Gospel but, at the end of the age, having been softened towards God once again, will look upon their Lord, whom they *pierced*, and *mourn greatly* for Him.

And how shall the Jews mourn? They shall mourn for Him as one mourns for a firstborn son. Just as the Egyptians mourned over the firstborn in Egypt, so too shall the Jews mourn for the Firstborn of God, the Passover Lamb who was sacrificed, as God's Firstborn, for their sins. Thus they shall mourn for Him as for a *firstborn* son, and also as for an *only* son:

> *"I will pour on David's house, and on the inhabitants of Jerusalem, the Spirit of grace and of supplication; and they will look on Me whom they have pierced; and they shall mourn for Him, as one mourns for his **only son**, and will grieve bitterly for Him, as one grieves for his firstborn."* (Zechariah 12:10)

Who mourns for an only son? In Israel's history, it was Abraham, that great man of faith, who *almost* mourned for his *only son*:

> *[The LORD] said, "Now take your son, **your only son**, whom you love, even Isaac, and go into the land of Moriah. Offer him there as a burnt offering on one of the mountains of which I will tell you."* (Genesis 22:2)

Yet God spared Isaac. Abraham did not have to mourn for his only son. Still, the people of Israel have sinned grievously against their God and Father. Therefore, they must mourn, as for an only son:

> *"It will happen in that day," says the Lord GOD, "that I will cause the sun to go down at noon, and I will darken the earth in the clear day. I will turn your feasts into mourning, and all your songs into lamentation; and I will make you wear sackcloth on all your bodies, and baldness on every head. I will make it **like the mourning for an only son**, and its end like a bitter day."* (Amos 8:9–10)

Yet who is this *"only Son"* for whom the Jews shall mourn? Is this not *God's only-begotten Son*, who is Christ, the Lord?

> *In this the love of God was manifested toward us, that God has sent **His only-begotten Son** into the world, that we might live through Him.* (1 John 4:9, NKJV)

And why shall the Jews mourn so bitterly over Him? Is this not because they themselves were the ones who pierced Him?

> [The Apostle Peter preaching at Pentecost:] *"Men of Israel, hear these words! Jesus of Nazareth, a Man approved by God to you by mighty works and wonders and signs which God did by Him among you, even as you yourselves know, Him, being delivered up by the determined counsel and foreknowledge of God, **you** have taken by the hand of lawless men, **crucified** and killed...."* (Acts 2:22–23)

There is much hope for the Jews because the Prophet Zechariah prophesies the coming repentance of the Jews. The natural olive branches, having been broken off of the olive tree, may, indeed, be grafted back into the tree, by God. There shall be grieving, mourning, and wailing over sins. They shall see Christ, at last, as the promised Son of David. For, the house of David is nothing without the Son of David. Yet who is the Son of David? Who is the Christ, the Son of David, who shall come to Jerusalem to restore her to glory? Jesus of Nazareth is the Son of David. He is the One whom the house of David should have worshipped, but instead pierced. He is the One for whom the house of David shall, in the future, mourn with a deep mourning:

> *Behold, He is coming with the clouds, and every eye will see Him,* **including those who pierced Him**. *All the tribes of the earth will* **mourn** *over Him. Even so, Amen.* (Revelation 1:7)

The Gospel, then, is concerned neither for Jews only, nor for Gentiles only. Rather, the Gospel is for both Jews and Gentiles; it is for all of those who would mourn for the One whom they pierced. The Jews pierced Jesus. The Gentiles likewise pierced Him. Therefore, all must mourn on account of Him, if they desire the hope of salvation.

So then, the Gospel is *a summons to mourn*. To be sure, the Gospel, due to its nature as the glad tidings of Christ, calls for shouts of joy and jubilation. It causes little lambs to leap for joy. Nevertheless, we must remember that before the Gospel ever calls for laughter, it first calls for tears. In the Gospel, weeping precedes rejoicing, even as sackcloth precedes garments of praise.

God says, in Zechariah, *"They will look* **on Me** *[that is, on God Himself]* **whom they have pierced**.*"* Every man is guilty. Every man has committed unthinkable crimes against God. There is no man whose sins are not responsible for piercing God, in the Person of the Son of God who took on flesh as the Son of Man, on the cross. We, each and all, spat at Christ, through sin. We, together as a collective humanity of depraved and wicked rebels, hated Christ. In doing so, *our sins pierced the Son of God.*

Me, Whom They Have Pierced

O dear Christian, how long has it been since you last looked upon the One whom you yourself pierced, by your sins, and thus mourned on account of Him? Do you remember seeing, by faith, the innocent, merciful love of God in His eyes as the Roman soldiers pierced His hands and His feet with those sharp, iron spikes? Do you recall His cries of agony and torment as they lifted His cross up from the earth? Did you not grieve the first time you saw, by faith, His blood poured out on your behalf, even you, who formerly denied Him? Did you not mourn when you first saw the light of the glory of God gushing out from the blood-pouring fountains of His wounds? O Christian, do you still mourn and weep in repentance before the One whom you pierced? Is not the Lamb of God worthy of your flowing tears of love and mourning for Him whom your sins have pierced?

Behold, He is coming with the clouds! Behold, every eye shall see Him! Behold, the Son of David shall be glorified when they who pierced Him mourn on account of Him! And thus the piercèd One shall be praised by the seemingly countless angelic hosts and by all of the seemingly innumerable saints of Heaven as God over all, blessed forever, ages unto ages, world without end. Amen.

14

AWAKE, O SWORD!
The Cross in Zechariah 13:7-9

"Awake, O sword, against My Shepherd, and against the Man who is close to Me," says the LORD of Hosts. "Strike the Shepherd, and the sheep will be scattered; and I will turn My hand against the little ones. It shall happen that in all the land," says the LORD, "two parts in it will be cut off and die; but the third will be left in it. I will bring the third part into the fire, and will refine them as silver is refined, and will test them like gold is tested. They will call on My name, and I will hear them. I will say, 'It is My people;' and they will say, 'The LORD is my God.'" (Zechariah 13:7–9)

None other than the Sovereign LORD[1]
Is He who shall arouse the sword
Turn not, O sword, against the foe
But at the Shepherd, strike the blow

He who neither slumbers, nor sleeps
Stirs the sword, and scatters the sheep
Turn not, O sword, against the foe
But at the Shepherd, strike the blow

Few are faithful, only a third
Remain to keep His holy Word
Turn not, O sword, against the foe
But at the Shepherd, strike the blow

Strike the Shepherd, God's Friend of old
Test the remnant, refined as gold
Turn not, O sword, against the foe
But at the Shepherd, strike the blow

---

[1] "Awake, O Sword!" a poem by Timothy L. Fan © 2015. All rights reserved.

GOD is He who slumbers not. It is He, who never sleeps, who shall *awaken the sword*. It is not as though God has been sleeping. The wicked prosper in their wickedness, yet God does not sleep. They feast in the temples of their gods, and they remain awake throughout the night drinking sweet wine and performing great acts of debauchery. Yet during this dark night of sin, in which the wicked trample upon the backs of the righteous, God does not sleep. Rather, at the proper time, He awakens His sword against them.

Is this not what we, the persecuted of the flock, are waiting for? Are we not holding on, with the desperate gripping of our fingertips, to the hope that a great sword will be awakened against those who unrepentantly hate God? The Prophet Isaiah, in his time, laid out before suffering, afflicted Israel this hope of the sword that will be awakened against the enemies of God's people:

> *Who has [awakened] one from the east? Who called him to his foot in righteousness? He hands over nations to him, and makes him rule over kings. He gives them like the dust to his* **sword***, like the driven stubble to his bow.* (Isaiah 41:2)

We hope in this. Even as we pray for our enemies, and thus for their repentance, our hope is that one day the sword of justice shall be awakened against all of the unrepentant oppressors of God's people. Yet the Prophet Zechariah's vision of the sword being awakened is quite different than that of the Prophet Isaiah. In fact, Zechariah's vision is quite disconcerting. It has within it an immediate ability to perplex us. For, in Zechariah's prophecy, the awakened sword is *not* aimed at the enemies of Israel. Rather, the sword of Zechariah's prophecy is aimed at *God's Shepherd*, and *God's faithful people*:

> *"Awake, O sword,* **against My Shepherd,** *and* **against the Man who is close to Me,***" says the* LORD *of Hosts. "***Strike the Shepherd***, and the sheep will be scattered; and I will turn My hand* **against the little ones***."* (Zechariah 13:7)

Awake, O Sword!

This is perplexing. Why would the Lord awaken the sword only to turn it against His own faithful Shepherd, and against the precious little ones of the flock? This does not seem to make any sense. We understand the sword being awakened to bring justice against the wicked. However, we do not understand the sword being awakened in order to strike the righteous. This is perplexing, even as perplexing as the prophecy that the aged Simeon prophesied over the infant Jesus when he held the Christ-babe in his arms, saying to Mary:

*"Yes, **a sword will pierce through your own soul**, that the thoughts of many hearts may be revealed."* (Luke 2:35)

O precious Christian, the sword of the sufferings of the cross is a mysterious sword. Does not God, your Shepherd, love you, O precious little Lamb? And yet you are pierced with the sharp sword of being persecuted for His name's sake. Is not Christ your faithful Protector? And yet your heart is broken within you. Are you bereaved, O little Lamb? Are you crying for your mother, who has fallen asleep in Christ? Are you weeping for your father, whom the wicked have cast into prison? Is the flock, with whom you once held sweet fellowship, now scattered by the winds of persecution? Do you flood your bed, and drench your couch with tears? O sweet and precious little Lamb, your Shepherd is He whom the sword first struck. *He was pierced for you.* Therefore, He whose wounds are life to you knows how to heal you who are pierced of heart, and how to bind up you wounds. Your Shepherd shall comfort you; it is He who shall carry you.

THE SWORD-PIERCED SHEPHERD

The turning of the sword against the Shepherd and against the little ones of the flock is perplexing, and even astonishing, yet we must hold the following two truths together, however much tension we may feel in doing so. First, God is the one who awakens the sword. It is His own doing. Yet second, the sword, at present, does not strike the enemies of God, but rather it strikes the Shepherd of God, the Good Shepherd, and even the little ones of the true flock of God. What, then, does this mean?

*"Awake, O sword, **against My Shepherd**, and against the Man who is close to Me," says the LORD of Hosts. "**Strike the Shepherd**, and the sheep will be scattered; and I will turn My hand against the little ones."* (Zechariah 13:7)

There are, to be sure, two very different shepherds that are struck by the sword in the book of Zechariah. Earlier in the book, we see the sword strike the Antichrist. He is a false shepherd, a worthless shepherd, and thus, being Satan's chosen shepherd, he is the very "Anti-shepherd." And so the sword of God strikes him:

*Woe to **the worthless shepherd** who leaves the flock! **The sword** will be [against] his arm, and [against] his right eye. His arm will be completely withered, and his right eye will be totally blinded!* (Zechariah 11:17)

This is quite understandable to us. It makes sense to us that God awakens the sword to strike *the Anti-shepherd*. Yet what does not makes sense to us is the difficult truth that the Sovereign Lord allows *the Good Shepherd* to be struck with the edge of the sword. Why would God allow this? Why would He awaken the sword, only to permit it to strike *the Good Shepherd*?

We must understand who this Good Shepherd is, in order to understand this mystery. God, speaking through Zechariah, calls this Shepherd *"My Shepherd"* and *"the Man who is close to Me."* He is, therefore, the Christ of God. He is the Son of David, anointed by God to shepherd His people and carry them forever. He is also God's *"Man who is close to Me."* That is, He is the eternal Friend of the Father. He is the Word of God, the One who was with God in the beginning, and who shared eternal divinity and glory with the Father before the world began. The Good Shepherd is the Son of God, the only true Shepherd over Israel. He, the eternal Shepherd who became flesh and dwelt among us, must be struck with the sword. *"Strike the Shepherd,"* says the Prophet Zechariah, and so He must be struck:

AWAKE, O SWORD!

I gave My back to those who [struck] Me, and My cheeks to those who plucked off the hair. I did not hide My face from shame and spitting. (Isaiah 50:6)

And also,

*Surely He has borne our sickness, and carried our suffering; yet we considered Him plagued, **struck by God**, and afflicted.* (Isaiah 53:4)

On the Roman cross at Golgotha, Jesus, our Shepherd, was *struck* with a horrible deathblow. He was *pierced* by the sword:

*For dogs have surrounded Me. A company of evildoers have enclosed Me. **They have pierced My hands and feet**.* (Psalm 22:16)

And,

*Deliver My soul **from the sword**, My precious life from the power of the dog.* (Psalm 22:20)

According to the opening verse of Zechariah chapter 13, in order for Israel's intolerable uncleanness to be washed away, God Himself must provide a miraculous fountain, a cleansing fountain.[2] Yet this cleansing fountain is now found to be a fountain of blood. Before God's holiness, only blood can atone for the grotesqueness of human sin.[3] And, therefore, *the sword* is awakened against God's own Shepherd, His only-begotten Son.

They pierced Him. The Jews struck their own Shepherd, compelling the Romans to pierce Him to death. Yet *we also* pierced Him. By our former mockeries and our former transgressions, we also pierced Him to death. All of humanity has raised the sword against Christ. Yet He was pierced for our

---

[2] *"In that day there will be **a [fountain]** opened to David's house and to the inhabitants of Jerusalem, **for sin and for uncleanness**."* (Zechariah 13:1)

[3] *"According to the Law, nearly everything is cleansed with blood, **and apart from shedding of blood there is no remission**."* (Hebrews 9:22)

transgressions. He was struck down with the sword, at the cross, for our iniquities. The Shepherd laid down His life for the sheep. The wages of our sin was death, but He paid those wages for us.

We thus plead with the unconverted: O lost, little Sheep! O wayward Ewe or wandering Ram! How can you continue to defy such love? Do you not see His wounds? Do you not see how His hands and His feet were pierced through for your own sins? Do you not see the marks and deep scars on His brow, where the crown of thorns once dug into His head? If He who awakens the sword, and controls the sword, allowed the sword to strike His only-begotten Son, piercing to death the only-begotten Son of the Father, how can you continue to spit in His face? Will you continue to blaspheme such a God of love? How long will you persist in rebelling against His holy commandments? O lost, little Sheep! Will you not turn away from your dark deeds of wickedness, confess your sins to Him, and look upon the One whom you pierced? Will you not pledge your loyalty, your life, and the fullness of your love to this great Shepherd, who bears the marks and scars of such divine and redeeming love for you?

THE SHEEP WILL BE SCATTERED

What, then, shall happen to the sheep? If the wicked shall strike the Shepherd, what shall become of His flock? If the sword is awakened to strike the Shepherd, will it also strike the sheep?

"Awake, O sword, against My Shepherd, and against the Man who is close to Me," says the LORD of Hosts. "Strike the Shepherd, **and the sheep will be scattered***; and I will turn My hand against the little ones."* (Zechariah 13:7)

What happens to sheep when they have no shepherd? Are they not very vulnerable without a shepherd?

Moses spoke to the LORD, saying, "Let the LORD, the God of the spirits of all flesh, appoint a man over the congregation, who may go out before them, and who may come in before them, and who may lead them out, and who may bring them in; **that the** *congregation of the LORD not be as sheep which have no shepherd."* (Numbers 27:15–17)

It is a terrifying thing for the sheep to lose their shepherd. And as the Prophet Zechariah has spoken beforehand, a people without a godly leader is like a flock of sheep without a shepherd:

For the teraphim have spoken vanity, and the diviners have seen a lie; and they have told false dreams. They comfort in vain. ***Therefore they go their way like sheep. They are oppressed, because there is no shepherd.*** (Zechariah 10:2)

This is why Jesus came. He came to have compassion upon a small, faithful group of people, the remnant of God's flock, who were like sheep without a shepherd:

Jesus came out, saw a great multitude, ***and He had compassion on them, because they were like sheep without a shepherd****, and He began to teach them many things.* (Mark 6:34)

Yet Jesus, the Good Shepherd, also knew the prophecy of Zechariah chapter 13. He knew full well that He, the Good Shepherd, would have to lay down His life for the sheep. In consequence, the sheep would be scattered:

Then Jesus said to them, ***"All of you will be made to stumble because of Me tonight****, for it is written, 'I will strike the shepherd, and* ***the sheep of the flock will be scattered.'"*** (Matthew 26:31)

And again,

Behold, the time is coming, yes, and has now come, ***that you will be scattered, everyone to his own place****, and you will leave Me alone. Yet I am not alone, because the Father is with Me.* (John 16:32)

Indeed, the disciples were scattered. They first deserted Jesus and fled. Their ranks were scattered. Then, after Jesus' resurrection from the dead, they were regathered at Jerusalem, and it was there, at Jerusalem, that they were commissioned by the Holy Spirit, on the day of Pentecost. Yet the sword of persecution awoke quickly in those earliest days of the Church, and came against them suddenly. And it was this *sword of persecution* that *scattered them abroad*:

> ***A great persecution*** *arose against the church which was in Jerusalem in that day.* ***They were all scattered abroad*** *throughout the regions of Judea and Samaria, except for the Apostles.* (Acts 8:1)

The sword awakens not only against the Shepherd, but also against His true sheep. If they pierced *Him* with the sword, then they also shall pierce *them* with the sword:

> *And those of the people who understand shall instruct many;* ***yet for many days they shall fall by sword*** *and flame, by captivity and plundering.* (Daniel 11:33)

Dear, faithful Christian, remember that persecution is quite difficult to understand. It oftentimes will come upon you when you least expect it to come. When you neither have been seeking it, nor have been provoking it, it nevertheless will come upon you suddenly. Without warning, your neighbor will lie about you and falsely accuse you, or else another professing Christian will start to slander you and attack your character. Moreover, oftentimes you will not be able to decipher any clear, circumstantial explanation for it. You will have loved them with gentleness and reverence before the Lord. Yet they, the very ones whom you will have tried to reach with the Gospel of God, will end up attacking you, suddenly, and without any lucid explanation for doing so.

Precious, faithful Christian, when the persecution comes—and it will come, for *"all who desire to live godly in Christ Jesus will suffer persecution"* (2 Timothy 3:12)—remember that the reason why it does not make sense, at least according to any biblical standards of justice and righteousness, is because it is *Satanic*. The enemy hates your evangelism. He despises your uncompromising fidelity to the commandments of Christ. Therefore, the enemy will assault you, and will awaken the sword of persecution against you.

When this happens, precious Brother or Sister, remember that that sword first was aroused against the Chief Shepherd, Christ Jesus the Lord. Your wounds will be His wounds. Your blows will be His blows. When they persecute you, they will be persecuting Him. You will be sharing in His earthly afflictions and sorrows, that one day you might also share in His Heavenly Kingdom and glory [Romans 8:17]. And since His wounds, upon His resurrection from the grave, became the marks of His triumph over sin and death, then you can rejoice in the hope that your wounds, received with groans and tears for the sake of His name, shall also prove to be your victorious marks of glory, on the Last Day.

A REMNANT WILL BE LEFT IN THE LAND

The purpose of the sword, however, is not only to prove the enduring faith of the elect even through fiery trials of persecution, but also to expose evil, and to make distinct separations within the flock. God is He who awakens the sword, and He uses it to differentiate between the true sheep and the false ones:

"It shall happen that in all the land," says the LORD, **"two parts in it will be cut off and die; but the third will be left in it."** (Zechariah 13:8)

The awakened sword is used by God to cut a line of separation between the wicked of the flock, and the faithful remnant of the flock. For, when God comes to judge His people, there shall be a remnant that will be spared. Yet it shall be *a small remnant*:

*Unless the LORD of Hosts had left to us **a very small remnant**, we would have been as Sodom; we would have been like Gomorrah.* (Isaiah 1:9)

The people of Israel are numerous. They are as numerous as the sand on the seashore. Still, at the Judgment, only *a remnant* of the people will be proved to have been faithful to their Lord:

*It will come to pass in that day that **the remnant of Israel**, and those who have escaped from the House of Jacob will no more again lean on him who struck them, but shall lean on the* LORD, *the Holy One of Israel, in truth.* ***A remnant will return, even the remnant of Jacob, to the mighty God. For though your people, Israel, are like the sand of the sea, only a remnant of them will return.*** *A destruction is determined, overflowing with righteousness. For the Lord* GOD *of Hosts will make a full end, and that determined, throughout all the earth.* (Isaiah 10:20–23)

And how big is the remnant? It is very small. Zechariah says that only *one-third* of the people shall be left in the land, which matches the prophecy of an earlier Prophet, the Prophet Ezekiel:

*You, son of man, take **a sharp sword** [is this not very much like Zechariah's "sword"?]; you shall take it as a barber's razor to you, and shall cause it to pass on your head and on your beard: then take balances to weigh, and divide the hair.* ***A third part*** *you shall burn in the fire in the middle of the city, when the days of the siege are fulfilled; and you shall take **a third part**, and strike with **the sword** around it; and **a third part** you shall scatter to the wind, and I will draw out **a sword** after them.* (Ezekiel 5:1-2)

And also,

*Yet will I leave **a remnant**, in that you shall have some that **escape the sword** among the nations, when you shall be scattered through the countries.* (Ezekiel 6:8)

Jesus did not come to bring peace on the earth, but a sword [Matthew 10:34]. This sword, once awakened, separates between true believers and false believers. It also separates between true teachers and false ones. The churches of the world may be big. There may be megachurches in many cities. The number of Christians may appear to be as many as the sand on the seashore. Yet in the end, *only a remnant will be saved.* Two-thirds shall be cut off by the sword. *Only one-third* shall remain after the sword has done its separating work:

> *"Before Him all the nations will be gathered,* **and He will separate them one from another, as a shepherd separates the sheep from the goats.***"* (Matthew 25:32)

And yet there is, even today, still a remnant of true, humble, and faithful believers. There is a portion of the flock of God that is strong, vibrant, holy, and unmoved by the threat of persecutions. God always has His remnant, and even now God's remnant is bright and luminous in holiness:

> *Even so then at this present time also* **there is a remnant according to the election of grace***.* (Romans 11:5)

In the year 1656, when Richard Baxter was invited to preach to a large gathering of fellow pastors in the Worcestershire Association of Pastors in England (which he never got to do, since he was struck with illness), he penned a message that later became known as his great book, *The Reformed Pastor*. At the beginning of this message to his *fellow pastors*, he took time to warn them that, in all likelihood, there were some pastors in their midst who were not on their way to Heaven. He called them to examine themselves, to see if any among them were, in actuality, on the road to Hell. Thus Baxter understood full well the severe implications of the awakened sword of the thirteenth chapter of Zechariah. He knew that only a remnant would prove to be true worshippers of the Lord God.

O little Flock of God, Christ's Word is like a double-edged sword, proceeding out of His mouth. It exposes false faith. On the Day of Judgment, it shall separate between true believers and false believers. Therefore, O little Flock, do not forget the biblical distinction between the Church visible and the Church invisible. That is, whenever you visit another local church, or go to a Christian conference, or else go to another form of gathering of the larger body of the Church, do not assume that the Church visible is the same as the Church invisible. There is a remnant, to be sure, and we praise God that there is, indeed, such a faithful remnant.

Yet the Church visible is oftentimes crowded with false believers. Therefore, it is not to be equated with the Church invisible, the true Church of the Lord. And we must remember this distinction. For, if we do not remember this truth, this dividing *"sword"* of Zechariah's prophecy, then we will blindly follow the Church visible, in all of her errors, off of the steep cliff of her current, moral compromise and her present, dangerously unsound doctrine.

"I WILL...REFINE THEM...AS GOLD"

The sword, then, is awakened against the Shepherd, Jesus Christ, and against the little ones of the flock, through persecution. It also cuts and separates between the Church visible and the Church invisible. It cuts off two-thirds of the flock and leaves only a third of the flock in the land. And yet even this remnant, this third of the flock, must undergo significant suffering:

> ***I will bring the third part into the fire****, and will refine them as silver is refined, and will test them [as] gold is tested. They will call on My name, and I will hear them. I will say, 'It is My people;' and they will say, 'The LORD is my God.'"* (Zechariah 13:9)

A sword is awakened to strike the Shepherd, and even the remnant of the flock will have to suffer. The remnant will be refined in the fire, as silver is refined, and it will be tested in the fire, as gold is tested. The suffering of the sword, then, is for the good of the remnant. It refines and purifies the true flock of God. Listen, then, to the crackling heat of the good, purifying fires of God in Scripture:

> *But He knows the way that I take.* ***When He has tried me, I shall come out like gold****.* (Job 23:10)

And,

> ***For You, God, have tested us. You have refined us, as silver is refined****.* (Psalm 66:10)

And also,

The refining pot is for silver, and the furnace for gold, but the LORD tests the hearts. (Proverbs 17:3)

And again, this time from the book of the Prophet Isaiah:

And I will turn My hand on you, ***thoroughly purge away your dross****, and will take away all your tin.* (Isaiah 1:25)

And yet again, in the Words of the Prophet Daniel:

Many shall purify themselves, and make themselves white, and be refined*; but the wicked shall do wickedly; and none of the wicked shall understand; but those who are wise shall understand.* (Daniel 12:10)

And, lastly from the Prophets:

And He will sit as a refiner and purifier of silver, and He will purify the sons of Levi, and refine them as gold and silver*; and they shall offer to the* LORD *offerings in righteousness.* (Malachi 3:3)

The persecuted Church in China has adopted a Chinese proverb in order to describe her unspeakable sufferings under the Communist government. Instead of being disheartened by their sufferings, the Chinese Christians say, triumphantly, "Real gold fears no fire." In saying this, they are merely speaking biblically:

Wherein you greatly rejoice, though now for a little while, if need be, you have been put to grief in various trials, that the proof of your faith, ***which is more precious than gold that perishes even though it is tested by fire****, may be found to result in praise, glory, and honor at the revelation of Jesus Christ.* (1 Peter 1:6–7)

O little Remnant, O little Flock, we do suffer, now. For, the prophecies of the cross of our Lord Jesus Christ are not only declarations of the divine glory of our crucified and risen Savior, but also invitations for us to carry our own crosses, so that, suffering with Him, now, we also might share in His glory, in His Kingdom, when He comes. Therefore, we become deathly ill, now. We are thrown into prison, now. Some of our brethren around the globe are put to death with sword for the sake of the name of Jesus, even now. Our loved ones die, now. Our children weep, now. The fires of suffering are hot, with searing heat, even now.

What, then, shall we say when these fiery trials come upon us, even each one of us? We shall say, by faith, even through tears, "It is good for us to be thus afflicted as we share in the afflictions of Christ. It is good. The Lord who brings His remnant through the fire is able to keep our souls from being scorched. Thus we will glorify God in the midst of this fiery furnace, even offering our bodies as living sacrifices, consumed with love for Him, and our blood and tears as drink offerings, poured out for Him. For, when we come forth from these fires, we shall be as silver, refined, and as gold, purified. Therefore, we rejoice in our sorrows and glory in our tribulations, since the day is fast approaching when God will answer us even before we call to Him, and He shall say, *'This is My people'*; and each one of us shall say, *'The LORD is my God.'*"

And thus in Heaven we shall join that countless multitude of saints, purified as gold and silver, and made priests and Levites in the service of His name, in bringing unto God the Father, and unto Jesus Christ the Son of the Father, our offerings in righteousness, to the praise of the glory of His grace, forever and ever, joy eternal, days beyond number, world without end. Amen.

Part Five:

THE GLORY
of the Cross of Christ

15

NOW THE SON OF MAN IS GLORIFIED
The Glory of THE CRUCIFIED CHRIST in John 13:31-35

When [Judas] had gone out, Jesus said, "Now the Son of Man is glorified, and God is glorified in Him. If God is glorified in Him, God will also glorify Him in Himself, and He will glorify Him immediately." (John 13:31–32)

GOD the Father shall be glorified in God the Son. At this point in the Gospel of John, Palm Sunday already has come and gone. The Son of David already has ridden into Jerusalem on a donkey, with the crowd waving the branches of palm trees and the people shouting, *"Hosanna in the highest!"* (Matthew 21:9). Also, as we learn from the other Gospel accounts, Jesus already has cleansed the Temple, cursed the fig tree, and silenced the Pharisees and Sadducees with His wisdom. In fact, at this point in the Gospel of John, the Passover supper already has been prepared and eaten. Jesus already has washed His disciples' feet. Judas already has eaten the bread that Jesus dipped in the dish, and already has gone out to betray Jesus. Here, at this point, with His betrayer gone—such that Judas will not be privy to this very special discourse that Jesus gives to His beloved disciples—Jesus announces the immediacy of His coming glorification:

*When [Judas] had gone out, Jesus said, "**Now** the Son of Man is glorified, and God is glorified in Him. If God is glorified in Him, God will also glorify Him in Himself, and He will glorify Him **immediately**."* (John 13:31–32)

Jesus' glorification is coming, immediately. The time for Him to be glorified finally has arrived. Also, Jesus' imminent glorification shall be a reciprocal one. That is, in this impending glorification, Jesus will glorify the Father, while the Father, simultaneously, will glorify Him. As Jesus will be glorified, so too will the Father be glorified, and vice-versa. The glory between God the Father and God the Son is a reciprocal glory.

Where did Jesus learn this? How does He know that His upcoming, immediate glorification shall be reciprocal with that of the Father? Obviously, His Father told Him so. Yet is it not most wonderful to think upon Jesus, who *is* the Word of God, reading about this very truth *in* the Word of God? Jesus Christ, the very Son of God, once read about this reciprocal glory between God the Father and His Son, the Servant, in the book of the Prophet Isaiah:

He said to Me, "You are My Servant; Israel, **in whom I will be glorified.***"* (Isaiah 49:3)

The Father, then, is glorified in the Son, His Servant. Yet the Son, His Servant, is also glorified in the Father:

Now the LORD says, He who formed Me from the womb to be His Servant, to bring Jacob again to Him, and to gather Israel to Him, **for I am [glorified] in the LORD's eyes**, *and My God has become My strength.* (Isaiah 49:5)

The glory of Jesus, the Son of Man, is reciprocal with that of the Father. Jesus Himself teaches this:

But when Jesus heard [that Lazarus was sick], He said, "This sickness is not to death, **but for the glory of God** *[that is, for the Father's glory],* **that the Son of God may be glorified by it***."* (John 11:4)

Moreover, in the Gospel of John, Jesus not only teaches that His glory is reciprocal with the Father's glory, but He also prays for this to be so. He prays not only for His own glorification, but also for His Father's glorification. He prays this way because the Father and Son possess a reciprocal glory:

> *Jesus said these things, and lifting up His eyes to Heaven, He said, "Father, the time has come.* **Glorify Your Son, that Your Son may also glorify You.** *...* **I glorified You on the earth.** *I have accomplished the work which You have given Me to do. Now, Father,* **glorify Me with [Yourself] with the glory which I had with You before the world existed.***"*
> (John 17:1, 4–5)

O Christian, have you, by faith, seen the Son of God glorified? Do you, by faith, yearn to see the Son of God glorified fully on earth, as He is glorified already in Heaven? As the world mocks the Son, even in the same manner in which it scorns the Father, do not we, His children, long to see the Father glorified, through the Father's glorification of the Son, at the final Judgment? Is this your greatest and most blessed hope, namely, that Christ would return in glory, and thus be glorified by the Father with all of the thunderous glory of the Lord of Heaven and earth? Do you pray, with tears, that God will be glorified, at last, in His Son, at the Judgment, so that all of the nations of the earth shall fear Him and give glory to Him? O dear Christian, fear God, and glorify His name, even as you pray that the Son of Man will be glorified, and that quickly!

GLORIFICATION ONLY THROUGH THE CROSS

Yet how does this come about? This is, to be sure, the greatest event in all of world history, wherein the brightness of the Father's glory is revealed through the glorification of His only-begotten Son. But how does this happen in real, tangible history? The glory of the Lord shall be revealed, a reciprocal glory between God the Father and God the Son, and all flesh shall see it, together [Isaiah 40:5]. Yet how, exactly, shall all flesh see it? Notice, again, the *immediacy* of this coming glorification:

> *When [Judas] had gone out, Jesus said,* **"Now** *the Son of Man is glorified, and God is glorified in Him. If God is glorified in*

*Him, God will also glorify Him in Himself, and He will glorify Him **immediately**."* (John 13:31–32)

What brings about this "now-ness," this immediacy? Is it not the cross? What, then, brings about the reciprocal glorification of the Father by the Son, and the Son by the Father? Is it not the cross? In history, then, the reciprocal glory of the Father and of the Son is revealed through the Son's passion on the cross:

[Returning once more to Isaiah's prophecy about the Father and Son's reciprocal glory:] *He said to Me, "You are My Servant; Israel, **in whom I will be glorified**."* (Isaiah 49:3)

How so? How is the Father glorified in His Servant, and His Servant in Him? This comes about through the sufferings of the Christ that are sandwiched between verses 3 and 5 of the prophecy:

*But I said, "**I have labored in vain. I have spent My strength in vain for nothing**; yet surely the justice due to Me is with the* LORD, *and My reward with My God."* (Isaiah 49:4)

It is the cross, and nothing less than the cross, which reveals the reciprocal glory of the Father and of the Son in real human history:

Jesus answered [Andrew and Philip, who were entreating Him on behalf of certain Greeks], *saying, "**The hour has come for the Son of Man to be glorified**."* (John 12:23)

What hour has come, that the Son of Man should be glorified? Is this not the hour of suffering? Is this not the hour of the cross?

*"**Now My soul is troubled**. What shall I say? 'Father, save Me from this hour?' But for this cause I came to this hour. **Father, glorify Your name!**" Then there came a voice out of the sky, saying, "**I have both glorified it, and will glorify it again.**"* (John 12:27–28)

O sluggish soul of mine, so slow to believe, do you not see how the Son's glorification is also reciprocal with that of the Father? And do you not behold how this reciprocal glorification cannot take place except through the cross? God the Father has willed it so. God the Son has accepted it as such. First comes the cross, and then, and only then, comes the glory:

[Jesus says to the disciples on the road to Emmaus:] *"Did not the Christ **have to suffer these things** and [then] **to enter into His glory?**"* (Luke 24:26)

Is this not how the Gospel works? Is not the Father glorified through the humiliation and punishment of the Son on the cross, all for no sins of His own, but for our own sins? And is not the Son glorified through the Father's good pleasure prospering in His own hand? Is not the Lamb first slain *before* He is honored with Heavenly glory and Heavenly blessing? And when the Lamb who was slain is glorified by all of the angels and saints of Heaven, is not the Father, who sits upon the Throne, also honored with Heavenly glory and Heavenly blessing?

God so loved the world that He gave His only-begotten Son. Therefore, the Father is glorified for His love, and the Son is glorified for His obedience to the Father's will. In the same way, the Son so loved His friends that He was willing to lay down His life for them. Therefore, the Son is glorified for His love, and the Father is glorified for His willingness to punish His beloved Son in our stead. At the cross, the righteousness of the Father, demonstrated by His wrath poured out against the horror of human sin, is revealed. At the same time, on the cross, the righteousness of Christ, demonstrated by His sinless obedience to the Father, is revealed. Therefore, God the Father is glorified at the cross, just as Jesus, His Son, is glorified at the cross. The Father and the Son are both fully eternal and fully divine. And the reciprocal glory that each possessed before the creation of the universe is revealed in human history through Christ's suffering for sins upon the cross.

Why, then, do we expect things to be any different for us, the servants of Christ? If He is our Master, is the servant greater than his Master? If the Master glorifies the Father through the sufferings of the cross, should we expect anything less than righteous suffering to follow our prayers for Christ to be glorified *in* us, and God to be glorified *through* us?

> [Jesus says to Peter:] *"Most certainly I tell you, when you were young, you dressed yourself, and walked where you wanted to. But when you are old, you will stretch out your hands, and another will dress you, and carry you where you do not want to go." Now He said this,* **signifying by what kind of death he would glorify God.** *When He had said this, He said to him,* **"Follow Me."** (John 21:18–19)

O precious Brother or Sister, are you praying that God would use your life to glorify Him? If so, do you not remember that the reciprocal glory of the Father and of the Son is only revealed to the world *through the sufferings of the Son*? How, then, shall God be glorified in you? Are you willing to be hated as He was hated? Hunted as He was hunted? Despised as He was despised? Falsely accused as He was falsely accused? Mocked as He was mocked? Beaten as He was beaten? Crucified as He was crucified? Are you willing to be a living sacrifice, set aflame by your persecutors, for the glory of God? Are you really desirous to be a drink offering, poured out, as a libation, for the glory of the Father and of the Son? If not, then pray not for God to be glorified in you. Sing not of such glorification.

Yet since the Spirit of God lives in you, and, therefore, you cannot help but pray such things, then carry this hope with you into your sufferings. That is, you must remember that even while you are suffering for the sake of His name, He shall be glorified in you. What is more, even as you share in His sufferings at the present time, so too, when He comes, shall you share, subserviently, in the Kingdom of Heaven, in His glorification:

> *...and if children, then heirs; heirs of God, and joint heirs with Christ;* ***if indeed we suffer with Him, that we may also be glorified with Him****.* (Romans 8:17)

CHRIST'S GLORY MANIFESTED ONLY FOR "A LITTLE WHILE"

Yet for how long will this glory be revealed? How long will this dark world be allowed to enjoy such a bright light? If the glory of God is revealed in the sufferings of His Son like a brilliant flash of lightning, how long will this marvelous demonstration last? Jesus says that it will not last long. God's glorious visitation of humanity in the flesh of Jesus Christ will be a very brief visitation:

> *"Little children, I will be with you **a little while** longer. You will seek Me, and as I said to the Jews, 'Where I am going, you cannot come,' so now I tell you."* (John 13:33)

The reciprocal glory of God the Father and God the Son, revealed in Christ's sufferings, both throughout His earthly life and especially on the cross, shall not be revealed to wicked humanity indefinitely. Instead, the revelation comes only with momentous brevity. Just as a brilliant rainbow, arcing in deep colors across the sky, is short-lived, and just as a shooting star, which is a meteor, lights up the night sky, but only for a short moment, so too does Jesus' light visit our dark, dark world with much brevity:

> *The Pharisees heard the multitude murmuring these things concerning Him, and the chief priests and the Pharisees sent officers to arrest Him. Then Jesus said, "I will be with you **a little while** longer, then I go to Him who sent Me. You will seek Me, and will not find Me; and where I am, you cannot come."* (John 7:32–34)

Also,

> *Jesus therefore said to them, "Yet **a little while** the light is with you. Walk while you have the light, that darkness does not overtake you. He who walks in the darkness does not know where he is going. While you have the light, believe in the light, that you may become children of light." Jesus said these things, and He departed and hid Himself from them.* (John 12:35–36)

The reciprocal glory between the Father and the Son is revealed to the world in the suffering, agonizing, persecuted, and dying flesh of Jesus Christ. He has come to His own, but His own have not received Him. He has come to reveal the Father's glory, but the Jews and Romans alike hate that glory. Therefore, the revelation of this reciprocal glory of God will last only *"a little while"*:

> ***"Yet a little while**, and the world will see Me no more; but you will see Me. Because I live, you will live also."* (John 14:19)

And,

> *"**A little while**, and you will not see Me. **Again a little while**, and you will see Me."* (John 16:16)

In Jesus Christ, God has revealed His glory to the world. When Jesus' disciples glorify the Son by confessing that the Son is sent from the Father, then the Father is glorified also. In the same way, when the disciples give glory to the Father, they do so by ascribing the Father's glory to the Son. However, only a few recognize and acknowledge this reciprocal glory. Only a few are true disciples. All of the rest of the people, from the pompously educated Greeks to the superstitiously idolatrous Jews, reject and refuse this reciprocal glory of God. Therefore, the light of this glory shall, in only a little while, be snatched away from them.

The call for men to repent in light of the Gospel always comes with urgency. The door of repentance and faith, for the forgiveness of sins, is open only for *"a little while."* The offer of divine pardon, extended even to the worst of spiritual criminals, is valid only for *"a little while."* There is an open invitation for all to enter, with violence, into the gates of the Kingdom of Heaven, but those gates are open only for *"a little while."* There is an open invitation for sinners to come to the Wedding Feast of the Lamb, and to be given wedding clothes for the Wedding Feast, but the doors of the Lamb's banquet hall remain open only for *"a little while."*

The great problem with the wicked is that they think that they have all of the time in the world before the Judgment Day. They deceive themselves into thinking that all things go on, uniformly, as they have since the creation of the world—willfully forgetting that God brought a global flood of judgment upon the world in the days of Noah [2 Peter 3:4-6]. They also deceive themselves by saying, "Tomorrow, we will go to such and such a place, and vacation there, or do business there," not knowing that tomorrow their very life may be taken from them [James 4:13-14]. These mockers, these self-deceivers, say to themselves, "I shall eat, drink, and be merry today, and, if needed, I shall repent later on." Yet later on will not come, for God's wrath comes upon them in just *"a little while"*:

> *The great Day of the* LORD **is near. It is near, and hurries greatly**, *the voice of the Day of the* LORD. *The mighty man cries there bitterly. That Day is a Day of wrath, a Day of distress and anguish, a Day of trouble and ruin, a Day of darkness and gloom, a Day of clouds and blackness, a Day of the trumpet and alarm, against the fortified cities, and against the high battlements.* (Zephaniah 1:14–16)

The Gospel is exceedingly urgent, since the reciprocal glory of God the Father and of God the Son is only revealed to the world for *"a little while."* After that, once it is refused, it is quickly taken away. Those who hate the light will have the light taken away from them in but a moment. Those who despise the preaching of the Gospel will see the godly preachers of the Gospel snatched away from them in but a moment. People who hate the salt of the earth will wake up, in just *"a little while,"* to find themselves living in a salt-less world. The wicked, who despise the grace of God by willfully pretending that it is a license to indulge their sinful flesh with myriads of revelries and fornications, will, in only *"a little while,"* discover themselves to have been cast into Hell, and to be living in a grace-less realm of conscious, everlasting torment.

The reciprocal glory of God the Father and of Jesus Christ, His only-begotten Son, is revealed to the world only for a little while longer. After that, this wicked world shall be plunged into an everlasting darkness, wherein there is no glory at all.

Yet for believers, the little-while-ness of Christ's sufferings is filled with hope. The truth that Jesus sufferings lasted only for *"a little while,"* is very hopeful for us. For, God's reciprocal glory is revealed through us, even us, His children, but only as we suffer as those who follow in Christ's footsteps of suffering. Therefore, it is hopeful for us to know that God's revelation of glory through us, which comes through our sufferings, will last only *"a little while"* longer. After that, we shall be caught up to our God and Father, and to our Lord Jesus Christ, and our suffering will be no more:

> *For our light affliction,* **which is momentary,** *works for us more and more exceedingly an* **eternal** *weight of glory.*
> (2 Corinthians 4:17)

And also, as the greatest of all of our hopes:

> ***In a very little while****, He who comes* ***will come****, and will not [tarry].* (Hebrews 10:37)

O precious Christian, have the tribulations of this present, weary life overwhelmed you, like the breakers of a raging river crashing over your head? Do your lips quiver with grief for those whom you love who already have fallen asleep in Christ? Does your heart bleed on account of the evil around you? Do you love God's commandments, such that you have learned to hate every path of deception, and also to hate the double-mindedness of sinful man, and yet do you find yourself all alone, like a sparrow on a rooftop, for doing so? O precious Christian, let this Gospel promise quiet your soul before God: in only a little while, it will all be over. In only a very little while, our Lord shall come like a thief in the night, and those who say, *"Peace and security!"* will be given over to sudden destruction, and shall not escape, but you, together with all of those who have died in Christ, shall be caught up to meet the Lord in the air. In only a very little while, dear, weeping Christian, you shall be with the Lord always [1 Thessalonians 5:2-3; 4:17], and He shall wipe away every tear from your eyes.

Now the Son of Man Is Glorified

Our Reciprocal Love for One Another

Let it be said, then, that the reciprocal glory of the Father and of the Son is revealed to the world through the sufferings of the Son. Let it also be said that this reciprocal glory, which is a warm, Heavenly light shining in a wicked, dark world, shall not sojourn amongst fallen man for long. The light is taken away. The reciprocal glory is received up into Heaven, and hidden away in Heaven. Yet there is still a witness on earth to this reciprocal glory. Even after Jesus ascends into Heaven, His disciples are left to bear witness to the reciprocal glory between God the Father and God the Son:

> *"A new commandment I give to you, that you love one another. Just as I have loved you, you also love one another.* ***By this everyone will know*** *that you are My disciples, if you have love for one another."* (John 13:34–35)

How do Jesus' disciples bear witness to the reciprocal, triune glory of God? What shall His disciples do in order to tell the world that the Father, the Son, and the Holy Spirit all possess an equal, reciprocal glory? The disciples shall announce this Gospel of the reciprocal glory of the three Persons of the Trinity *through the disciples' love for one another*:

> *"A new commandment I give to you, that you* ***love one another****. Just* ***as I have loved you, you also love one another***. *By this everyone will know that you are My disciples,* ***if you have love for one another****."* (John 13:34–35)

This is both a new commandment, and an old one, all at the same time. It is an old commandment, since it is has been around since the beginning:

> *Now I beg you, dear lady,* ***not as though I wrote to you a new commandment, but that which we had from the beginning, that we love one another****.* (2 John 5)

God's children are to love one another. Even when they are sinned against, a child of God is to love his brother, and to love his neighbor. This is an old commandment:

You shall not hate your brother in your heart. You shall surely rebuke your neighbor, and not bear sin because of him. You shall not take vengeance, nor bear any grudge against the children of your people; **but you shall love your neighbor as yourself. I am the LORD**. (Leviticus 19:17–18)

Yet this also is a new commandment. It is new, not only in that it is a summing up of the entirety of the Law and Prophets in just a single commandment, but also new in that it comes only through the blood of Jesus Christ. That is, without the shed blood of Jesus, His death for our sins, His resurrection from the grave, His ascension into Heaven, and His sending of the Holy Spirit to indwell the hearts of true believers, we would be powerless to obey this command. We could not love one another, with distinctly biblical love, without the power of God's Spirit at work in us. Therefore, this supernatural love that we have for one another, a love that comes only through the Spirit of the living God, bears witness to the reciprocal glory that is contained within the Godhead. We bear witness to the glory of God the Father, the glory of God the Son, and the glory of God the Holy Spirit *by loving one another*:

Owe no one anything, **except to love one another; for he who loves his neighbor has fulfilled the Law**. (Romans 13:8)

How so? How does our reciprocal love for one another bear witness to the glory of Christ Jesus? It does so because Christ Jesus first loved us. In other words, our love for one another is a reciprocal love. Jesus first loved us; therefore, we must love one another:

By this we know love [that is, the reciprocal love of the Gospel], *because* **He laid down His life for us. And we ought to lay down our lives for the brethren**. (1 John 3:16)

And,

*"If I then, the Lord and the Teacher, **have washed your feet**, you also **ought to wash one another's feet**."* (John 13:14)

Our love for one another is a reciprocal love. We love one another even as Jesus first loved us and gave His life for us:

*"This is My commandment, that you love one another, **even as I have loved you**."* (John 15:12)

How, then, do we bear witness to the reciprocal glory of God the Father, God the Son, and God the Holy Spirit? We do so through our love for one another. We possess, as true, Spirit-born believers, a reciprocal love for one another:

***In love of the brethren be tenderly affectionate to one another**; in honor preferring one another.* (Romans 12:10)

And again,

*Seeing you have purified your souls in your obedience to the truth through the Spirit in sincere brotherly affection, **love one another from the heart fervently**.* (1 Peter 1:22)

Jesus is not here, on earth, in the flesh, at present. He is omnipresent in His deity, but He is, in His resurrected body, presently in Heaven. He is sitting at the Father's right hand, waiting for His enemies to be made His footstool. In Heaven, His glory, which He shares equally with the Father, is known to all. Yet what about here on earth? If the people of the world can no longer look upon the incarnate Son of God with their physical eyes, how can they ever see the glory of God revealed in the face of Christ Jesus? The sobering, astounding truth is that the world will see the reciprocal glory of the Godhead through our love for one another:

*Beloved, if God loved us in this way, we also ought to love one another. **No one has seen God at any time. If we love one***

another, God remains in us, and His love has been perfected in us. (1 John 4:11–12)

    Do you see it, dear Brethren? Those who are appointed to eternal life—being those who have eyes of faith to see the Kingdom of God—will, in truth, see glimpses of the glory of the invisible God *in our love for one another*. They will see, spiritually, the reality of the incarnate Christ, who sits at His Father's right hand in radiant glory, *through our love for one another*.
    That is, they will see husbands loving their wives by sacrificing themselves for the sake of their wives' protection and sanctification, and wives submitting themselves to their husbands, in meekness, as unto the Lord. They will witness fathers teaching the Scriptures to their children in their living rooms at home, and mothers singing psalms, hymns, and spiritual songs over their nursing infants, and also homeschooling their older children, amidst much hardship, in the goodness of the fear of the Lord. When they see Christians loving one another in these ways, such that they witness those who are rich in this present world offering glad gifts to those who are the persecuted poor amongst the churches, they—the ones who have eyes to see it—will exclaim, with great jubilation, "The Lord and Christ of these Christians, indeed, must be the one, true God!"
    Moreover, we pray, they will see our children loving one another. They will see them rejecting both the filthy allurements of the world and the selfishness of modern child psychology, and, instead, loving one another, even with Gospel admonitions and Gospel tears, in truthful, sacrificial love. And, we pray, they thus will say of our children, "These children are not like the children of the world. These must be the children of the Most High God!"
    Do you have eyes to see it, dear Brethren? Can you see the reciprocal glory that both God the Father and God the Son possess in Heaven? Are you able to see the way in which we will love one another, in perfection, in Heaven? Can you see Christ's blood covering over the sins of the Christian father, so that the Christian father can live in sinless perfection in Heaven, and thus love his Christian son, whom he formerly sinned against, with a perfect

love in Heaven? Do you see Christ's resurrection raising a Gentile Christian from the grave, spotless and sinless, such that his former sins against his Jewish-Christian brother are forgiven, and his love for his Jewish-Christian brother is perfected? Can you see the Christian martyr in Heaven, who gave his lifeblood in order to witness to the uncoverted, extending his hand of greeting to the very one who approvingly sanctioned his martyrdom, and yet who subsequently become a believer? Do you have faith to see a Christian husband, now in Heaven, looking into the eyes of the woman who, in this life, was his Christian wife, and, having been cleansed of all of his former sins committed against her, now loving her, at last, with a *sinless, perfectly purified* love?

    Do you see the Church, the Bride of Christ, looking upon the One who was slain for her salvation, and saying of Christ, the King of Heaven, "Now is the Father glorified in the Son! Now is the Son glorified in the Father! For, the Father gave His Son, and the Son willingly gave Himself to the Father's will. Therefore, now, and for eternity, to Him who sits upon the throne, and to the Lamb, be a reciprocal glory, unto all ages, forever and ever!"? For, in Heaven, thus shall be the praises of our immutable, ever-glorious God, and of His ever-glorious Christ, unto eternal days, glory unceasing, world without end. Amen.

PROPHECIES OF THE CROSS

16

PEACE BE TO YOU
The Glory of THE RISEN CHRIST in John 20:19-29

When therefore it was evening, on that day, the first day of the week, and when the doors were shut where the disciples were assembled, for fear of the Jews, Jesus came and stood in the midst, and said to them, "Peace be to you." When He had said this, He showed them His hands and His side. The disciples therefore were glad when they saw the Lord. Jesus therefore said to them again, "Peace be to you. As the Father has sent Me, even so I send you." When He had said this, He breathed on them, and said to them, "Receive the Holy Spirit! If you forgive anyone's sins, they have been forgiven them. If you retain anyone's sins, they have been retained."

But Thomas, one of the twelve, called Didymus, was not with them when Jesus came. The other disciples therefore said to him, "We have seen the Lord!" But he said to them, "Unless I see in His hands the print of the nails, and put my hand into His side, I will not believe." (John 20:19-25)

GOD comforts His children when they are afraid, even when the doors are shut for fear of their enemies. The men of Sodom may be outside, clamoring for Lot's blood, yet behind the locked doors Lot is safe, and the angels of the Lord are present within the house both to blind Lot's attackers and to bring comfort to Lot. Similarly, the impoverished widow of one of the sons of the prophets, the widow who petitions Elisha the Prophet for help, may find herself inside of her home, doors bolted shut for fear of the creditor who is coming to take away her two sons to be his slaves. Yet within the house, behind the locked doors, God comforts her by miraculously filling her empty vessels with valuable oil, such that she can sell the oil, pay off her debt, and still have a modest living leftover for herself and her sons.

The world hates Christ, and so the world hates true Christians. Thus in this world we do, indeed, have many tribulations. There are fierce enemies who rise up to persecute us, and ravenous wolves who seek to devour us. Yet when we are in danger, and thus hiding behind shut doors, the Lord our God visits us with the comfort of His holy presence. Whenever we go into our room, and shut our door behind us, and pray to our Father in secret, He who sees us seeking Him in secret also visits us, and comforts us in secret:

Come, my people, enter into your rooms, **and shut your doors behind you.** *Hide yourself for a little moment, until the indignation is past.* (Isaiah 26:20)

The Apostles, then, are meeting together with the doors shut behind them. They have heard the report of Mary, namely, that the Teacher, raised from the dead, has appeared to her and to the other women in the new light of the morning. However, since the Apostles themselves, perhaps Peter excepted, have not yet seen Jesus, they are filled with doubts and unbelief. Yet it is here, while trembling together in fear behind shut doors, that they first see the risen Lord. He appears to them, rebukes them for being so slow to believe, and then comforts them with His divine comfort.

O precious Church, O little Flock, remember that the very first Resurrection Sunday was a dangerous day for the Apostles. Realistically, any one of them could have been arrested, tried, and crucified under the false accusations of the Jews, in league with the Romans, in like manner with Jesus, their Master. Thus, since they had not yet believed in Christ's resurrection, they had every human reason to be afraid, and so were wise to meet with the doors shut behind them.

Precious Brothers and Sisters, our current work and sufferings within our small, persecuted churches in America are labors of love that, in our small, mustard-seed way, seek to prepare the larger American Church for the coming persecutions of true believers in America. For, since our nation has now turned so far away from the Law of Christ and all of His righteous statutes and judgments, the question is no longer, "Shall serious persecutions come upon those American Christians who truly fear God?" but rather, "How soon, and in what malicious forms shall serious persecutions come?"

To be sure, when fierce persecutions come upon American Christians, there shall be many churches that keep their doors wide open, and operate persecution-free. This is because they shall bow down to the demands of the persecutors, justifying themselves without the slightest prick or sting of conscience for doing so. For, those pastors and deacons who even now are unwilling to be persecuted for speaking boldly against the *societal horrors* of Secularism in the public schools, or the *abominable nature* of homosexuality and transgenderism, or the *monstrous nature* of the practice of contraception even by married couples within the churches,[1] shall not have the moral backbone to withstand the wily word games and legal intimidation tactics of those who seek to annihilate the Gospel of Jesus Christ in America. Instead, such pastors and deacons shall betray the Gospel while simultaneously quoting the Bible as a justification for their actions of betrayal. They may even take the witness stand against their fellow pastors

---

[1] Thus says Calvin: "The voluntary spilling of semen outside of intercourse between man and woman is a *monstrous* thing. Deliberately to withdraw from coitus in order that semen may fall on the ground is *doubly monstrous*. For this is to extinguish the hope of the race and to kill before he is born the hoped-for offspring. This impiety is especially condemned, now by the Spirit through Moses' mouth, that Onan, as it were, by a violent abortion, no less cruelly than filthily cast upon the ground the offspring of his brother, torn from the maternal womb. Besides, in this way he tried, as far as he was able, to wipe out a part of the human race. If any woman ejects a [preborn baby] from her womb by drugs, it is reckoned a crime incapable of expiation and deservedly Onan incurred upon himself the same kind of punishment, infecting the earth by his semen, in order that Tamar might not conceive a future human being as an inhabitant of the earth." (John Calvin on Genesis 38:10, qtd. in Charles D. Provan, *The Bible and Birth Control* [Monongahela, PA: Zimmer Printing, 1989], 15, emphases added. Note that Calvin's anti-contraception exposition of Genesis 38:10 is *curiously omitted* in all of the modern editions of his commentary on Genesis.)

and deacons who refuse to fall down and worship before the gold image—that selfsame antichrist ideology—which the voting nation will have set up.

Yet do not fear, O little Flock, for it is your Father's good pleasure to give you the Kingdom. So when you take your stand against the blasting horns, flutes, harps, lyres, and psaltry of a new Nebuchadnezzar—let the reader understand—then do not worry about how you shall obtain food to eat or clothing to wear. Instead, go into your room, shut the doors behind you, and pray to your Father in secret. For there, even where you find yourself trembling in fear behind closed doors, your risen Lord will draw near to you with His Word and His Spirit, in order to comfort you.

HIS WORD OF PEACE

He comforts His disciples, no doubt, only *through His Word*. It is *through His Word* that He comforts us. Thus when He comes to the Apostles on the evening of the first day of the week, as they tremble together in fear of the Jews with the doors shut behind them, what does He say to them? With what Word does He comfort them? He comforts them with His divine Word of *"peace"*:

When therefore it was evening, on that day, the first day of the week, and when the doors were shut where the disciples were assembled, for fear of the Jews, Jesus came and stood in the midst, and said to them, **"Peace be to you."** (John 20:19)

And again,

Jesus therefore said to them again, **"Peace be to you.** *As the Father has sent Me, even so I send you."* (John 20:21)

And, once more,

After eight days again His disciples were inside, and Thomas was with them. Jesus came, the doors being shut, and stood in the midst, and said, **"Peace be to you."** (John 20:26)

Peace Be to You

This is a greeting of comfort, *"Peace be to you."* It is the same greeting that the steward of Joseph's house used when the brothers of Joseph were trembling with fear on account of being falsely accused of stealing money from the lord of the land of Egypt. The steward of Joseph's house spoke to them, seeking to comfort them, by saying, *"Peace be to you"* (Genesis 43:23).

Yet in the Bible, God Himself also uses this greeting. When Gideon is trembling with fear, knowing that he has seen the Angel of the LORD, the LORD comforts Gideon in this very same manner:

*Gideon saw that He was the Angel of the LORD; and Gideon said, "Alas, Lord GOD! Because I have seen the Angel of the LORD face to face!" The LORD said to him, **"Peace be to you!** Do not be afraid. You shall not die." Then Gideon built an altar there to the LORD, and called it **"The LORD is Peace."** To this day it is still in Ophrah of the Abiezrites.* (Judges 6:22–24)

This, indeed, is for our comfort. Whenever someone extends God's true peace to someone else, this is for the purpose of comfort. Thus when men of the sons of Judah and Benjamin come to join David's band of soldiers at the stronghold in the wilderness, David is unsure whether they are friends or enemies. Are they sincere in wanting to serve him, or do they come as spies, sent from Saul, in order to betray David into Saul's hands? Yet when Amasai, chief of the captains, prophesies in the Spirit and says to David, *"We are yours, David, and on your side, you son of Jesse.* ***Peace, peace be to you, and peace be to your helpers****; for your God helps you"* (1 Chronicles 12:18), then David is comforted by them and receives them, even making them captains of the troop.

How does our Lord comfort us when we are in serious danger of persecutions for the sake of His name? He comforts us with His Word of peace. And the Eleven recognize this Word of peace, since Jesus also spoke this same Word of peace to them prior to His death on the cross and subsequent resurrection from the grave:

"Peace I leave with you. My peace I give to you*; not as the world gives, give I to you. Do not let your heart be troubled, neither let it be fearful."* (John 14:27)

And,

> *"These things I have spoken to you, **that in Me you may have peace**. In the world you will have tribulation; but be of good cheer, I have overcome the world."* (John 16:33, NKJV)

Yet the resurrection of Christ from the grave is the greatest comfort of all of God's miraculous comforts. Therefore, when Jesus says, *"Peace be to you!"* to His disciples, even as He appears to them behind the shut doors, He also says, *"As the Father has sent me, even so I send you"* (John 20:21), thus designating Himself as the only *divine* Apostle (for, the Father Himself sent Him from Heaven), and yet also designating His disciples as the true Apostles of His Church (since He also now sends them). Furthermore, the peace of Jesus Christ resting upon His Apostles means that they now have the delegated authority to bind and to loose sins, such that if they forgive the sins of any, they are forgiven them, and if they retain the sins of any, they are retained.

Yet all of this is built upon the very Gospel that Christ Jesus has commissioned them to preach, and that Gospel is the Gospel of peace. Thus Jesus reveals Himself to them in His resurrected body and says to them, *"Peace be to you!"* in order to commission them to be His ambassadors to all nations. And as His ambassadors, they are to preach this glorious *Gospel of peace*:

> *"I create the fruit of the lips: **Peace, peace, to him who is far off and to him who is near**,"* says the LORD; *"and I will heal them."* (Isaiah 57:19)

Still, what kind of peace is this which the Gospel proclaims? Is it not a new-creation peace? Is it not a restoration of man to his former peace with God in the Garden of Eden? Is this not fully supernatural, such that spiritually dead men are raised to spiritual life, just as Christ's physical body, being dead, now has been raised to physical life and immortality?

Jesus says to the disciples, *"Peace be to you!"* and having said this, He *breathes on them* and says to them, *"Receive the Holy Spirit!"* (John 20:22). Is this not, then, a new-creation peace, which is the peace of re-created life in Him? For, in the book of Genesis, after the Lord God formed man of the dust of the ground, He *breathed* into his nostrils the *breath* of life, and the man became a living being [Genesis 2:7]. In the same manner, when the Prophet Ezekiel bemoaned the vision of a valley in Israel full of bones, very dead and very dry, the Lord God asked His Prophet if those bones could live. Then the Lord God said to Ezekiel:

*Then He said to me, "Prophesy to **the [breath]**, prophesy, son of man, and tell **the [breath]**, 'Thus says the Lord GOD: Come from the four winds, **O breath**, and **breathe on** these slain, that they may live.'"* (Ezekiel 37:9)

Therefore, Jesus *breathes* upon the disciples in order to commission them to preach this Gospel of *new-creation peace*. The *peace* of Christ's resurrection is a new-creation peace. It gives life to the dead; it makes all things new. And this is why the Apostolic greetings to the churches throughout the New Testament are oftentimes greetings of *"peace."* They greet the churches with the peace of the Gospel, which is a new-creation peace:

*...but I hope to see you soon, and we will speak face to face. **Peace be to you**. The friends greet you. Greet the friends by name.* (3 John 14)

And,

*Now **the God of peace be with you all**. Amen.* (Romans 15:33)

Do you perceive, then, just how much comfort such a Gospel of peace brings to persecuted and troubled Christians? For, this Gospel peace is inseparable from the resurrection of Jesus Christ from the grave, and His resurrection is inseparable from the promise of a new creation. Currently, we groan and lament in these mortal bodies. Under the wounds and sicknesses of the Gospel, we outwardly are wasting away. Under the persecutions of the enemies of the Gospel, we die daily, being like sheep led to the slaughter. *"Blessed are you who weep now, for you shall laugh"*

(Luke 6:21), and so, in accordance with those Words of our Lord, we do weep now, and oftentimes in torrents of tears.

Yet the resurrection of Christ Jesus from the grave seals for us the promise that one day the Lord our God will create New Heavens and a New Earth. He who breathes new life into once dead souls—that is, souls that were once dead in their sins and transgressions—is also He who shall turn deserts into lush river valleys, and this present, filthy, sin-polluted world into the New Paradise of God. And how do we know these promises of God to be trustworthy? We know them to be faithful and true only by Jesus' resurrection from the dead. That is, since He showed the disciples His hands and His side, and thus His resurrection was physical, tangible, and, therefore, truly historical, we have every confident comfort in believing that He who breathed life into Adam will also breathe new life into the bodies of those who have died in Him, at the resurrection on the Last Day. For, Christ is, indeed, risen from the dead, and thus as in Adam all die, even so in Christ all shall be made alive! But each one in his own order: Christ the firstfruits, and afterward those who are Christ's at His coming [1 Corinthians 15:20-23].

THE TEMPORARY UNBELIEF OF THOMAS

However, there is one who is absent from this first appearance of the resurrected Christ to His disciples. This is Thomas, called Didymus, which means "Twin":

*But Thomas, one of the twelve, called Didymus, was not with them when Jesus came. The other disciples therefore said to him, "We have seen the Lord!" But he said to them, "Unless I see in His hands the print of the nails, and put my hand into His side, **I will not believe**." (John 20:24–25)*

Now, neither should we be too hard on Thomas, since many of us would have responded in the same way, nor should we overlook his unbelief, as if it is a light matter. For, Thomas has many compelling reasons to believe. He has, for example, not only the testimony of many eyewitnesses to the risen Lord, but even eyewitnesses whom he knows, loves, and trusts:

> *Jesus said to [Mary], "Do not hold Me, for I have not yet ascended to My Father;* **but go to My brothers, and tell them**, *'I am ascending to My Father and your Father, to My God and your God.'"* **Mary Magdalene came and told the disciples that she had seen the Lord**, *and that He had said these things to her.* (John 20:17–18)

And, again,

> *The other disciples therefore said to him,* **"We have seen the Lord!"** (John 20:25)

Not only does Thomas have eyewitnesses whom he loves and trusts, but he also has every reason to believe in Christ's bodily resurrection from the dead *on account of the many Old Testament prophecies concerning the resurrection of the Christ*. For, not only did God use the witness of the earliest disciples to testify to the resurrection of Jesus, but He also set down the resurrection of the Christ in stone, as it were, in the immutable prophecies of the Old Testament. Thus we hear David prophesying:

> *For You will not leave My soul in Sheol,* **neither will You allow Your Holy One to see corruption**. (Psalm 16:10)

And, as Isaiah prophesies:

> *[On account of the anguish of His soul,* **He shall see light**, *He shall be satisfied.]* (Isaiah 53:11)[2]

And, according to the Prophet Hosea:

> *After two days He will revive us.* **On the third day He will raise us up**, *and we will live before Him.* (Hosea 6:2)

---

[2] The present author's own translation.

PROPHECIES OF THE CROSS

Even the Prophet Jonah was in the belly of the fish *three days and three nights*. And Thomas himself had been present to hear Jesus, his Master, explain how Jonah's time in the belly of the fish prefigured Christ's time in the tomb:

But He answered them, "An evil and adulterous generation seeks after a sign, but no sign will be given it but the sign of Jonah the Prophet. **For as Jonah was three days and three nights in the belly of the [great fish], so will the Son of Man be three days and three nights in the heart of the earth."** (Matthew 12:39–40)

Moreover, Thomas, who is called the Twin, had been present to hear Jesus make explicit prophecies about His upcoming crucifixion and subsequent resurrection on the third day:

From that time, Jesus began to show His disciples that He must go to Jerusalem and suffer many things from the elders, chief priests, and scribes, and be killed, **and the third day be raised up**. (Matthew 16:21)

And also,

[Jesus speaking directly to the Twelve, including Thomas:] "They will scourge and kill Him. **On the third day, He will rise again.**" (Luke 18:33)

Foolish unbelief it is in the heart of any disciple that is slow to believe these things! Yet even the disciples on the road to Emmaus were guilty of such slowness of heart:

*He said to them, "**Foolish men, and slow of heart to believe in all that the Prophets have spoken!** Did not the Christ have to suffer these things* **and to enter into His glory?**" (Luke 24:25–26)

Thomas, then, is not diabolically guilty, for he eventually does come to believe, and then goes on to be a most extraordinary

Apostle of Christ Jesus. Yet he is guilty of being slow to believe, especially in the face of so many godly reasons to believe. His is not the unforgivable sin, yet it is a sin nonetheless. For, he who once waxed bold in saying, *"Let us go also, that we may die with Him"* (John 11:16), is now unwilling to receive both the eyewitness and the Scriptural testimony to Christ's resurrection.

Skepticism towards God's Word is never a virtue, but always a vice. It is not virtuous to have doubts about the veracity of God's holy Word. The wicked may say that it is smart, intelligent, and wise to reserve intellectual doubt towards all things, even the Bible itself, and yet to do so is neither smart, nor intelligent, nor wise. Rather, doubting skepticism towards God and towards His Word is always sinful.

It is the sin of pride, since the doubting skeptic haughtily blinds himself to his own wickedness of heart and the sheer vileness of his own sins against God. It is also the sin of idolatrous ignorance, since the man who doubts God's holy Word is ignorant of all of the multitudinous lines of evidence that God has provided for those who have eyes to see them, and such ignorance comes from his idolatry of knowledge—at the least the kind of knowledge that is severed from God Himself.

Thus the skeptic finds himself in a vicious cycle of pride and blindness, pride and blindness, which increases both pride and blindness with each passing cycle. Therefore, doubting skepticism, being a willful sin, is not, in the end, rooted in the intellect, but rather in the heart. It is unholy and unthankful to God, since it does not fear God and love God. For, if a man were to fear God and love God with his whole heart, then such a man would never entertain skepticism towards the very Word of God.

Yet we are in no way saying that Thomas has committed all of these sins to the extreme. He only has committed them in part, for his is merely a temporary lapse into the pride and hardness of heart that produces such doubting skepticism. Yet we are saying that true unbelievers, the ones who never repent before God in spiritual sackcloth and ashes, are guilty of such sins to the full measure. In Hell, in the midst of the torments of the worm that does not die and the fires that are not quenched, all unbelievers will weep and gnash their teeth at what was, in this life, their own foolish skepticism towards God.

They will bemoan that they had the audacity to drag Jesus before the judges, when in truth they themselves were right on the brink of falling into the hands of the living God, and thus being dragged, justly condemned, before the High Court of Heaven, on account of their evil deeds. When He offered His blood for them, they spit at Him. When He rose from the dead, they scoffed at the eyewitnesses to His resurrection, and also at the Scriptural witnesses of Moses and the Prophets. Therefore, dying in their wicked unbelief, they will serve an everlasting sentence in the flames of Gehenna, having defied and blasphemed the Father by scoffing at the divine testimony to the resurrection of His only-begotten Son from the grave.

"My Lord and My God!"

We are called, then, to believe: not a story, but a true history; not a myth, but an accurate account; and not a legend, but a true, historical Person, complete with the marks of His historical identity. Jesus of Nazareth is that Person, and He shows the marks of His historical identity to Thomas by allowing Thomas to touch the sights of His former mortal wounds:

> *After eight days again His disciples were inside, and Thomas was with them. Jesus came, the doors being shut, and stood in the midst, and said, "Peace be to you." Then He said to Thomas, "**Reach here your finger, and see My hands. Reach here your hand, and put it into My side**. Do not be unbelieving, but believing."* (John 20:26–27)

Again, Thomas should have been willing to believe even without this gracious condescension from the Lord Jesus. For, the same Scriptures that foretold the piercing of the Messiah's hands and feet also foretold His resurrection from the grave on the third day. Yet the Lord is gracious, and thus, knowing the wavering nature of our hearts, offers His disciples physical proofs of His glorious resurrection from the tomb:

When He had said this, **He showed them His hands and His side.** *The disciples therefore were glad when they saw the Lord.* (John 20:20)

And also,

"See My hands and My feet, *that it is truly Me.* **Touch Me and see,** *for a spirit does not have flesh and bones, as you see that I have."* (Luke 24:39)

All of the Apostles, and not just Thomas, were allowed to see the marks on His hands and the spot where the spear had pierced His side. Not only that, but all of them were allowed to touch Him, and to feel with their own hands that He had flesh and bones, even in His resurrected state. A ghost or spirit does not eat fish, and yet He ate fish. He was truly raised in bodily form:

That which was from the beginning, that which we have heard, ***that which we have seen with our eyes, that which we saw, and our hands touched,*** *concerning the Word of life (and the life was revealed, and we have seen, and testify, and declare to you the life, the eternal life, which was with the Father, and was revealed to us)....* (1 John 1:1–2)

However, Jesus reserves a special blessing for those who, unlike Thomas and the others, have not been made privy to such wondrous things. He says to Thomas, *"Because you have seen Me, you have believed.* ***Blessed are those who have not seen, and have believed"*** (John 20:29). This, of course, includes us, for none of us have seen the risen Christ with our eyes, or touched the marks of His former wounds with our hands. And yet, by the miracle of the revelation of the Spirit of Christ within us, we most certainly believe!

How, then, does Thomas respond to Jesus?

Thomas answered Him, **"My Lord and my God!"** (John 20:28)

Is this not the only truly orthodox response to the Gospel of Jesus Christ, who, by His resurrection from the dead, according to the Spirit of holiness, has been declared to be the Son of God with power [Romans 1:4]? Should not all of the redeemed of the Lord think upon the glory of Christ's resurrection from the grave and say only this, *"Our Lord and our God!"*? Is not Jesus Christ fully God? Is He not eternally God, eternally uncreated, and nothing less? Thomas makes the good confession. He cries out, *"My Lord and my God!"* even as he will later travel abroad with this Gospel about the incarnation of the Son of God, travelling possibly to China, but most assuredly to India,[3] wherein he will die as a martyr, possibly pierced through with spears, bearing witness to the certain divinity of Jesus Christ, crucified for sinners, and risen from the dead.

Beloved Christian, you who have not seen and yet have believed, what is your own response to the truth of Jesus Christ? When you see Him crucified, having breathed His last and yielded up His spirit to the Father, and having been pierced through His side with the soldier's spear, such that blood and water flowed out, what do you say of this Man, hanging dead on the cross? Do you not weep over your sins against Him and cry out, *"My Lord and my God!"*?

What, then, do you say when you see Him, by faith, risen from the dead? When you hear Peter say, *"…whom God raised up, having freed Him from the agony of death, because it was not possible that He should be held by it"* (Acts 2:24), what do you say? When He, the risen Lord, says to you, *"Do not be afraid. I am the First and the Last, and the Living One. I was dead, and behold, I am alive forever more. Amen. I have the keys of Death and of Hades"* (Revelation 1:17–18), what do you say in response? Do you not fall down before His fiery brilliance and soul-piercing eyes of fire and cry out, *"My Lord and my God!"*?

And what, then, shall the whole Church, the whole great multitude which no one can number, of all nations, tribes, peoples, and tongues, cry out and say with one, harmonious shout, once He comes on the clouds with the holy angels to gather His elect from the four winds of the earth? When He comes like lightning, flashing across the whole horizon, and His chariot sounds like

---

[3] For the church-historical evidence for this, see, among several other sources, Gregory of Nazianzus *Orations* 33.11 (*NPNF*[2] 7:332).

thunder—the kind of divine thunder that shakes the heavens and the earth—and sends forth great hailstones before Him, with burning coals of fire, such that He renders His anger against the wicked with fury, and His rebuke with flames of fire, what will the roaring shout of His elect children be? Will we not shout, with a roar, the very confession of the Apostle Thomas, that this risen Christ, now returning to execute the divine vengeance upon the earth, is both our Lord and our God? Will not the Church sing, *"Our Lord and our God!"* even as she sings, thunderously, that great song of Moses, the servant of God, and the song of the Lamb, saying:

> *"Great and marvelous are Your works, O Lord God, the Almighty! Righteous and true are Your ways, O King of the nations. Who would not fear You, O Lord, and glorify Your name? For You only are holy. For all the nations will come and worship before You. For Your righteous acts have been revealed."* (Revelation 15:3–4)

Thus we shall sing, with never ceasing praises, and with exuberant joy, unto the glory of the risen Christ, who is our Lord and our God, and unto the glory of the eternal Father, time without measure, everlasting days unto everlasting days, world without end. Amen.

17

THE SEVEN-SEALED SCROLL
The Glory of THE LAMB, SLAIN in Revelation 5:1-14

I saw, in the right hand of Him who sat on the throne, a book written inside and outside, sealed shut with seven seals. I saw a mighty angel proclaiming with a loud voice, "Who is worthy to open the book, and to break its seals?" No one in Heaven above, or on the earth, or under the earth, was able to open the book, or to look in it. Then I wept much, because no one was found worthy to open the book, or to look in it. (Revelation 5:1-4)

GOD gave certain portions of the book of Revelation to the Apostle John in the form of a scroll, with writing upon it both on the front and the back. How infinitely precious, then, is this scroll, since it contains the final revelation given in God's holy Word! At first, it is closed, and very much *"sealed,"* even with *"seven seals,"* which means a complete sealing. Yet in the end, at the unfolding of the final, climactic judgments of the wrath of Almighty God, it shall be found opened. Here, then, is how John first sees it:

*I saw, in the right hand of Him who sat on the throne, **a book** written inside and outside, **sealed shut with seven seals**.* (Revelation 5:1)

The scroll, which contains certain portions of the book of Revelation, is sealed. It is sealed up, even with seven seals. Yet as time moves forward, the Lamb who stands in the midst of the throne of Heaven opens the book by unsealing the scroll, and thus the book is later found *"open"* in the hands of the risen Christ:

*He had in His hand **a little open book**. He set His right foot on the sea, and His left on the land.* (Revelation 10:2)

Part of the climactic glory of the book of Revelation, then, involves the *"opening"* of *"books."* There are books that were once closed and sealed up, which, at the end of all things, shall be found to have been opened by God. The books, once opened, signify that the time for the Final Judgment has arrived at last:

*I saw the dead, the great and the small, standing before the throne, and they **opened books**. **Another book was opened**, which is the Book of Life. The dead were judged **out of the things which were written in the books**, according to their works.* (Revelation 20:12)

The *sealing up*, and subsequent *opening up* of the books of God, then, signifies the times of the very end of the age. If God's books are sealed, then His wrathful judgments are still future. Yet if His books are opened, then His wrathful judgments are impending, even looming on the horizon.

What, then, dear Reader, is your spiritual posture towards the book of Revelation? Do you try to ignore it, wishing that it were not there, sitting on your bookshelf, beckoning you to read it? Do you pretend that it is too difficult, too sealed up in confusing imageries and opaque metaphors, for you to understand? Do you thus prefer to think about plans for your future, always meditating on earthly gains and pleasures, rather than having to face the unsettling message of the book of Revelation? Do you not know that the *book* lies before you *unsealed*, and thus very much open? Are you not aware that, whether you like it or not, God shall hold you accountable to the message of this open, unsealed book?

Pray, then, dear Reader, that the Lord of glory and light will enlighten your eyes to give you an obedient faith in understanding this precious book—the book of Revelation. For, your response to its contents shall determine your everlasting reward in the

Kingdom of Heaven—or else, your everlasting punishment in the unending judgments of Hell. Pray, therefore, with all fervency, for a God-fearing obedience, empowered only by the blessed Spirit of Christ, through the Gospel of the Lamb, to the book of Revelation:

Blessed is he who reads and those who hear the Words of this Prophecy, **and keep those things which are written in it;** *for the time is near.* (Revelation 1:3, NKJV)

SEALED WITH SEVEN SEALS

There was a time when the book of Revelation was completely sealed. It was unopened, and unable to be opened. It was, at the time of the Apostle John's vision, very much sealed up. And this caused the beloved Apostle much grief and anguish:

I saw, in the right hand of Him who sat on the throne, a book written inside and outside, **sealed shut with seven seals.** (Revelation 5:1)

At the beginning of the fifth chapter of Revelation, the book is still very much sealed. God has sealed up its message, just as He formerly sealed up many Old Testament prophecies:

"Is this not laid up in store with Me, **sealed up** *among My treasures"?* (Deuteronomy 32:34)

The Lord is He who seals His holy Word and keeps it hidden from the eyes of wicked, adulterous men:

Wrap up the Testimony. **Seal the Law among my disciples.** *I will wait for the LORD, who hides His face from the house of Jacob, and I will look for Him.* (Isaiah 8:16–17)

This is God's holy prerogative. He has the sovereign, divine right to seal up His Word according to the mystery of His will. The clay cannot demand of the Potter a full revelation of His judgments and plans. Rather, the Potter has the right to keep His decrees to Himself, and especially when the clay is hardened and rebellious.

Therefore, God seals up matters that He desires to conceal. And, at the proper times, God opens up those same matters, the ones He now chooses to reveal:

> *Pause and wonder! Blind yourselves and be blind! They are drunken, but not with wine; they stagger, but not with strong drink. For the LORD has poured out on you a spirit of deep sleep, and has closed your eyes, the prophets; and he has covered your heads, the seers. All vision has become to you **like the words of a book that is sealed**, which men deliver to one who is educated, saying, "Read this, please"; and he says, **"I cannot, for it is sealed."*** (Isaiah 29:9–11)

In particular, the times of the end were sealed up under the ministries of the Old Testament Prophets. The Prophet Daniel, for example, was commanded by God to seal up his prophecies until the allotted time for mankind to repent had run its course:

> *"But you, Daniel, shut up the Words, **and seal the book**, even to the time of the end: many shall run back and forth, and knowledge shall be increased."* (Daniel 12:4)

And again,

> *I heard, but I did not understand: then I said, "My lord, what shall be the issue of these things?" He said, "Go your way, Daniel; **for the Words are shut up and sealed until the time of the end**. Many shall purify themselves, and make themselves white, and be refined; but the wicked shall do wickedly; and none of the wicked shall understand; but those who are wise shall understand."* (Daniel 12:8–10)

Even in the book of Revelation, some things are sealed up, kept from the ears of all people, including Christians. Not all things are revealed to God's saints. The secret things still belong to the Lord:

THE SEVEN-SEALED SCROLL

When the seven thunders sounded, I was about to write; but I heard a voice from the sky saying, **"Seal up the things which the seven thunders said,** *and do not write them."* (Revelation 10:4)

And yet, the time of the end has come. The end times have begun. For, the book of Revelation, itself, is no longer sealed. The Old Testament prophecies have been unlocked. The Revelation given to the blessed Apostle John is now *unsealed*, and *very much opened*. Therefore, the time of the end is near, even at the door:

He said to me, **"Do not seal up the Words of the prophecy of this book,** *for the time is at hand."* (Revelation 22:10)

The unsealing of the book of Revelation is both grave and urgent, for this is what ushers in the final events and judgments of world history. Once the book of Revelation is unsealed, the final judgments of the wrath of God against the wickedness of the nations can commence. In other words, the glorious coming of our Lord Jesus Christ must follow, not precede, the unsealing of the book. Therefore, the Apostle John was, upon receiving this initial vision of the fifth chapter of Revelation, filled with grief and sorrow. Having such a deep yearning for the final judgments of God to come upon the earth, he wept and wept, since nobody in Heaven, or on earth, or under the earth, was found who was worthy to open the book and to break its seven seals:

Then I wept much, because no one was found worthy to open the book*, or to look in it.* (Revelation 5:4)

The Apostle John did not have his affections set upon the question of which sports team would win the championship game, or upon the question of which godless film would win the best picture award. Such ideas would have been seen by John as being wholly dishonorable—completely sordid and very much unworthy of a Christian's time and attention. Rather, his affections were set upon *this great book*, the book of Revelation, which he saw in the right hand of Him who sat upon the throne of Heaven. He loved *this book*, and yet it was sealed with seven seals, unable to be opened, and thus he wept, with a great weeping.

Does anyone weep anymore? Is there anyone in our own day who weeps, as the Apostle John wept? Have all hearts today grown cold to the Word of God? Does anyone weep over whether or not the book of Revelation is opened? Is there anyone out there, in the churches of today, who longs for the coming of the Kingdom of our God and of His Christ the way in which the Apostle John longed for it? Does anyone today still weep for the events prophesied in the book of Revelation to come to pass, in real, human history? Shall not God bring justice for His elect, who have been so murderously slain by the wicked? Shall not God's righteous judgments be revealed? Are these things considered worthy of being *wept over* by anyone anymore? Does anyone today weep for the future revelation of Christ the way in which John himself wept for the future revelation of His glory?

Dear Christian, where are your affections? Are they set upon the world, or are they fully invested in the final events of the book of Revelation that will unfold both prior to, and at the Second Coming of Christ Jesus? The Lord Jesus is coming soon. And yet the question is: when He comes, shall He find faith upon the earth? When He comes, *how much faith* shall He find in your own heart?

THE LION OF THE TRIBE OF JUDAH

The Apostle John did not weep in vain. He loved *this book*. He desired, with tears, for the full wrath and glory of the Lamb to be revealed. And so he wept. Yet he did not weep in vain:

> *One of the elders said to me, "Do not weep.* **Behold, the Lion who is of the tribe of Judah, the Root of David, has overcome: He who opens the book and its seven seals.***"* (Revelation 5:5)

There are twenty-four elders seated on twenty-four thrones, all of them encircling the great throne of God. One of them—and who was it? Was it Moses? Was it Elijah? Was it Paul, who had been beheaded under Nero? Was it Peter, who had been crucified upside-down? Could it have been James, the very brother of John, who had been killed with the sword under wicked King Herod?—we do not know who it was, but one of them said to John, *"Do not weep. Behold, the Lion who is of the tribe of Judah, the Root of David, has overcome: He who opens the book and its seven seals."*

At last! The sealed book shall be unsealed. At last! The closed book shall be opened. How so? No one else is worthy to do it, but *the Lion of the tribe of Judah has conquered*. He has unsealed the dark tomb of sin and death, and thus loosed the power of Satan over God's elect. Therefore, He alone is worthy to open the book, to unseal its contents, and to loose its seven seals.

There is a Lion in the room! As if the presence of the four living creatures, and the twenty-four elders, all surrounding the One who sits on the throne—as if all of this is not terrifying enough! Now, there is a Lion! And yet this is a comforting Lion. This is the Lion who shall open the book and loose it seven seals. He is the Lion of the tribe of Judah, just as the patriarch Jacob prophesied just prior to his death:

> **Judah is a lion's cub**. *From the prey, my son, you have gone up. He stooped down, he crouched* **as a lion**, *as a lioness. Who will rouse him up?* (Genesis 49:9)

Who is this Lion of Judah? He is a king. For, Solomon built his throne of ivory, overlaid with gold, and the throne had six steps leading up to it, *with a pair of lions on each of the six steps* [1 Kings 10:20]. Solomon thus prophesied that there would be a future King, a Christ, who would rule the world like a great lion. And, of course, when the wicked rage against such a lion-like King of Righteousness, He, the King, shall roar against them in His lion-like wrath:

> **The terror of a king is like the roaring of a lion**. *He who provokes him to anger forfeits his own life.* (Proverbs 20:2)

Who is the Lion of Judah? In the Old Testament, *God is the Lion of Judah*. He comes to judge the nations, to the very ends of the earth, with the terrifying roar of His wrath:

The peaceful folds are brought to silence because of the fierce anger of the LORD. **He has left his [lair], as the lion**; *for their land has become an astonishment because of the fierceness of the oppression, and because of His fierce anger.*
(Jeremiah 25:37–38)

    Yet the roar of this fierce Lion of Judah is not always terrifying. Sometimes it is comforting. For, whenever the Lion of Judah is on one's side, one can feel very safe and protected, indeed.

    The present author's two eldest sons, his beloved eldest boys, did not grow up in the safest neighborhood in the world. In their neighborhood, sirens went off regularly. Police cars visited their street regularly. Together with their father, mother, and other siblings, they viewed several arrests through the lens of their living room window, and on one occasion, their mother needed to call the police herself, in order to report a neighborhood crime. On another occasion, just past midnight, the present author was compelled to scare off two young men who were trying to break into his house through the front door. Therefore, his two eldest boys did not always feel safe, and especially when they were little toddlers.

    However, the boys' grandmother, who since has gone ahead of them to worship the Lion of Judah in His Heavenly courts, once gave them a plush, toy lion when they were both still quite little. She wanted them to look upon the plush, toy lion and think of the Lion of Judah. And this comforted both of them greatly. For, whenever the toddling boys were frightened by something or someone in their neighborhood, they would place the plush lion in their bedroom window sill. For, they knew that the true Lion of Judah, the Lord of Heaven and earth, was guarding them.

    Sometimes when the Lion of Judah roars, it is extremely comforting. For His beloved children, His chosen ones of the covenant, the Lion's roar is, indeed, greatly comforting:

They will walk after **the LORD, who will roar like a lion; for He will roar**, *and the children will come trembling from the west. They will come trembling like a bird out of Egypt, and like a* *dove out of the land of Assyria;* ***and I will settle them in their houses,*** *" says the* LORD. (Hosea 11:10–11)

The Apostle John was found weeping. He was found weeping because no one was found who was able to open the book, and to loose its seven seals. But then he heard the roar of the Lion of the tribe of Judah. He heard the Lion roar, and he was greatly comforted. For, the Lion, who has conquered death, is able to open the scroll and to loose its seven seals.

O weeping Christian, weep no longer over the seven-sealed scroll. O frightened and afflicted Christian, be terrified no longer by Satan. For, the Lion of Judah has conquered. He has vanquished Satan. He has cut through the seal that enclosed Him in the tomb. Risen from the dead, descended from David, the Lion of Judah has conquered! Therefore, Satan shall be cast into the abyss. The wicked, who terrorize the righteous, shall be slain by the sword that proceeds from His mouth. The Kingdom of our God and of His Christ *shall* come, and He *shall* reign forever and ever. Therefore, O weeping Christian, O terrified Christian, weep and be terrified no more. For, the Lion has roared. His roar has announced the opening of the scroll, the breaking of its seals, and thus it is a comforting roar. Be comforted, O you who are dearly loved by Your Father in Heaven, for the Lion roars in order to comfort you. He roars in order to bring you safely into His Kingdom, where sickness shall no longer strike you, and where the wicked shall terrify you no more. His roar is powerful, even powerful enough to shake both the heavens and the earth, and yet it is to you your Bridegroom's shout of salvation, even the roaring shout of divine, covenantal love with which He comforts you.

THE LAMB WHO WAS SLAIN

The Apostle John, however, does not actually *see* the Lion of the tribe of Judah. He may hear His comforting roar, but when he looks, he does not see a lion at all. Instead, to His great surprise, the Apostle John looks and sees *a Lamb*:

> *I* **saw** *in the middle of the throne and of the four living creatures, and in the middle of the elders,* ***a Lamb*** *standing, as*

*though **it had been slain**, having seven horns and seven eyes, which are the seven Spirits of God, sent out into all the earth. Then He came, and He took it out of the right hand of Him who sat on the throne. Now when He had taken the book, the four living creatures and the twenty-four elders fell down before **the Lamb**, each one having a harp, and golden bowls full of incense, which are the prayers of the saints. They sang a new song, saying, "You are worthy to take the book and to open its seals: **for You were [slain]**, and bought us for God with Your blood out of every tribe, language, people, and nation, and made [them] kings and priests to our God, and [they] will reign on the earth."* (Revelation 5:6–10)

The book is sealed. The scroll needs to be opened. Yet who is worthy to open the scroll and to loose its seven seals? The Lamb alone is worthy. *The Lamb was slain*, and so He is worthy.

This imagery of the Lamb, no doubt, is a reference to the Passover Lamb. The Jews were to celebrate the Passover Feast by always remembering *the slaying of the Passover Lamb*:

Your lamb *shall be without defect, a male a year old. You shall take it from the sheep or from the goats. You shall keep it until the fourteenth day of the same month; and the whole assembly of the congregation of Israel **shall [slay] it at evening**.* (Exodus 12:5–6)

Jesus is the Lamb who was slain. He has redeemed us by His blood. He is God's Servant, who became the sacrificial Lamb of God on our behalf:

*He was oppressed, yet when He was afflicted He did not open His mouth. **As a lamb that is led to the slaughter**, and as a sheep that before its shearers is silent, so He did not open His mouth.* (Isaiah 53:7)

Who, then, is worthy to take the scroll and open its seven seals? Only the Lamb is worthy. For only He purchased redemption for His elect, with the purchase price of His own blood, from every tribe, tongue, people, and nation. Thus He alone is worthy to open the book, and to bring world history to its climactic end. He alone is worthy to bring His wrath upon the wicked nations that rage against Him. And He alone is worthy to gather His elect from the four corners of the earth. He alone is the Lamb of God. He alone can open the scroll, for He alone is *worthy*:

*They sang a new song, saying, "**You are worthy** to take the book and to open its seals...."* (Revelation 5:9)

This is the greatest question of Heaven. The greatest question of Heaven is, *"Who is worthy?"* There is no greater question in all of Heaven:

*I saw a mighty angel proclaiming with a loud voice, "**Who is worthy** to open the book, and to break its seals?"* (Revelation 5:2)

And again,

*Then I wept much, because **no one was found worthy** to open the book or to look in it.* (Revelation 5:4)

The Lamb, therefore, is the greatest answer of Heaven. He defines Heaven, for He alone answers the greatest question of Heaven. The greatest question of Heaven is, *"Who is worthy?"* And here, then, is the greatest answer of Heaven:

*They sang a new song, saying, "**You are worthy** to take the book and to open its seals: for You were killed, and bought us for God with Your blood out of every tribe, language, people, and nation, and made [them] kings and priests to our God, and [they] will reign on the earth." I saw, and I heard something like a voice of many angels around the throne, the living creatures, and the elders. The number of them was ten thousands of ten thousands, and thousands of thousands; saying with a loud voice, "**Worthy is the Lamb** who has been [slain] to receive the power, wealth, wisdom, strength, honor, glory, and blessing!" I heard every created thing which is in Heaven,* *on the earth, under the earth, on the sea, and everything in them, saying, "To Him who sits on the throne, **and to the Lamb** be the blessing, the honor, the glory, and the dominion, forever and ever! Amen!" The four living creatures said, "Amen!" Then the elders fell down and worshiped.* (Revelation 5:9–14)

How worthy is the Lamb? The answer to this question defines Heaven for us. If we cannot answer this question, we cannot know Heaven. But if we understand that the worthiness of the Lamb, a worthiness that unseals the scroll in its entirety, is what it truly is, then we shall understand Heaven. For, the worthiness of the Lamb in the unsealed book of Revelation is equal to, is as high and exalted as, and is as glorious and majestic as the worthiness of God Himself:

*"**Worthy are You, our Lord and God**, the Holy One, to receive the glory, the honor, and the power, for You created all things, and because of Your desire they existed, and were created!"* (Revelation 4:11)

Do you see it? Is the book, the scroll, now unsealed and opened before the eyes of your soul? Do you see that the worthiness of the Lamb is equal to, is as high and exalted as, and is as fearsome and divine as the worthiness of the Father in Heaven? If so, then why should any of us be baffled at all at the thought of dear Henry Martyn, that God-centered missionary from England, sacrificing career, prestige, health, comforts, and even marriage to the one whom his heart loved, in order to die a thousand deaths of persecutions, sufferings, and sorrows on the mission fields of India and Persia, and all so that countless men and women of India and Persia might rise up on the Last Day, having been redeemed, through the practical means of Martyn's preaching and Bible translations, by the blood of the Lamb, and thus join so many countless others from every tribe and tongue and people and nation in proclaiming the worthiness of the Lamb?

Do you see the scroll opened before your eyes? Do you see the worthiness of the Lamb? If so, dear Christian, how is your holiness? How is your willingness to be scorned by the world for the sake of holiness? How is your willingness to suffer for the sake of the Gospel? Are you willing to live the kind of holy life—utterly dedicated to God in holiness—that is *worthy* of the Gospel of Christ? Are you crucifying the world daily, and being crucified to the world daily, and thus hating sin and idolatry daily, and daily living the kind of life that is *worthy of the blood of the Lamb who has redeemed you*?

Only let your way of life **be worthy of the [Gospel] of Christ***....* (Philippians 1:27)

They sing a new song in Heaven. This is no longer the song of Moses only. This is the song of Moses and of the Lamb. In Heaven, the book is fully unsealed and fully opened. In Heaven, they spend eternity singing, **"Worthy is the Lamb who was slain!"**

This is your identifying mark as a Christian. This is what defines you as a Christian. God made you for this singular purpose: to proclaim, with everything you have, the worthiness of the Lamb. Your job is not to get caught up in the cares and worries of this world. Rather, your always painful, yet exceedingly joyful job is to herald the worthiness of the Lamb who was slain for the sins of the world. So dear Pilgrim, whenever you lose your way, and find your mind and heart wandering astray, return to this singular purpose: to make known, with all of your might, the worthiness of the Lamb of God.

This is the voluntary employment of the saints in Heaven. Heaven is where the saints make the everlasting confession and sing the everlasting exaltation of the worthiness of the Lamb. And this is why there is an everlasting Hell. For, Hell is reserved for all of those who hate the Lamb, and who refuse to acknowledge the worthiness of the Lamb. In doing so, they condemn themselves as being *unworthy* of eternal life, and thus thrust themselves headlong into to the everlasting *unworthiness* of fire that burns with brimstone, and of weeping and gnashing of teeth.

Yet Heaven is, indeed, prepared for God's saints. In Heaven, the saints will proclaim the everlasting praise of the worthiness of the Father's own Lamb. We know that we are bound for Heaven if we yearn, in our hearts, to enter into this perfected praise of the worthiness of the Lamb. We, who are saved, long to be in Heaven, where we shall see the Lamb, face to face, shall be warmed in the Lamb's shepherding arms, and shall be illuminated in the light of His countenance. And we shall know that we have arrived in Heaven when we hear, not the Lion's roar, but rather the roar of a great and seemingly countless multitude, of angels, to be sure, but also of glorified saints, of all of those who fear Him, small and great—all of them wearing white robes, washed in the blood of the Lamb—singing, with a unified and blaring voice, *"Salvation be to our God, who sits on the throne, and to the Lamb!...Worthy is the Lamb!"* (Revelation 7:10; 5:12). And thus we shall proclaim the eternal worthiness of Him who sits upon the throne, whose appearance is like that of a jasper and of a sardius stone, and of the Lamb, by ascribing to our God all blessing and honor and glory and power, forever and ever, eternal jubilation, days beyond number, world without end. Amen.

Conclusion:

"I Have Finished the Work"

*"I glorified You on the earth. **I have [finished] the work** which You have given Me to do."* (John 17:4)

JESUS prays to the Father, with His eyes upon the impending sufferings of the cross, and says, *"I have [finished] the work which You have given Me to do."* God is His eternal Father. He is God's eternal Son. Together, they have shared eternal, divine glory before the creation of the world. Yet the Father has sent His Son to earth, in the flesh, to do the Father's *work*. The Son is one with the Father. He shows that He is one with the Father by doing the *works* of the Father, the very *works* which the Father gave Him to do.

How, then, does the Son do the Father's work? How does He perform the works of His Father? He, as a dutiful Son, imitates His Father, and works under the gaze of His Father, all in order to please His Father. Just as the son of a carpenter learns his trade by imitating his father's work, developing balance on the ladder and swiftness with the saw, and just as the son of a scholar learns to read on his father's knee, with a pen in one hand and an ancient manuscript in the other, so too does the Son of God learn His Father's work by doing only what He sees His Father in Heaven doing.

However, the work that the Father has given His Son to do is a most painful work. It is a work of hardship and suffering. The Father has assigned His Son the job title of *"Man of Sorrows."* This is the work that the Father has given His Son to do—that of suffering for the sins of the world. Thus the Son has a baptism to be baptized with, and He is distressed until it is finished. He casts out demons and performs cures today and tomorrow, and the third day His work of suffering shall be finished. His strength shall be perfected and finished in weakness. His patient endurance shall have its finished work, and He shall be shone to be finished and complete in His sinless obedience to the Law, and to the Father's will. He, the Author of our salvation, finishes His work through sufferings.

And yet, the Son still loves His Father's work, for by it He pleases His Father. His food is to do the will of the Father who sent Him, and to *finish His work*. Again, He loves this work, for *the works which the Father has given Him to finish*—the very works that the Son does—bear witness of Him, that the Father has sent Him. Thus He prays to the Father, *"I glorified You on the earth. I have **[finished] the work** which You have given Me to do."*

In Him, in the Son of God, the Writings of the Prophets are fulfilled. As He reveals the Father's glory to the world, and as He suffers for the iniquities of us all, the prophecies of the Scriptures concerning the Son of Man are fulfilled, and finished. At Golgotha, Jesus fights the perfect fight, and runs and finishes the perfect race. He finishes His work first by suffering the things foretold by the Prophets, and only afterwards by entering into His glory.

Again, Jesus prays to His Father in John 17:4, *"I glorified You on the earth. I have **[finished] the work** which You have given Me to do,"* and, in many ways, *we* are the fruits of His work. For, He also prays to the Father in John 17:22-23, *'The glory which You have given Me, I have given to them; that they may be one, even as We are one; I in them, and You in Me, that they may be **[finished in oneness]**; that the world may know that You sent Me and loved them, even as You loved Me."*

For true believers, Christ's work of regeneration in us is already finished. His work has exposed our sins as devilishly dark, and horribly condemning. It has brought our consciences to the brink of Hell, and, in turn, caused our hearts to flow with tears of repentance. His work, through our faith in Him, has quickened our hearts, giving us life and breath in the Holy Spirit, and has caused us to be born again into the living hope of His resurrection. This is the work of redemption that He has finished in us. We are bought with a price. We are sealed with the everlasting seal of His Holy

Conclusion: I Have Finished the Work

Spirit. Therefore, our salvation is assured. Our adoption into sonship is finished.

Yet our sanctification is not yet finished. Nevertheless He, our God and Savior, who has begun *a good work* in us, shall *finish it*. This great, sanctifying work of Christ in us has begun conforming us to His image, and reshaping us into His likeness. And it shall be finished, one day. He who has redeemed us, also shall perfect us. He who has foreknown us, also shall glorify us. For, in the Heavenly City of Zion, we shall join the Church of the firstborn who are registered in Heaven, and we shall behold the spirits of just men made perfect. We shall keep His Word, perfectly, in Heaven. Therefore, His work of love shall be perfected and finished in us. He shall look upon the saints of Heaven, and He shall say to His Father, "Behold! My finished work."

Jesus prays to the Father, *"I glorified You on the earth. I have **[finished] the work** which You have given Me to do."* Thus the work is finished. Jesus, bleeding from the back, and pierced through in the wrists and ankles, wearing the crown of thorns, His face bludgeoned beyond recognition, and gasping for breath as He suffocates on the cross, finishes the work that the Father has given Him to do. He becomes sin for us. He bears the weight of our sins in our stead. He endures the fiery storm of God's wrath in our place. He makes an end of sins; He finishes the transgression of His people. Thus, knowing that all things are now finished—that all of His Father's work of redemption is now finished—that the Scripture might be fulfilled and finished, He cries out, *"I thirst!"* And after they fill a sponge with sour wine, put it on hyssop, and put it to His mouth, He receives the sour wine, and says, **"It is finished!"** And bowing His head, He gives up His spirit.

Christ Jesus, therefore, has finished the work that His Father has given Him to do. He has pleased His Father by humbling Himself unto death, even death on a cross. Therefore, God has exalted Him to the highest place, giving Him the name which is above every name, that at the name of Jesus every knee should bow, of those in Heaven, and of those on earth, and of those under the earth, and that every tongue should confess that He is Lord, to the glory of God the Father.

At the time of the end, He shall come down for us, with a shout, with the voice of an archangel, and with the trumpet of God. He shall slay the wicked with the sword that proceeds from His mouth, and He shall cast the beast and the false prophet into the lake of fire that burns with brimstone. And then, at last, His final work shall be *finished*, and the mystery of God shall be *finished*, as He declared beforehand to His servants the Prophets. And we shall see His face, and His name shall be on our foreheads, and His tabernacle shall be with men, and He will dwell with us, and we shall be His people. And, unto an unending eternity of bliss, forever, and ever, world without end, God Himself shall be with us, and be our God. Amen.

About the Author

When grace abounds to the chief of sinners, Christians learn to boast only in the cross of the Lord Jesus Christ. Awed by the grace of God and the majesty of the cross, Timothy Fan serves, pastorally, to remind Christ's people that they are God's image bearers, His craftsmanship, created in Christ Jesus for good works, and are, therefore, very precious to Him.

Raised in a Southern Baptist church in Denver, Colorado, Timothy studied chemistry in college and completed his seminary training in biblical studies. He most recently served as the pastor of Genesis Family Church in Westminster, CO, and is the author of *Divine Heartbeat: Listening to God's Heartbeat for Preborn Children*, *The Babes of Christmas*, and *God's Ordinary Tinker: The Life and Doctrine of John Bunyan*. He and his beloved wife disciple their children through Christian home education, and pray for a "Malachi 4:6 revival" in the waning, contemporary Church.

Timothy's historic-Christian "mentors" include John Chrysostom, Balthasar Hubmaier, William Tyndale, John Knox, Richard Baxter, John Bunyan, and William Wilberforce. From Tyndale he has learned that "we be called unto a Kingdom that must be won with suffering only, as a sick man winneth health....Who ought not rather to choose and desire to be blessed with Christ in a little tribulation, than to be cursed perpetually with the world for a little pleasure?"

Soli Deo Gloria. Glory to God alone.

"For of Him, and through Him, and to Him, are all things. To Him be the glory forever! Amen." (Romans 11:36)

TO OBTAIN FREE MP3 AUDIO SERMONS BY PASTOR TIMOTHY FAN, PLEASE VISIT HIS MINISTRY WEBSITE AT:

www.godcentereduniverse.com

www.ingramcontent.com/pod-product-compliance
Lightning Source LLC
Chambersburg PA
CBHW020150090426
42734CB00008B/765